THE
ROAD
TO
SHALIMAR

THE
ROAD
TO
SHALIMAR

BY CARVETH WELLS

WITH A FOREWORD BY

LOWELL THOMAS

ILLUSTRATED WITH PHOTOGRAPHS

Doubleday & Company, Inc., Garden City, N.Y., 1952

LIBRARY OF CONGRESS CATALOG CARD NUMBER: 52-5219

DEDICATED TO MY WIFE, ZETTA,
MY CONSTANT COMPANION
IN ARCTIC, DESERT, AND JUNGLE

FORE-WORD

Ever since I read his first book I've been a Carveth Wells fan. That was long ago when first he emerged from the Malay jungle and wrote the story of his adventures in the equatorial forest, that weird land of pygmies, jungle animals that hunt the hunter, and fish that climb trees. Even when I fail to agree with him I thoroughly enjoy his infectious and rather uproarious sense of humor. In his books, on the platform, and over the radio, Carveth has built a reputation as a spinner of yarns. One obvious reason for his success is his contagious enthusiasm. Whenever he is around, either in person, in print, or as a disembodied voice, there is excitement and entertainment.

In this new Wellsian opus he starts kicking Socialism around in the first few pages. I expected that, for he's been at it ever since he wrote that book, *Kapoot,* the account of the jaunt he and Zetta took to Russia some years ago. This time he also comes up with a novel suggestion for solving the thorny problem of who is to control the fabled Vale of Kashmir. The more I think about his proposal, the better I like it. As a possible bond between India and Pakistan it might be even more miraculous than the rope trick.

One reason why I am always stimulated by a Carveth Wells book is the hearty way in which I can disagree with him on many points. That's one of the sources of interest between friends, enthusiastic differences of opinion on about half the things that come up, and just as enthusiastic agreement on the other half.

On the subject of India and Pakistan, for example, there are some points about which I say—"Carveth, you're all wet." But

8

he replies that on these topics I am simply drenched. The reader of this book will get the point when he comes to some statements not too favorable to the great subcontinent of southern Asia.

A Carveth Wells book, like one of his sparkling and informal platform efforts, is made doubly interesting by his many asides. In fact, if Carveth has anything on his mind besides the book he is writing, he's almost certain to include it, which is the reader's good luck. To him there is nothing incongruous about taking us to Lapland on the way to the Vale of Kashmir.

In addition to his enthusiasm, another reason why he is a gifted storyteller is that he sees the little things that most travelers miss. When I meet a woman I usually come away with a general impression. But not Carveth. He can give you a complete description of her expression, her costume, her jewels. He has a similarly observant eye for foreign scenes and gets many times more fun out of travel than many who roam this world. Yes, even if he makes you mad now and then, it is always stimulating to journey with Carveth Wells, whether it's to the Mountains of the Moon or along *The Road to Shalimar*.

Lowell Thomas

CONTENTS

ILLUSTRATIONS

following page 156

INTRO-
DUCTION

Late one night when I was attempting to sneak by my parents who were sitting in our parlor, I heard my father reading to my mother:

"O! best of delights as it everywhere is,
  To be near the loved One, what rapture is his,
Who in moonlight and music thus sweetly may glide
  O'er the Lake of Cashmere with that One by his side!
If woman can make the worst wilderness dear,
  Think, think what a Heaven she must make of Cashmere!"

I was then at the romantic age of seventeen and I promised myself that one day I would go to Cashmere.

Forgetting all about having stayed out too late, I walked into the room where my father and mother were sitting. Before they had a chance to speak I began to ask my father about the poem.

Father then told me that the author of those beautiful lines from *Lalla Rookh* was the famous Irish poet, Thomas Moore, and that he had once lived in Bermuda, my father's birthplace.

Mother was wearing an exceedingly beautiful and soft shawl which she took off and pulled through her wedding ring. Then, as though reading my thoughts, she said, "One day you will go to Cashmere, where this shawl was made." (In those days Kashmir was spelled Cashmere.)

Henceforth I read and thought so much about it that Kashmir became my "Shangri-La."

In my early twenties I applied for a job in the Colonies that would get me to Singapore, whence I hoped eventually to reach Lake Dal and glide to Shalimar, the "Abode of Love." But the road to Shalimar was destined to be long and filled with many

15

disappointments and heartaches. For six years I lived in the Malay jungle surveying and constructing the railroad from Singapore to Bangkok, until, worn out by various tropical diseases, I was sent to America to die.

But that is another story. Years passed, and in 1931 I met my "loved one." In 1932 we were married and I planned to set out for Shalimar on our honeymoon. But my publisher had other ideas.

For the first time in fifteen years Russia had opened her borders to visitors, so off we went to the land of the "Great Experiment."

Instead of a honeymoon, that journey was a nightmare.

More years passed, and in 1939 we set out for Shalimar via Japan and China. Stopped at Peking by Japan's war with China, we turned back and headed for India via Hong Kong. The very day we arrived at Hong Kong, World War II broke out and all thought of "gliding over the Lake of Cashmere side by side" had to be abandoned.

Eleven years passed before I again set foot on the soil of Asia, but by that time war between India and Pakistan put Kashmir out of bounds.

Back again in the United States, I almost gave up hope of ever seeing the Vale of Kashmir. India and Pakistan continued to growl at one another across a cease-fire line, and from the look of things in 1950, neither Nehru nor Liaquat Ali Khan intended to budge an inch.

"We can at least try to get there," said Zetta. "Let's go around the world again on a President liner like we did in 1939. Those boats stop at Karachi, and now that you know the Prime Minister of Pakistan, perhaps he can help us get to Kashmir from there."

All our plans were made for this trip when the Korean war started. Our round-the-world voyage via Kashmir had to be canceled.

"You give up too easily!" said my indefatigable wife. "Why don't we try to reach Kashmir via Europe?"

And that is how it happened that instead of sailing from San Francisco we set out from New York on board the S.S. *Stockholm* of the Swedish American Line, bound for Gothenburg, Stockholm, arctic Lapland, and Hammerfest, the most northerly town in Europe.

It may seem a queer route to take to Kashmir, but we finally made it.

Just how we did so is told in the following pages.

"The Dugway"
Stockbridge, Mass.
September, 1951

THE
ROAD
TO
SHALIMAR

CHAPTER ONE

One wintry afternoon in February 1950, I found myself looking at a rather inconspicuous brass plate at the entrance to No. 12 East Sixty-fifth Street, New York City, upon which was the name "Pakistan House."

Except for the brass plate, the exterior of the building was just like the rest of the houses, drab and uninteresting.

I rang the bell. The door was opened by a swarthy individual dressed in European clothes and wearing a gray woolen muffler around his throat. He was obviously cold, but instead of shivering and shrinking from the icy blast that accompanied me into the house, he threw out his chest and faced it.

"Yes, sir. Mr. Shaffi is in," he said as he ushered me into the very remarkable vestibule of the consulate general of Pakistan.

But it was not the colorful murals that caused me to wonder, nor the large pictorial map of the world's largest Moslem state. It was the vibrant electrical atmosphere of the place, the constant ringing of the telephone, the cultured English accent of the girl in charge of the switchboard, the Cockney accent of the chief clerk, and the frequent goings and comings of smartly dressed young women, all of whom had that same telltale accent of the well-educated British college girl.

Fascinated, I listened to the telephone operator, who not only managed her switchboard expertly but at the same time carried on conversations with various departments by means of an interoffice communication instrument at her side.

"No, sir. The Ambassador is in Washington." . . . "Pakistan House. You wish to speak to Mr. Murton? I'll connect you." . . . "Yes, Mr. Shaffi. I told him the Ambassador was in Wash-

19

ington. . . . There's a gentleman here to see you, Mr. Shaffi. Mr. Carveth Wells. . . . Yes, sir. I'll send him up. . . . Two coffees, did you say? Yes, sir, I'll have them sent up."

Then with a pleasant smile, "Mr. Shaffi will see you now. Upstairs, large doors on the left."

As I walked up the well-carpeted stairs I wondered what kind of personage this man Shaffi could be, who could apparently carry on several conversations at once, talk on long distance to an ambassador one minute, order coffee the next, and so inspire the members of his staff that they all worked like beavers, willingly and with smiles on their faces. I didn't know it at the time, but I was soon to find out that Shaffi was the symbol of Pakistan, enthusiasm, boundless energy, and hard work.

I was in the same position as a newspaper reporter who remarked at a press party, "How in hell can I be expected to know anything about Pakistan? It isn't even mentioned in the Encyclopaedia Britannica."

When I entered his office, Shaffi was seated behind a large desk smoking a cigarette in a very long holder. The only thing dark about him were his eyes, which positively glittered. His face was whiter than mine, and when he spoke his accent was typically Oxford, not in the least lah-de-dah, and completely devoid of that peculiar accent known in the East as "chee-chee" that marks most people who have learned to speak English in India.

Somehow I felt as if I had known Shaffi all my life.

"Where have you been hiding yourself?" he said with a laugh. "We've been looking for you on three continents! Hadow told us months ago that you were thinking of going to Kashmir."

Hadow was the British consul general in Los Angeles. Born

in Kashmir, he had very kindly offered to help me with all kinds of introductions.

Hadow was a man of his word. He had advised the Pakistan Embassy to expect me, but I had allowed three months to elapse before I took any steps to pay my respects.

"We have a job for you," said Shaffi. "How soon can you go to Karachi?"

The suddenness of the whole proposition took my breath away. "Would I be able to visit Kashmir as well?"

"Forget about Kashmir for the present," he said. "You can go to Karachi and be back here in a couple of weeks. How about it?"

Then turning to his interoffice communication instrument, Shaffi said, "Get me the Ambassador!"

"His Excellency on the wire, sir."

"Shaffi speaking, Your Excellency. He's turned up. . . . Carveth Wells. . . . Yes, he's here in my office. . . . I'll ask him."

Turning to me, "Can you accompany me to Washington at once?"

I nodded.

"Yes, Your Excellency, we'll leave right away."

Was I dreaming? Shaffi must have read my thoughts.

"We do things quickly in Pakistan." He laughed. "Now, let's drink that coffee."

Noticing that Shaffi was wearing an old school tie which was very familiar, I inquired, "Aren't you wearing an Old Pauline tie?"

"I certainly am. Why not? I went to St. Paul's."

"So did I," I said eagerly.

"Then why aren't you wearing your tie?"

I explained that old school ties had gone out of fashion in America.

21

"Well," said Shaffi, "they are still in fashion in Pakistan. I suggest you start wearing one yourself!"

That night I found myself in Washington in conference with Ambassador Ispahani, a charming man, who is the Thomas Lipton of Pakistan. From him I learned that President Truman had invited Prime Minister Liaquat Ali Khan* to pay a state visit to the United States, that he would be leaving Karachi in about three weeks, and that my job was to go to Karachi, meet the Prime Minister and his family, return to America one week ahead of him, and then precede him on his transcontinental tour of the United States.

As the Prime Minister had never visited America before, I was to confer with him and his wife, Begum Liaquat Ali Khan, answer their questions, give them a few tips on what they might expect on their tour of the United States of America.

Only a few weeks had passed since Nehru had paid a similar visit to America, making speeches and receiving honorary degrees, so that it was most important to our own government that Liaquat Ali Khan's visit should not be overshadowed by Nehru's. It looked to me as if it was going to be a hard job. As a result of about fifty years' work of dozens of Hindu lecturers, poets, authors, and mystics, Americans were decidedly pro-Indian, and the name Nehru was almost as well known as Gandhi.

Not many Americans had ever heard of Pakistan, still less of

*As this book was going to press, news came from Karachi of the dastardly murder of Liaquat Ali Khan, by a hired assassin, while he was making a speech at Rawalpindi. There seems to be no doubt that the Prime Minister was killed because of his moderation, his friendship for the West, and his strong adherence to the principles of the United Nations. Although he was an ardent exponent of Pakistan's claims with regard to Kashmir, he refused to be swept away by the fanatical demand for a "holy war" against India.

Prime Minister Nehru himself, in a eulogy of Liaquat Ali Khan, was prompt to acknowledge that he was "a great steadying influence."

Liaquat Ali Khan. In fact, many people were so confused that they often asked me whether he was going to bring Rita Hayworth with him!

However, I needn't have worried about either Liaquat or the Begum. I found them both born ambassadors of good will. Both were good mixers and just the opposite of the proverbial "stuffed shirt." But I didn't know this until I met them in Karachi, or I might have talked myself out of one of the most interesting assignments I have ever been given.

Having obtained the blessings of our State Department, I secured a round-trip ticket to Karachi via Pan American World Airways for the modest sum of $1120.50 and left New York at 4 P.M. on the sixteenth of March on a Boeing Stratocruiser. As I planned to be back in New York within two weeks, I took only a suitcase containing my tropical clothing, my Contax, my Bell and Howell motion-picture camera, and a good supply of Kodachrome film.

The fly in the amber was having to leave my wife behind.

"Don't worry, darling," said Zetta as she kissed me good-by. "This trip to Pakistan is just the reconnaissance survey for our long-overdue expedition to Kashmir. I have a feeling that we'll be gliding over Dal Lake together this summer."

One of the last things I did before leaving New York was to buy some presents for the Prime Minister and his family. For Liaquat I got a set of Kodachrome slides of America's wonderlands and a viewer. For the Begum, Zetta bought a set of plastic jars and bottles with gold-plated stoppers. For the two young sons of the family I decided to buy a steam engine, the kind I used to love as a boy, that had a real fire, a whistle, and a safety valve.

But such an engine was not to be had at any of the stores I

tried in New York. "Too old-fashioned!" I was told. I found plenty of steam engines, but in every case, instead of having a real fire to heat the boiler, they had to be plugged into an electric-light socket and "boiled" just like an electric coffee percolator.

To me, half the fun of the engine was lighting the fire and, incidentally, running the risk of setting the house on fire too. So I decided to look for the right kind of steam engine in England, where children and their toys are less sophisticated than they are in America.

A surprise awaited me when I reached the International Airport at Idlewild. There was a Pakistani deputation to see me off, all of them wearing smart Jinnah hats made of karakul. But even more picturesque was the most popular member of the Explorers Club, the chief of Clan Fhearghuis of Strachur, in full Highland dress and carrying the flag of the club, which he presented to me. It was Flag No. 50. The very same flag which I had carried with me to Russia in 1932.

The flight across the Atlantic to England was much smoother than riding in a Pullman. Moreover, champagne and orchids were free, so everyone arrived in Socialist England in a very happy frame of mind. It was March 17, and despite contrary propaganda, the English were wearing shamrock or some kind of green in honor of St. Patrick. King George himself presented bunches of shamrocks that day to the officers of his Irish Guards. In fact, to judge from the green everywhere, London might have been Dublin.

I was met by my brother and sister-in-law, whom I had not seen for some time. Both had that unmistakable look that I saw in Russia during the famine of 1932; a look that denoted inadequate nourishment: too many potatoes and not enough meat and vitamins. They told me that they were still on strict rations, such as an ounce of cheese a week, a small pat of butter per week, and an occasional egg. Yet as I rode in a taxi to the Savoy Hotel, I noticed that the store windows were filled with all kinds of wonderful-looking meats, fruit, eggs, and mountains of butter.

Somebody got plenty of good food in England, but it was certainly not the average citizen.

I found myself thinking of the days of our United States Neutrality Act, when the British were on a cash-and-carry basis and fought alone; of the terrible days of the blitz, when the people themselves battled under the most frightful conditions and saved England from falling into the hands of our enemy. Never has a people who deserved so much received so little. It was shocking to find that the people of England had less than our former enemies.

Outwardly the Savoy Hotel was just the same as it had been in bygone days. Assistant managers in frock coats, plenty of diminutive bellboys, and the usual porter who was a walking encyclopedia of knowledge.

I entered the dining room and ordered luncheon. Printed on the menu were the words, "Cost of meal may not exceed five shillings." Then on the opposite side of the menu were the words, "Service charge six shillings." So the cost of service was more than the meal served. As for the meal itself, there was a choice of soup or fish, some kind of stewed meat, plenty of potatoes, and bread pudding for dessert. In addition there was one slice of bread, one disk of what-was-supposed-to-be-butter--but-wasn't, and three very small lumps of sugar. The disk of butter was about the size and thickness of a quarter or an English shilling. I arose from the table hungry and angry. But if the food was poor and inadequate, the accommodation was palatial. Such iniquities as rationing, priorities, and permits had never been dreamed of when the Savoy Hotel had been furnished. Not even the finest bathroom in New York's Waldorf could excel the luxurious equipment I enjoyed at the Savoy, with its full-length porcelain bath, twin washbasins, French bidet, jumbo-sized fluffy bath towels, and glittering electrically heated towel racks to dry them on. As for electric bells for room service, there was a regular switchboard of them.

I rang for the waiter. Almost instantly a distinguished individual looking more like a cabinet minister than waiter appeared.

"That was a dreadful luncheon they gave me downstairs!"

"Really, sir," said the waiter with a pained look. "What can I get you?"

"What have you got?"

"Anything you wish. Anything!" he answered with emphasis. "May I suggest that in future you take your meals in your room?"

Evidently good food was obtainable in London just as it had been in Moscow when we were there, provided you knew the ropes and could pay black-market prices.

That afternoon I hired a taxi and drove to Gamages, which always used to be and still is London's most remarkable store for almost anything under the sun, especially sporting goods and toys. The store hadn't changed a bit, nor had the steam engines.

Having bought exactly the same kind of engine that I had owned as a boy, I spent the rest of the afternoon cruising about in the taxi, much to the delight of the driver, who told me that he had once driven a hansom cab and longed for the good old

26

days before austerity. London was a very different city from the one it had been in 1932, when Zetta and I had stayed at the Savoy after our journey through Russia to Mount Ararat. There was of course a good excuse for the vast areas of ruins that surrounded St. Paul's Cathedral—Hitler.

But I wondered what excuse there was for London's appearance of general dilapidation and neglect. Some districts which used to look so smart made me think of Leningrad when paint was unobtainable. The people looked different also. Just pull out their shirttails and you might have mistaken a London crowd for Moscow!

But not even in Moscow had I seen such long queues waiting for busses. Some of them were blocks long. Iron railings had even been erected along the curb for people to lean against. There they stood uncomplainingly, many of them reading their evening papers while they waited and waited for a bus to carry them home.

In my London days Londoners would have demanded and got more busses. But apparently present-day Londoners do what they are told and accept with resignation what they are given. Many of them undernourished, yet with money in their pockets, just look hungrily at the display of food in the stores.

Just to see what would happen, I entered one of those well-stocked grocery stores and asked for a pound of butter and a dozen eggs.

The shopkeeper looked at me as if I were crazy.

"D'you shop 'ere?" he inquired belligerently.

"I'm trying to. I want some butter and eggs," I answered. "I'm an American."

The shopkeeper's manner changed completely. "Very sorry,

sir, but we can only sell to our regular customers. You can obtain anything you wish at your hotel."

I had already discovered that, but as I didn't wish to get into
an argument, I went out of the shop. Just where the regular
customers were I do not know, but they certainly weren't shopping that day. Presumably they were black marketeers. Even
under Socialism the rich fare much better than the poor.

That evening I invited my brother and his wife to dinner at
the Savoy, but not in the public dining room.

"Order whatever you want. To hell with rationing!"

"Haven't had a meal like this for ten years," remarked my
brother with a sigh of satisfaction. Porterhouse steak, French-
fried potatoes, aparagus, deep-dish apple pie with lots of thick
cream, an assortment of cheese, celery, and olives. We had
sparkling burgundy with the steak and port with the almonds
and raisins.

As for the cost, it was very expensive for English purses, but
not unusually so for American. The bill came to just under four
pounds, which was only about ten dollars.

"That's what cleaning women get for one day's work in Los
Angeles," I remarked.

"That's what they paid you for one week's work when you
were an assistant professor at London University," chuckled my
brother, which started us off reminiscing.

After sending them home to Ealing by taxi I opened my
diary to make a few entries. There, in Zetta's writing, was this
little note: "Welcome to London. Don't let Socialism give you
high blood pressure!"

The next morning, after a delicious English breakfast in bed,
I hurriedly packed and asked for my bill.

In America the bill clerk would have pressed a few keys in

her calculating machine and given me my bill in two minutes. But not so at the Savoy Hotel.

"Bill at once!" said the room clerk in horror. "I'm afraid you will have to go to the accounting department. When does your plane leave?"

"Twelve o'clock and it's ten-thirty now and I have to drive all the way to your London airport at Windsor," I said with a grin.

"Don't worry, sir. Pay the bill when you come back. No hurry!"

"But I'm going to Pakistan! I won't be back for ten days."

"Remarkable!" said the assistant manager. "We'll have your bill ready for you when you return."

Good old Savoy!

The plane for Karachi was packed. But not with people going to the ends of the earth. About half the passengers were well-to-do English people going to Belgium to get a decent meal and spend a happy, carefree week end.

The plane took off at noon. In a matter of minutes we were flying over the English Channel and could easily see both sides.

At one o'clock we landed in Brussels, where we were served a good luncheon, including steak and all the butter and sugar we wanted.

Belgium, with free enterprise, was a paradise compared with Socialist England. Most of the people I saw in the airport restaurant were English filling their shrunken stomachs with enough good food to maintain them until the next week end.

I couldn't help thinking of the time Zetta and I got out of Russia and entered Finland. I had lost thirty pounds in weight and Zetta eighteen. The boundary between Russia and Finland was a small river about fifty yards wide. On the Russian side there was a government-made famine. On the Finnish side was a lovely restaurant with all the food in the world. But unlike England, Russia didn't permit her citizens to go to Finland for lunch. Better to die of starvation than become contaminated with capitalism.

On thinking the matter over, I have come to the conclusion that as far as food is concerned there is a remarkable similarity between Russia and England with regard to the treatment of their citizens. Both countries export food for the sake of American dollars, while their citizens suffer dire austerity. As any American knows who has been in the habit of sending food packages to England, a great many of the items bought in the United States were originally exported from England.

It is difficult for a layman to understand why the English have to exist on starvation rations when Belgians appear to have all the food they want. But those who understand the workings of Communism know that so long as a government controls all sources of food it controls the people who must do what they are told or starve.

Ultimately, under Communism, the state controls all sources of production, the state regulates all consumption, the state is the only employer of labor, and the state owns all means of transportation and communications. The result of all this is that the people become servants of the state instead of the state being the servant of the people as it is in a democracy.

In Russia, this process being complete, down has come the Iron Curtain. In England, where the Socialist government was rapidly nationalizing everything, the people were being deprived more and more of the fruits of their labor and their precious liberty. For the wealthy, escape was still possible. Yet there were still those in England who threw up their hands in horror if it were suggested that they were on the road to Communism and slavery. Such people would do well to remember the words of Lenin: "That which is generally called Socialism is termed by Marx, 'the first or lower phase of communistic society.'"

Socialist Bernard Shaw said, "Communism is the same as Socialism, but better English." Comparisons are odious, but having just experienced Belgium and England, it was only natural that the conversation among the passengers on Pan American's Constellation when it left Brussels and headed for the Far East should turn to Communism.

Like an arrow we flew over Germany and Austria, apparently so peaceful and beautiful but full of tragedy. As we flew over the Bavarian Alps there was a rush to try to glimpse Hitler's hide-out, Berchtesgaden, which was directly beneath us. We were then given the exciting news that we were behind the Iron Curtain as we flew the entire length of Yugoslavia. Suddenly the plane made a right-angle turn and flew ten miles before resuming its proper course. "That was to avoid Belgrade," explained the captain, who then informed us that ours was the first commercial airplane that had been permitted to fly across Yugoslavia since the war.

Then darkness fell. Dinner was served while we were flying over Athens. Not even the lights of New York or Los Angeles can compare with those of Athens because of the city's extraordinary shape. It seemed like only a matter of minutes until we were over Beirut, Lebanon. I thought of the last time I had been there, in the dear gone days of unrestricted Mediterranean cruises when Americans were welcomed with open arms anywhere in Europe instead of being arrested as spies and left to rot for months in Communist jails.

The day may come when, instead of flying at eighteen

31

thousand feet with nothing to look at but clouds, commercial planes will fly low enough so that passengers may see the wonders below them.

I was still thinking of the wonders of Lebanon when suddenly the plane started to descend in great circles. Round and round we went, lower and lower, until, emerging from the clouds, we saw beneath us the lights of the oldest city still inhabited and one of the holiest cities of Islam, Damascus. When we landed it was 10:45 P.M. London time but 12:45 Damascus time.

While the plane was being serviced we were conducted to the airport dining room for a midnight snack. There, to the raucous playing of a third-rate jazz orchestra, about fifty people were dancing rumbas, sambas, and finally a slow waltz to the tune of "Auld Lang Syne"!

"I wonder what St. Paul and John the Baptist would say if they were here!" remarked a passenger who was obviously shocked.

It was quite a relief to get back into the air again.

"Our next stop will be Karachi, 2075 miles. Better take a nap," said the voice of the captain over the plane's loudspeaker.

Three hours later I was awakened by the sun shining on my face.

Through a break in the clouds I saw two steamers. We were flying over the Persian Gulf. Then the clouds closed in and I went back to sleep.

About midday I felt the plane descending. I looked at my diary. It was Sunday, March 19, and written in Zetta's hand were the words, "Welcome to Karachi, darling!"

From the air Karachi and the surrounding countryside looked

32

brown and parched. West Pakistan looked anything but inviting. One hundred years ago Sir Richard Burton had called this region where the river Indus wends its way to the sea "the Unhappy Valley," yet so far, every Pakistani I had met seemed to wear a perpetual smile.

Almost everyone except Pakistanis had told me that Karachi was a stinking hole and that only a miracle could ever change it.

But the miracle has happened, and the "miracle man" was the late Mohammed Ali Jinnah, known to all Pakistanis as the Quaid-i-Azam, the "Great Leader." Before our plane had rolled to a stop I saw, scampering across the runway, a mongoose. It was "Rikki-tikki-tani" in person. I had arrived in the stamping ground of Rudyard Kipling.

CHAPTER TWO

Karachi boasts that it has the finest airport in Asia. This is just as well, for it is certainly one of the busiest, with planes arriving at all hours of the day and night from many different points of the compass.

The arrangement for handling baggage and passengers was extraordinarily efficient and might well serve as an object lesson for New York. A brand-new nation, Pakistan is not handicapped by old ideas. The officials, all young, seemed eager to do everything they could to give newcomers a good impression, and this especially applies to the customs, immigration, and health officers.

Almost simultaneously with our arrival, planes off-loaded passengers from India and Indonesia, so that the scene in the waiting room was most colorful. I saw one elderly Moslem arrive with three ladies, all of whom were veiled so completely that only their eyes were visible. From the look of their tiny bare feet, however, almost milk-white and loaded with gold and silver anklets, they must have been wealthy and of high class.

"Not many of our Pakistani women veil nowadays," remarked Dr. Hassan, the government representative who had been sent to meet me. "We have to thank Begum Liaquat Ali Khan for that. Veils interfere with work, and every Pakistani works. And the Begum works hardest of all."

Apparently the airport officials had been tipped off that I was the guest of the government, a V.I.P. Long before one of our own government officials had started through the customs, my baggage and I had been whisked away like magic. In less than

35

ten minutes I was seated beside Dr. Hassan in a fine automobile, speeding across the desert toward the city.

"You will be staying at the Beach Luxury Hotel!" he said with a smile. "Nice cool sea breeze there. Better take a rest while you can. You're going to be a busy man, if all I hear is correct."

"From the look of things around here, I shan't be the only busy person." I laughed, pointing to swarms of workers, male and female, digging holes, sifting sand, mixing concrete, making bricks, erecting bamboo scaffolding, and carrying goatskins filled with drinking water for the sweating laborers. "What are they building?"

"Just another new apartment house. You'll see lots of them. Karachi is growing like a mushroom."

My companion then explained that the population of Karachi had grown from 400,000 in 1947 to about 1,250,000 in 1950.

"You date your progress from your revolution in 1776," he said. "We date ours from August 14, 1947, the date of the Partition of India."

Just then a camel cart passed us.

"First time I ever saw a camel gallop like that. What's the hurry?"

"He's just a Pakistani camel," chuckled Dr. Hassan.

I must have seen hundreds of camels working like mad. Most Pakistani camels are hairless and have black shiny hides.

"That's because the sea air doesn't agree with them," explained the doctor. "They have skin trouble, so their owners anoint them with oil."

You have to see a camel cart going full speed to believe it. As all four wheels have rubber tires and the camel's feet have cushions, the progress would be noiseless were it not for the

36

numerous little bells that are attached to the animal's anatomy.

A wag who was accustomed to the place before Partition once called Karachi a one-camel town. Nowadays it would be more aptly termed the "City of a Thousand Camels." But this doesn't mean that there are no other means of transportation. Karachi's traffic is about as heterogeneous as it is possible to imagine. Trucks, busses, taxis, donkey carts, droshkies, bullock carts, pushcarts, push bikes, motorcycles, and motorcars all compete with His Lordship the Camel. But unlike the great cities of India, there are no meandering holy cows to slow things up. Hustle and bustle are the order of the day in Karachi. Anybody who says that you cannot hurry the East just hasn't been in Pakistan.

Neighboring India is very different. Indians don't have to hurry, for at the time of Partition they inherited ready-made the very efficient Indian Civil Service with all its buildings, equipment, and highly trained personnel. While a minority of these civil servants were Moslems, the majority were Hindus, so that as far as government buildings, office equipment, and such important white-collar workers as clerks, typists, stenographers, and secretaries were concerned, Pakistan had to start from scratch. It is related that this new nation of eighty million people, the fifth largest nation in the world, had only one type-writer and one good typist. She was Begum Liaquat Ali Khan herself, one of whose first jobs was to teach stenography.

For months, during the organization of government, officials had to live in tents and use empty packing cases for tables and chairs. Nobody thought of hours of labor. Everybody, from the highest to the lowest, set to work willingly, following the example of their great leader, Mohammed Ali Jinnah, who worked himself into an early grave.

37

By the time I arrived at the Beach Luxury Hotel I realized that I was about to have an entirely new experience. I was to play my small part in the performance of the miracle of Pakistan.

Dr. Hassan had been right when he said that there would be a fine breeze. The moment I opened the door of my bedroom I was almost blown off my feet by the wind which came straight from the sea at the bottom of the hotel garden.

"Sahib would like luncheon?" inquired the bearer who had been assigned to look after me. "I will unpack Sahib's suitcase. Have you any clothes for the dhobi [washerman]?"

This courteous attention made me think of the old days of Singapore when servants called us "tuan" (master) and country people saluted Westerners with a smile instead of murdering them.

In Malaya, when we wanted service, we called "Boy." In Pakistan you call "Bearer." But there is no cringing or subservience before Westerners in Pakistan. The lowly Pakistani treats his superiors, regardless of race, with manly respect and in turn expects to be treated as a man.

Before taking his leave my friend Dr. Hassan said, "A car will be at your disposal day and night. You will find it parked outside the hotel."

When I looked out of my bedroom window I was delighted to see a lovely old English garden ablaze with hollyhocks. It was high tide, and the smell of the sea was mixed with the perfume of spices and flowers.

But at low tide, just as it had been in Singapore and Penang, the pleasant perfume changed to the characteristic stench which came from the mud flats. It took me back many years to the day when, as a young engineer, I had arrived in the Malay

38

Peninsula and saw my first tree-climbing fish scampering over the same kind of mud flats. Believe it or not, that characteristic stink of sulphureted hydrogen renewed my youth.

My bearer was a fine-looking man with a large black mustache. He told me that he had once looked after an English army officer in Peshawar, not far from the Khyber Pass. He certainly looked after me. He pressed my clothes, shined my shoes, turned down my bed, and brought me early-morning tea at 7 A.M. regularly. When or where he slept I never discovered. All I knew was that, regardless of the hour, if I called "Bearer" he appeared in a twinkling.

I didn't have to be told that the room clerk and hotel manager were Parsees. They were eternally working on their accounts and counting money.

"Sorry, sir. We do not cash checks," said the cashier.

"But," I expostulated, "this is an American Express Company's traveler's check."

"No checks! Only cash," he demurred.

I gave up. I don't believe those Parsees would have cashed a check for God. But I had forgotten. I was a guest of the Pakistan Government. I could sign all the chits I liked.

Luncheon was served in a lovely airy dining room to the strains of a quite passable orchestra. The food was excellent, but I passed up the salad and instead of water I drank lemonade made with imported soda water.

I had scarcely returned to my room for an afternoon siesta when there was a knock at the door and in walked a middle-aged American. He looked terribly distressed, pale as a ghost, and was obviously in pain. "I wonder if you can help me. I arrived here from Denver three days ago. I'm supposed to be doing a special job for the Pakistan Government, but I've had a

39

stomach-ache ever since I came. I don't even have time to go downstairs to the telephone. I think I'm going to die!"

It appeared that this was his first time out of the United States. No one had oriented him on how to keep well in the tropics. The night he arrived he had eaten salad and lots of delicious fruit, none of which should be eaten without being washed in permanganate of potash.

"Don't worry!" I reassured him with a smile. "Take a dose of this. You've got what most newcomers always get, 'Delhi Belly.'"

Taking from my well-worn medicine chest a small blue bottle which was labeled "Dr. Collis Brown's Chlorodyne," I gave my visitor twelve drops in a glass of water. Almost immediately his pain stopped. An hour later I gave him another dose and left him dozing blissfully.

That evening my friend from Denver came down to dinner with a broad grin on his face. "Never felt better in my life!" he said genially. "Why in hell didn't I get a bottle of that stuff in the States?"

"Because you cannot buy it there." I laughed. "It's dope. It's full of opium and other wonderful ingredients. Some people would swill the whole bottleful and die in their sleep."

I then gave him a few pointers on what to eat and drink if he wanted to keep well. I also gave him half my bottle of Chlorodyne, and he went his way rejoicing.

Some of my doctor readers will probably turn up their noses at Dr. Collis Brown's Magic Medicine. But as far as I'm concerned, I wouldn't dream of traveling in the tropics without it. It stops a headache, stomach-ache, or any other kind of ache. It is the tried and true friend of explorers ever since the days of David Livingstone. Just follow the directions on the bottle, and if it doesn't work, then your illness is serious enough to consult a doctor.

It was nine o'clock at night. I remembered my car. What could be better than a moonlight drive?

I went to the front of the hotel. There were several taxis waiting for business, but none offered themselves for hire. Instead, a fine new car rolled up, and out jumped a man wearing white baggy trousers. On his head he wore a Jinnah cap, which is the shape of a fez but made of karakul. It is the hallmark of all good Pakistanis.

"Have you been waiting for me since this morning?" I inquired apologetically.

"I work for my country," said the chauffeur proudly. "Unless you tell me, I shall be here always."

"Wonderful! I want to buy one of those hats you're wearing."

It was quite a long drive from the hotel to the downtown part of Karachi. As we passed the railroad yards I noticed that the sheds were packed to the eaves with sacks of wheat. Stacked in the open were immense piles of cotton, all baled with steel bands as they are in our South. Heavily laden camel carts were going and coming just as they had been at midday, but the construction work had stopped for the night and the streets were crowded with people laughing and chattering. Restaurants were doing a roaring business. Motion-picture theaters were brilliantly illuminated, and in the middle of one busy intersection was a revolving pedestal on which stood a shiny new American automobile. It was the latest-model Kaiser car.

Soon we stopped outside a small hat shop in which were displayed hundreds of Jinnah caps, some black, but most of them gray karakul.

I tried one on. "How much?"

"Thirty-five dollars American," said the shopkeeper in perfect English.

"Good God! You mean thirty-five rupees, don't you?"

"No, sir. Thirty-five dollars. This is genuine karakul."

I settled for an imitation karakul for which I paid six dollars, but I defy anyone but an expert to detect the difference.

Having donned my Jinnah cap, I re-entered the car.

"Drive to the grave of the Quaid-i-Azam," I said.

The chauffeur looked very pleased. I had evidently done the right thing.

"Here we are!" said the driver as we stopped before a large vacant lot in the middle of which a tent had been raised. Crowds of people were waiting patiently and reverently to enter. I took my place in the queue. No one took any particular notice of me.

Inside the tent the people passed by reverently. All that could be seen was a large blanket of fresh flowers which covered the grave of the man who is just as revered by the people of Pakistan as George Washington is by Americans.

As we drove back to the hotel that night I had to pinch myself to be sure that I wasn't dreaming. Three nights before I had been in New York. Last night I had had my dinner over Athens, yet here I was in Karachi, on the very threshold of Kashmir, waiting to meet the Prime Minister of the largest Moslem nation in the world, Pakistan.

Incidentally, the names Muslim, Moslem, and Mohammedan all mean the same thing, "belonging to the Faith of Islam and followers of the prophet Mohammed," but in the Indian subcontinent they are always known as Muslims.

Thanks to that lovely cool sea breeze, I slept like a top. At 7 A.M. I was awakened by my bearer, who placed beside the bed some tea, a couple of tiny but delicious bananas, and the morning paper. Said the leading editorial of the *Civil and Military Gazette:* "The eagerly awaited joint declaration by the Premiers of Pakistan and Bharat regarding measures to ensure security of minorities in both countries has unfortunately not been forthcoming."

"Bearer," I called, "where's Bharat?"

"India, sahib," he explained with a smile. "Same place."

It was then that I learned for the first time that the correct name of the neighboring dominion, as adopted in its new constitution, is the ancient name Bharat. "India" originated with the East India Company, and as it smacked of Britain, it was discarded. But the youthful Hindu nation quickly discovered that it had made a mistake. The whole world knew India. Nobody had ever heard of Bharat except a handful of Hindu intellectuals, so that every effort, except changing their constitution, is now made to retain the name India.

Pakistanis, who are blessed with a good sense of humor, take a delight in capitalizing on India's mistake and insist on speaking of Bharat. I searched that newspaper, but not once did I find the name India mentioned. However, in that one editorial alone, the name Bharat was used twelve times.

In the same newspaper it was announced that Liaquat Ali Khan was paying a visit to Nehru and was not expected back in Karachi for four days. But that did not mean a holiday for me. Oh no! Before I had finished breakfast I was called to the telephone. I was to have a conference with top officials to discuss the policy for the forthcoming visit to the United States of the Prime Minister. It was then decided that if the visit was to be a success it was essential that the people of America should be given all information possible on Pakistan, and that

43

the best way to accomplish this would be by means of motion pictures, television, radio, lectures, and the preparation of an attractive booklet which could be distributed in advance of the Prime Minister; a booklet which would be treasured by recipients as a souvenir of Liaquat's visit.

I knew now why I had been chosen for the job. I had produced several travel films, I had been in radio and television since the very beginning of both, and I had written fifteen books on foreign countries.

That I should be able to make a film of Karachi and write a fairly comprehensive book on Pakistan, both in a week, did not seem to be anything unusual to people who could perform such a miracle as the creation of a brand-new nation almost overnight.

"All I need is plenty of co-operation and not too many questions asked," I said as I popped on my Jinnah hat and took my leave.

"Go and see Mr. Ikram," said several voices simultaneously. "He can work wonders."

"Yes, sir. Mr. Ikram is expecting you," said a secretary when I entered some government offices a few minutes later.

Dressed in a spotless white linen suit and seated beneath a slowly revolving electric fan was Mr. Ikram, the wonder-worker.

Before I had finished telling him what I wanted he started using the half dozen telephones with which he was surrounded.

"Is that Mr. Douglas? . . . Mr. Ikram speaking. Mr. Carveth Wells is in my office. He is leaving for New York in one week. He will take with him a finished manuscript of a new booklet and a motion-picture film of Karachi. He will need the services of our historian, Mr. Rajput, our photographer, Mr. Barni, and

44

as many stenographers and assistants as required. Let everything else go. The matter is urgent."

In fifteen minutes I was in the office of Mr. Douglas. Rajput and Barni were already there. All three were young men. Douglas, as his name implies, was a Scot and sandy. But to judge from his accent, he had spent most if not all of his life in India. Rajput was a very quiet little man, an M.A., and an expert research worker. I afterward discovered that he was the author of a number of books. Modest to the nth degree, he never mentioned his authorship until he was saying good-by to me a week later, when he gave me one of his books, *Punjab Crisis and Cure,* which he had inscribed: "To Carveth Wells, the man whom I would like to make my intellectual master." He knew perfectly well that he could run rings around me when it came to intellect. Without his assistance I couldn't possibly have produced *Pakistan Today.*

Barni was the official photographer for the Pakistan Government.

A first-class cameraman who had made motion pictures in every part of Pakistan, he might easily have got his back up at being directed by a man who hadn't been in Karachi twenty-four hours yet had been commissioned to produce a film of his own home town. But Barni was a good sport. He knew what I wanted, and for the first time in his life he had all the Kodachrome film he wanted and didn't have to be economical with it. From morning until night he worked like a Trojan, usually all by himself, but occasionally with me to direct him.

The only time he really needed my assistance was when I wanted to photograph the Pakistan Navy. Cameras were not permitted inside the navy yard. I was with him when he tried to get past the guard at the gate. Leaving my camera behind,

I walked past the sentry toward a small shed on which I had seen painted: "Lieutenant Comm. England, R.N."

I found the officer seated at a desk. He was dressed in white shorts and beside him was a tall glass of liquid refreshment.

Having introduced myself and stated my business, before he could say "No!" I inquired brightly, "Oh, by the way, d'you happen to know any Garnetts in the Royal Navy?"

"Did you say Garnett? Of course I know the Garnetts. Fine naval family, the Garnetts."

"Teddy Garnett married my daughter," I replied.

The English ice was broken. Garnett proved to be the password for taking motion pictures of one of the smallest navies in the world. Only about six ships, it is true, but they were armed with the very latest weapons and manned by sailors who were just as smart and snappy as Britannia's finest.

"Make yourself at home!" said my new-found friend. "Take all the pictures you like, there's practically the whole Navy. The *Pipu Sultan*, the *Tariq*, the *Shamsher*, and a motor torpedo boat." Then, handing me the same kind of telescope that Nelson probably used at the Battle of Trafalgar, he said, "You can read their names. The two big ones are destroyers. The *Tariq* is a frigate, and the torpedo boat is No. H.D.M.L. 1266. Sorry I cannot go with you, but stick up your cameras anyplace you wish."

Beckoning to Barni to come in with all our equipment, we were about to take the Navy by storm when suddenly a motor launch drew alongside the wharf where we were standing and out jumped an English naval officer who might have passed for old man Neptune himself, except that he was wearing shorts. A giant of a man with a long beard and a barrel-like chest covered with black hair, he strode toward us.

"I say! What the devil are you doing with those cameras?"

"I was just about to photograph your Navy. I have permission."

Before he could explode again I used the password.

"D'you know any naval chaps named Garnett?"

Neptune's manner changed instantly. "Good God, man. Of course I know the whole family. I knew Teddy and Jimmie in Bermuda."

By this time a lady had disembarked from the launch and joined us. "Meet my wife, Mrs. Maud. I'm Captain Colin Maud. I teach these blighters how to shoot."

Mrs. Maud, rather pale but pretty, was wearing a white linen dress and carried a parasol.

"May I give your wife a present?" I inquired, taking from my pocket a cellophane envelope containing three pairs of the finest-quality nylon stockings. "I bought them for the Begum, but I find that protocol forbids a gentleman giving stockings to the wife of a prime minister. I've been wondering what on earth to do with them."

"Is it all right, darling?" inquired Mrs. Maud hopefully. "I haven't a decent pair of nylons to my name."

We all burst out laughing as I handed over the gift which I had intended to present to another.

"Damned extraordinary, the whole thing," chuckled Neptune. "Trespassers, movies, Garnetts, and silk stockings. Take all the pictures you like. I'm going to have a drink!"

Leaving Barni to his movies, I hurried back to the Beach Luxury Hotel, where I found my bedroom converted into an office. Squatting on the floor was a stenographer, and beside him Rajput, the historian, working like mad. Work had already started on *Pakistan Today*. It was already Tuesday. I had five

47

more days to finish the job before submitting the manuscript to Mr. Ikram.

To judge from the piles of manuscript beside him, Rajput had enough material for an encyclopedia on Pakistan. All I had to do was edit, Americanize it, and try to make it interesting as well as informative.

Day and night we stuck to the job. Meals were served in the room and coffee was consumed by the gallon.

Meanwhile Douglas was accumulating mountains of photographs for the illustrations. From more than a thousand I selected fifty for the text and twelve for a montage for the cover.

How many different government departments were engaged in keeping me supplied with material I have no idea, but there were plenty.

I certainly blessed the day I was taught précis writing at college, although at the time I used to wonder what possible use there could be for me, an engineer, to learn how to condense some government report covering fifty pages into one or two pages without ruining it.

Précis writing is just the opposite of ordinary writing. A novelist will take a plot and expand it into a book. A good précis writer can take such a book and after a rapid scanning of its contents extract the plot and tell the essential story in a few paragraphs.

In between bouts of dictating I would take my camera and take motion pictures. It helped to drive away the cobwebs.

One afternoon I decided to get some pictures of Government House and its lovely sunken garden. Except for the sentries at the gate, there didn't appear to be anyone around, so I strode across the velvety lawn, set up my tripod, and was in the act of photographing when a voice behind me said, "Can I be of any assistance?"

Turning, I saw a rather portly gentleman with a broad smile on his face. He was dressed in tightly fitting white trousers and a long white coat that reached to his knees.

"I hope I'm not intruding, but I'm very anxious to get some good pictures of the governor general's house and grounds," I explained. "He must be quite a gardener."

"I am the governor general! I should be most happy to show you around."

Instantly my thoughts flew back more than twenty years to Sweden.

The scene was the cathedral at Uppsala. I was taking a photograph when a voice behind me said, "Can I be of any assistance?"

Without looking up I said jokingly, "Yes. Get me an introduction to the archbishop."

"I am Archbishop Soderblom! I should be most happy to show you the cathedral!"

Both men had used exactly the same words. Both were extremely democratic, and both had the same faculty of putting a person at ease with their courtly manners and graciousness. Neither was a "stuffed shirt."

So it happened that with His Excellency Al-Haj Khwaja Nazimuddin,* governor general of Pakistan, as my guide I

---

*Within a few hours of the death of Liaquat Ali Khan, a meeting of the Cabinet was held at which it was decided that His Excellency Khwaja Nazimuddin would become Prime Minister, thus demonstrating the strength of Pakistan's organization as a democracy.

Prime Minister Khwaja Nazimuddin was educated at Cambridge University. He entered politics when he was twenty-eight and has held important government positions ever since. Before the Partition of India he was Minister of Education in Bengal. He was also a member of the Indian Food Delegation to the United States and represented India at the last session of the League of Nations held in Geneva in 1946. A devout Moslem, he performed the pilgrimage to Mecca in 1936.

At the same meeting Pakistan's Finance Minister, the Honorable Mr. Ghulam Mohammed was chosen to become Pakistan's third governor general.

toured the grounds of one of the most impressive mansions in Asia.

When I took my leave the governor turned to me and said cordially, "My niece is to be married here next Sunday. You may expect an invitation. Better bring your camera. It will be a colorful ceremony."

That evening when I returned to the hotel I saw in the lobby the familiar flag of the Rotary Club, which was to meet in the main dining room that night.

The last time I had attended a Rotary Club meeting in Asia had been in Tokyo before Pearl Harbor, when Dale Carnegie had been announced as the speaker of the day. Unfortunately Dale didn't turn up then and I had to substitute for him. That was one time when the absent-minded author of *How to Win Friends and Influence People* forgot to practice what he preached. He'll never forget Tokyo, nor will the Tokyo Rotary Club forget Dale.

When I went up to my bedroom Rajput and the stenographer were still working feverishly. But there was no talk of stopping. Instead, Rajput unpacked his little night case and donned a pair of extraordinarily shaped pajamas which must have been far more comfortable than they looked.

"Only four more chapters! I think we'll make the deadline!" he said cheerfully.

The Karachi Rotary Club meets at night. Instead of the usual luncheon, they stage a very impressive dinner. Evening dress, while not compulsory, is customary, and as the members bring their ladies, all wearing their prettiest dresses, it is quite a gala occasion.

A few of the men wore tuxedos, but most wore Pakistani dress, consisting of white baggy trousers and long, tight-fitting black coats with high collars. Many of the women wore Indian saris, but more wore Pakistani dress, so that the variety and color of their trousers were remarkable. None was veiled, and I was told that a good many of the younger women were expert rifleshots, being members of the Women's National Guard.

Without a doubt, Pakistani women are among the prettiest I have ever seen. Many have milky-white complexions and beautiful slender hands that would be the envy of any Hollywood star. Yet before Partition most, if not all, of these girls had been kept in strict seclusion.

As I had been asked to make a speech, I decided that the best subject I could choose would be "American women as compared with the women of Pakistan." I think they must have been expecting some sort of propaganda speech about the necessity of friendship between America and Pakistan. So when I started describing my impressions of Pakistani girls, a subject that presumably was usually taboo at such public gatherings, at first they appeared shocked and then they burst into delighted laughter as they saw themselves as others see them.

After the meeting was over there was dancing. Whether it was so or not, I could not determine, but it looked to me as if the girls danced only with the men who had brought them. There were several with whom I would have liked to dance the light fantastic, but I didn't have the courage to ask them and nobody offered to introduce me. Besides, there were those fierce-looking six-foot husky Pakistanis with curly black mustaches who stood around the dance floor watching. They made me think of my Chautauqua days in Utah, when open-air dancing always followed my lectures in the tent. Only once did I attempt to dance with one of those pretty Utah blondes. She was willing, but before we got halfway round the dance floor a husky Mormon tapped me on the shoulder. "Are you a Mormon boy?" he inquired rather menacingly. "No? Then you'd better get off the floor."

"Who's that fellow?" I asked.

"He's a bishop. He watches the girls!" I was told.

When I got to my room Barni, the official photographer, was waiting for me with the news that Liaquat Ali Khan had returned from his meeting with Nehru and had invited me to attend and photograph a meeting of the Cabinet in the morning. "*Life* magazine's photographer will be there," said Barni. "We can use his lights."

The Lord had his arms around me. Things were happening fast.

I had met the governor general and been invited to his niece's wedding. Now I was going to meet the Prime Minister and his Cabinet and be permitted to take movies. But I still hadn't met Begum Liaquat Ali Khan, nor had I been invited to meet the Prime Minister *en famille*.

As that was the main purpose of my going to Karachi, I decided to broach the matter at the cabinet meeting. I was anxious to deliver those presents, the Kodachromes of America, the plastic bottles, and, above all, the steam engine.

CHAPTER THREE

The meetings of Pakistan's Cabinet are held in the private residence of the Prime Minister. I had been tipped off to arrive ahead of the ministers so that I could have a few minutes' conversation with the man whom Jinnah had called "my right hand." As I entered the house at 10 A.M. the sentries snapped smartly to attention. It must have been my jaunty Jinnah cap that did it.

Liaquat (pronounced Lee-ah-kut) himself met me at the door. He couldn't have been more gracious. I knew immediately that he would make a hit in the United States. Tall, clean-shaven, rather thickset, dressed in a well-cut blue pin-stripe suit, smoking a cigarette and wearing old-fashioned round-lensed spectacles, the Prime Minister bore a striking resemblance to another man of dynamic energy, Henry Kaiser.

Descended from a long line of rulers, one of whom was a Persian king, Liaquat Ali Khan bore a royal title. But he had long since dropped that as being unsuited to the Prime Minister of a country dedicated to democratic principles. An Oxford graduate, Liaquat spoke beautiful English and had a vocabulary that was the envy of many an Englishman. But when he toured Pakistan, as he constantly did, he spoke Urdu, which is the language understood by the masses of his country.

It would be difficult to imagine two more dissimilar characters than Liaquat the Moslem and Nehru the Hindu; Liaquat, a chain-smoking, hardheaded businessman who liked his roast beef rare, and Nehru, a mystic, a master politician who wouldn't touch a tenderloin steak with the end of a barge pole. About the only characteristic Liaquat.had in common with Nehru was

53

that he was not a "holy man," yet, like Nehru, was the idol of his followers.

Looking at Liaquat Ali Khan, you wouldn't dream that he was the kind of man who could cope with the catastrophe which occurred in 1947 immediately after Partition, when about seven million Moslems who lived in India suddenly abandoned their homes and property and set out for Pakistan, while approximately five million Hindus and Sikhs who lived in what is now Pakistan pulled up stakes and set out for the land of their people.

Liaquat had a telling way of describing what happened to his country in its birth pangs: "It's just as though seven million New Yorkers—switchboard operators, lawyers, doctors, nurses, and subway employees—were moved out and replaced by the same number of farmers from upstate New York and Pennsylvania."

Liaquat himself was one of the refugees. He told me that when he left New Delhi for West Pakistan all he had was a bundle of rugs.

When he reached Lahore, great areas scarred by burning rubble were surrounded by the primitive encampments of the moving masses of refugees. Hundreds of thousands were wounded or sick. Then, to add to the general misery, cholera broke out. Hospitals were jammed; there were very few doctors and scarcely any nurses. At that time the nursing profession was not regarded as suitable for young girls of gentle families, much less the daughters of the wealthy, whose lives were even more sheltered.

It was then that Begum Liaquat Ali Khan made her nationwide appeal for Moslem girls of good family and education to volunteer without delay for training. Old prejudices and customs were swept away, with the result that untold lives were saved and the women of Pakistan suddenly emerged to take their place in the social and political framework of the newborn nation.

Meanwhile, Jinnah, the "Great Leader," having selected the once despised town of Karachi to be the nation's capital, sent Liaquat to do the job and organize a government. Men and women from all parts of the country were called upon to become officers in it. They arrived by plane, train, and boat, many of them at the risk of their lives. At first they established themselves either in tents or crude huts, which they shared with the crows that nested in the roofs. Worktables bought in the bazaar were their desks, empty boxes their chairs, but they carried on zealously. "Sufficient unto the day is the evil thereof" was their motto.

Today those same officials are housed in fine public buildings and provided with the very latest equipment and comfortable furniture.

A reporter once asked Liaquat, "What do you do for recreation?" "I do some different kind of work!" replied the Prime Minister.

Just before ten-thirty the different members of the Cabinet began to arrive, so Barni and I took up our positions with our cameras in an alcove which was directly opposite the chair which the Prime Minister would occupy. Blessings on the photographer from *Life* magazine, for had it not been for his battery of powerful electric lights, photography would have been out of the question.

As far as I can remember, there were fourteen men present. One notable absentee was Sir Mohammed Zafrullah Khan, Minister of Foreign Affairs, whose face is well known to America's television audiences as Pakistan's champion in the Kashmir dispute before the United Nations.

The only non-Moslem member of the Cabinet was Mr. J. N. Mandal, Minister of Law and Labor, who, in the days before Partition, was president in Bengal of Dr. Ambedkar's Scheduled Castes Federation. Like his famous leader, Dr. Ambedkar, who was a member of Nehru's Cabinet, Mr. Mandal is an "untouchable." He was the only one dressed à la Gandhi. The rest were in ordinary business suits or Pakistani dress, consisting of white trousers and smart knee-length black coats known as "sherwanis."

Having seated themselves at a long table with the Prime Minister in the middle on one side, the ministers spent five minutes in animated conversation and banter while we photographed them. They were all good actors, and as this was a historic occasion, Pakistan's debut in the March of Time, they put on an excellent show. Then, at a nod from Liaquat Ali Khan, we withdrew and left them to proceed with more important matters of state, presumably a report on Liaquat's conferences with Nehru.

As I was leaving the house Liaquat's private secretary informed me that I was expected to spend the morning and have luncheon with the family the following Sunday.

They were certainly early risers, for when I reached the house at 10 A.M., expecting to look over the situation with a view to selecting the most suitable locations for colored photography, they were all waiting on the veranda. Liaquat was dressed as usual in European clothes, dark blue suit, black karakul Jinnah cap, and one of the flashiest neckties I have ever seen. Collecting flashy ties and cigarette lighters were his hobbies, and with regard to the lighters, it was said that it was quite useless to give the Prime Minister one because he owned every kind that had ever been invented.

Begum Liaquat Ali Khan, a very pretty woman, was seated on a divan with her two sons on either side of her. The two boys, Ashraf, aged twelve and Akbar, aged eight, wore pale blue shorts with shirts and socks to match. I noticed that they rolled their socks down to the tops of their black oxford shoes. Both were sturdy young chaps with excellent manners and unquestionably obedient to their parents. It was quite refreshing to observe that neither of them was "fresh." They made me think of Swedish boys. They bowed when they shook hands and, except when I produced the steam engine, were very formal and spoke only when spoken to.

Begum Liaquat was exquisitely gowned in coral-fuchsia silk. She wore a very full divided skirt that reached so low that her feet were invisible except when she lifted it to walk. The top part of her dress was a kind of loose jumper that almost reached her knees, and over her head she wore a silk scarf with a gold-embroidered edge.

Her only jewelry consisted of earrings. These were of native gold, fan-shaped with little gold tassels. From the lobes of her ears they fanned out until they touched her shoulders and must have been about five inches long. I also noticed that her black eyebrows were beautifully arched, her cupid-bowed mouth, lipsticked, turned up at the corners, and that she had dimples. Her hands were small and expertly manicured. Altogether she was a most attractive personality, with a gay and gracious manner that I knew at once would make a hit in America.

"Be sure you wear trousers when you go to the States," I said laughingly, "and let the newspapermen take all the pictures they want."

"Be sure you explain that my husband is not Aly Khan and

57

that he is not related to the Aga Khan," she said with a chuckle.

That put us all at our ease, and from then on we talked and laughed like old friends.

I then produced the set of plastic bottles and jars which Zetta had sent her. She had never seen such things before and was delighted when she found that they were flexible.

"I shall certainly take these to America. They will be most useful."

Then I presented the set of Kodachromes and the viewer to Liaquat and showed him how to use it. Instead of just accepting the gift and putting it aside as I had expected, nothing would do but for the whole family to look at those lovely views of America's wonderlands.

I wish our Director of National Parks could have heard the ohs and ahs as they gazed enraptured at the beauties of Yosemite and Grand Canyon.

As there was only one viewer and four people to use it, about an hour was taken up just getting the preview of what was in store for them when they arrived in the United States.

But the climax of the morning was reached when I produced the steam engine. Never have I seen a couple of boys so thrilled. As I had foreseen, the thing they liked best of all was the engine's firebox and the little spirit lamp that was to provide the fire.

"Let's start it at once!" they exclaimed eagerly.

"You think of everything," laughed the Prime Minister when I produced a bottle of methylated spirits.

No more interview! No photographs! They could wait while the boiler was filled with water and the furnace lighted!

Then Ashraf carried the engine, which was already hissing and eager to go, to the far corner of the veranda, where a manservant took the boys in tow. Did Liaquat Ali Khan now settle down to discuss his forthcoming visit to America? He did not. He went along with the boys. He wanted to run the engine himself. This gave me a few minutes with the Begum.

"Wear your prettiest dresses. Take along lots of different kinds and colors. Always wear Pakistani dress. Knock their eyes out!" I advised. And that is exactly what Begum Liaquat Ali Khan did.

Fortunately she is not the beautiful-but-dumb type. Socially she is very vivacious and an excellent conversationalist. On the platform, before a mike and television, she proved to be quite professional in her performance.

This is not at all surprising when you know her background.

Her early childhood was spent at Almora and Naini Tal, two little hill stations in the lofty Himalayas. Her mother recalls her as a restless child, intelligent, sharp-witted, always ready to lead her three sisters and five brothers into some childish mischief. In America she would have been known as a tomboy. Hard to manage at school, nevertheless she graduated with honors with an M.A. in economics and sociology. In 1933 she married Liaquat Ali Khan, who then used his title Nawabzada; more familiarly, Nabob. His constant companion and helpmate, she realized that he needed a good secretary, so she learned to typewrite.

During the tragedy that followed Partition, when more than seven million refugees swarmed into Pakistan, many of them diseased and dying, she left her home and two sick boys in Karachi and proceeded again to Lahore, where she made her famous appeal for nurses. Every night she drove a truck touring the streets and bylanes of that crowded city, tending the sick, distributing food and clothing, and talking personally to those who, after frightful sufferings, had reached their "Land of Hope."

But she realized that relief was not the only necessity. The women of Pakistan had to be trained in physical fitness and methods of defense. They must be taught how to shoot as well as care for the wounded. It was then that she organized the Pakistan Women's National Guard, in which she now holds the rank of brigadier.

Then, very much as Molly Huggins, the wife of the governor, organized the women of Jamaica, Begum Liaquat Ali Khan founded the All-Pakistan Women's Association, which is open to all women regardless of caste, creed, or color. Entirely non-political, this organization has for its aim the social, educational, and cultural uplift of women. It is affiliated with the Federation of Women's Clubs of America.

It was the Begum who arranged for the visit and panel discussion with the women members of the Town Hall of America when that organization made its round-the-world tour.

Thanks to the Begum, there has been a great revival in the indigenous cottage industries of Pakistan, so that now there is a Cottage Industries Emporium in Karachi where tourists can purchase a large variety of beautiful work, from silver to scarves.

Yet with all her public duties Begum Liaquat found time to raise a family and maintain a very happy home. A talented musician herself, she sees to it that her sons study the piano and violin. Her hobby is gardening, and her favorite reading consists of biographies and autobiographies.

Stories of her spirit, her energy and vivacity have become legendary in Pakistan. When the American Ambassador was solemnly presenting the Prime Minister with President Truman's invitation to visit the United States, Liaquat, burly and inclined to be phlegmatic, was accepting it with equal solemnity. But not the Begum. To her such a visit represented one of the great experiences of her life. A pace or two behind her husband, she was literally dancing up and down, her eyes sparkling with excitement, when in a stage whisper she said to him, "Oh, do show some enthusiasm! Show some enthusiasm!"

But he didn't need to. The Begum had enough for both.

Having started the steam engine himself and watched it work, Liaquat left the boys to their own devices and rejoined us. Leaving the Begum on the veranda, where she could keep an eye on her boys, Liaquat and I strolled together through the house. Unfurnished when the family first occupied it, the Prime Minister's mansion, thanks to gifts which arrived from all parts of the Moslem world, was not only beautifully furnished but filled with priceless works of art, many of them treasures that the Metropolitan Museum of Art would be proud to own. But every now and then as I expressed my admiration of some particularly lovely object, Liaquat would say wistfully, "I managed to salvage some of my best rugs, but most of my household possessions had to be left behind."

He then explained that at the time of Partition most of the prominent Moslem families gathered together just what personal belongings they could carry and migrated to Pakistan. Houses that they had been occupying since the days of the Moguls, lavishly furnished and filled with treasures, were quickly abandoned. But they were abandoned gladly, for to them, what was more precious than any earthly possession was the knowledge that their beloved Quaid-i-Azam, Mohammed Ali Jinnah, had succeeded in securing the two large areas of northern India in which they were to be free and independent, and where they could help in the work of founding what has since become the largest Moslem nation in the world.

"These carpets we are walking on," said Liaquat, "are at least fifty years old, and they have been walked upon by thousands of people, many of whom were not too careful, yet they look like new!"

Noticing that I was admiring a very large carpet which adorned one of the walls of the drawing room, Liaquat explained, "The Shah of Iran gave that to me on his recent visit to Pakistan. It is much too beautiful to place on the floor." About ten feet wide and twenty feet long, the carpet was by far the most exquisite example of weaving that I had ever seen. "Look at the back," said Liaquat. "That is almost as beautiful as the front." I was afterward informed by an expert that this one carpet alone was worth at least thirty thousand dollars.

"I bet I know what hurt most to leave behind," I said.

Liaquat read my thoughts at once. "Ah yes, the Taj Mahal! I hope they take care of it."

Luncheon was served in the dining room, with Liaquat and the Begum at opposite ends of the table, the two boys on one side, and Mr. Mohammed Ali, secretary general of Pakistan, and I on the other.

"I see you know one another," said the Prime Minister as Mohammed Ali and I greeted each other cordially. I had met him only a week before in New York. Like Sir Zafrullah Khan, Mohammed Ali commutes between New York and Karachi.

"I hope you like Pakistani food," said the Begum. "Everything on the table was produced here. We are fond of pilau."

A pilau is a favorite dish with Moslems, especially Persians. According to the dictionary, a pilau is a mixture of boiled rice, raisins, spices, and some kind of meat or fowl. However, there is nothing mushy about a pilau. Each grain of rice is separate, and as it is always colored with some kind of spice, a pilau is pretty to look at as well as delicious to taste.

My Cornish upbringing caused me to recognize immediately the taste and color of saffron.

"How about the saffron? Do you grow that here too?"

"Certainly," replied the Begum. "It comes from Kashmir, and so does all this fruit," indicating a huge bowl of mixed fruit.

Few people who use saffron know what this precious spice is or how it is made. The saffron plant looks very much like a crocus. It is grown in large quantities on some of the plateaus of Kashmir. When in blossom, the large areas of mauve and purple color add a strikingly beautiful effect to an already beautiful landscape. The flowers are dried in the sun, and the pollen is extracted by hand. It is this pollen and the pollen-bearing portion of the blossom which constitute the saffron of commerce, often selling for as much as seventy-five dollars a pound. When mixed with water it forms a rich yellow dye. Kashmir's saffron is famous for its bouquet and is used not only as a spice but also as a pigment for the forehead marks of Hindus. Buddhist monks dye their robes with it.

Luncheon over, we adjourned to the veranda for coffee and the serious business of photography. To break the tension that so often exists when a posed portrait is to be taken, I produced the flag of the Explorers Club and explained that this was the flag that Admiral Peary had planted at the North Pole. Then, as I told them of the different places where I myself had carried the flag, they plied me with questions. I couldn't have asked for a better audience as I mentioned the countries and the strange people and animals I had encountered during my travels. The two boys, Ashraf and Akbar, listened wide-eyed

63

to my stories of Red Indians, Eskimos, Lapps, Hairy Ainus, Giants, and Pygmies. Meanwhile Liaquat puffed cigarettes and Barni took candid pictures with his Contax.

For the motion pictures the Begum chose a corner of her garden where a very lovely flowering vine made a perfect background. There the family stood while I directed them.

"More action, please. Begum, please pick a flower and hand it to Akbar," I shouted. I had no idea that the particular blossom which the Begum hastily chose was inhabited by a nest of pepper ants. Disturbed by this unwarranted intrusion of their privacy, the ants swarmed over Akbar, biting and stinging.

"That's wonderful!" I shouted. "Don't move out of the picture."

Poor Akbar was jumping about madly, but he stuck to his ground while his brother Ashraf swatted the ants, only to get them all over his own clothes. Then the Begum tried brushing the furious insects away, getting bitten herself in the process. Meanwhile Liaquat roared with laughter until a wandering pepper ant found its mark and started the Prime Minister swatting with the rest of them. It made a good movie.

"You asked for action," laughed the Begum. "You certainly got it."

When I looked at my watch it was three o'clock. I had been with the family five hours, and there hadn't been a dull moment.

"I suppose you're going to the wedding," said Liaquat as I bade them good-by. "I trust there won't be any pepper ants at Government House."

The guests were already arriving when I reached there. The lawn which had been deserted when I had been surprised by the governor general was now covered with hundreds of tables in readiness for more than a thousand people. There must have been at least a hundred waiters all dressed in spotless white with scarlet sashes and scarlet-and-gold turbans. A maître d'hôtel was rushing about inspecting the tables and ordering the waiters to cover the food with white cloths which would be removed as soon as the wedding ceremony was over.

At one side of the lawn was a raised dais about ten feet square on which were two chairs and a microphone on which was the name "ANSARI," presumably the name of the broadcasting company.

By special permission I was allowed to place my camera within ten feet of the dais, so that I had a wonderful view of the proceedings. It was a lovely afternoon, with a fresh cool breeze blowing that caused the flag over Government House to fly out straight from the flagstaff, much to the delight of about a dozen mynah birds which took turns trying to perch on the edge of the fluttering flag. Every now and then one of the birds succeeded, a difficult feat that was greeted by much appreciative squawking and chattering from its companions.

The time for the actual ceremony to take place was five-fifteen, but by five o'clock the lawn was packed with the elite of Pakistan as well as the entire diplomatic corps with their ladies. The only unaccompanied male that I noticed was the Ambassador from Saudi Arabia.

I felt sorry for the European diplomats in their striped trousers, frock coats, and top hats. They were hot and they looked it.

A more colorful crowd it would be hard to imagine. Every rainbow hue was represented in the dress of hundreds of gorgeously gowned women, many of whom wore jewels that sparkled and glittered in the setting sun. Except for the European ladies, not one of the guests wore an ordinary skirt. Divided skirts or tightly fitting pajamas were the order of the day, although there were quite a number of very beautiful saris, which are more commonly worn by the women of East Pakistan than those of the West.

By five-fifteen everyone was seated at the tables when a sudden hush came over the crowd. It made me think of the two-minute silence on Armistice Day. The quiet was so profound that the rippling of the flag could be heard distinctly. Suddenly the sound of bagpipes filled the air as Pakistan's famous regimental band of pipes and drums marched onto the lawn. Led by a giant drum major who strutted and tossed his glittering baton high into the air, those Pakistani pipers would have warmed the heart of the coldest Highlander. I've seen many a parade of Shriners, but few were so smart and snappy as this one.

An American crowd would have gone wild at such an exhibition of marching and playing. Yet in Pakistan the people are so accustomed to it that it is not considered unusual at all. It wasn't the band that the guests were interested in, but the man who was walking by himself behind it, followed by about fifty people, men, women, and children. It was the bridegroom and his relatives.

Tall, slim, and handsome, he was dressed in tightly fitting white satin trousers and a three-quarter-length white coat. On his head he wore a pale blue turban with long streamers behind. Around his neck were several long necklaces of bejeweled flowers.

Smiling and nodding to his friends, the bridegroom walked to the dais, where he took his seat in the very center. To one side sat an elderly gentleman, the most respected elder of the Moslem community, who was to pronounce his blessing and orate on the sanctity and duties of marriage.

"Where's the bride?" I whispered to Barni.

"Five miles away!" he answered.

Meanwhile the bridegroom was engaged in conversation with three gentlemen, who handed him a document to sign.

"That is the marriage contract," explained Barni. "One of the men is a lawyer and the others are the witnesses."

Put in a nutshell, the gist of the conversation between the bridegroom and the lawyer was as follows:

"We have just interviewed Miss So-and-So, who has expressed her willingness to accept you as her husband. Are you willing to marry her?"

"I am," said the bridegroom, who thereupon signed on the dotted line.

The wedding ceremony was over. It didn't take three minutes. Nothing religious about it. Just a straightforward contract, signed and sealed in the presence of witnesses.

Looking very pleased with himself, the bridegroom crossed his knees and looked over the assemblage, as much as to say, "It's My Day."

For the next five minutes the elderly Moslem recited by heart long passages from the Koran that dealt with the sanctity of marriage, while the guests bowed their heads in silent attention. The moment he stopped speaking everyone looked up, smiling. The tables were uncovered and the refreshments were served.

As for the bridegroom, I saw him walking rapidly toward his waiting automobile. The chauffeur stepped on the gas and he was gone.

"I suppose he is hurrying off to claim his bride!"

"Oh no," said Barni, "he's going to a big stag party first."

"What about the bride?" I asked.

"She's giving a big party herself tonight, but it's for women only."

He then explained that sometime during the evening the bridegroom, having taken leave of his men friends, would go to the bride's party to claim his wife and take her home with him.

It was dark by the time I got back to the Beach Luxury Hotel. Rajput, the historian, and his stenographer were still working on the booklet *Pakistan Today*.

"How's she coming?" I asked hopefully.

"Almost finished." Then with a worried look Rajput added, "But we need a little more color in the chapter on the women of Pakistan."

"Damn it," I said, "if only they'd let me go to that party the bride is giving tonight I'd be able to write something colorful firsthand."

"Not a chance in the world," laughed Rajput, "unless you can disguise yourself as a little boy. Ten years is the age limit for males at that party."

There was a knock at the door. It was my bearer with a note from Government House. "If Mr. Carveth Wells will be ready, a car will call for him at eight o'clock to take him to the bride's party."

"What luck! I'm going to the party!"

"Don't be too sure," said Rajput. "Those women will tear you to pieces if they catch you. Better wear your Jinnah cap."

I had just fifteen minutes to change my clothes. The car was waiting: a shiny new limousine with drawn blinds.

68

In I hopped beside a strange man.

"The governor general has arranged for you to attend the bride's party tonight. But I must warn you not to make yourself conspicuous in any way. You must keep moving. Stay in the shadows and be sure to keep close to me. The police are expecting us, but that will only get us into the garden."

Talk about being excited, my heart must have been beating as fast as the bridegroom's as we arrived at the gates of a large private house which was illuminated with colored lights. Hundreds of people were crowded around the entrance trying to get a glimpse of the goings-on within. The car stopped. A policeman opened the door, looked us over, saluted, and told us to drive in.

"Now let's stand behind these bushes," said my companion. "Ask me if you want anything explained."

"Where's the bride?"

"Upstairs where you see that window. She is being dressed by her relatives. It will be a couple of hours before she comes down."

"Who are those women?" indicating six stalwarts, all dressed in bright colors, who had stationed themselves at the gate where we had just entered.

"I think you would call them chucker-outers." He grinned. "Good thing we got here first. Their job is to keep men out."

Apparently part of the fun was for men friends of the bridegroom to try to crash the gate. Even as we watched, a car drove up and two well-dressed gentlemen stepped out. But they didn't get very far before the women seized them and amid screams and laughter hustled them out of the garden and outside the gate.

Then a band started playing as the women guests began to arrive.

"You will notice that we cannot see the band, nor can the band see what's going on," explained my friend.

If you can imagine the kind of party a wealthy young American girl would throw for her girl friends on the night before her marriage, then you will know what this one was like. Almost all were young debutantes wearing their most beautiful clothes. Occasionally I saw an elderly lady, but not often. A Hollywood scout would have gone crazy if he could have seen what I did. Talk about glamour girls! These Pakistan ones were beauties. Any one of them would have made the cover of *Life*, not to mention a whole succession of pin-up girls for the pages in *Esquire*.

Every style of Moslem dress was to be seen, as well as a few saris. But generally speaking, trousers held sway. Some were skin-tight from ankles to well above the knees. Others were just like men's trousers. Some were tight around the ankles but baggy from there up. Others were so wide and baggy that they are best described as divided skirts. Most of the girls wore elaborately decorated sandals that showed their pretty feet and brightly colored toenails. None was barefoot and none was veiled.

On they came, laughing and chattering as they made their way past the house and into the garden beyond. In my enthusiasm I must have stepped out too far from the shadows, for one of the girls gave a scream and pointed in my direction.

"Hurry, we must get out of here. Follow me."

Like a couple of prowlers, we dashed around the house into the darkness beyond. Along came the chucker-outers, screaming and laughing as they searched the bushes. But they missed us. Then two little boys spotted us and were about to rush off and give the game away when my companion shouted to them in Urdu. What he said I don't know, but the effect was magical. The boys joined us and remained with us for the rest of the evening.

From where I stood I could see the garden beautifully. At one end of a very long lawn was a raised platform in front of which were rows of folding chairs, at least five hundred. Behind the back row of chairs was a large expanse of lawn on which were set long wooden tables loaded with good things to eat.

Surrounding the whole lawn were bushes and tall trees, all of them decorated with colored lights very much like Christmas trees. But in addition to the lights, long streamers of colored silks and brocades hung from the branches. By ten o'clock every seat was occupied, the chattering died down, and all heads turned toward the house.

"Come on! The bridegroom is about to arrive. Let's get back to the gate!"

Just in the nick of time we arrived to see his limousine stopped by the policeman. Up rushed the chucker-outers. Okay, let him in. But this time the bridegroom had no bagpipe band to precede him. His was anything but the triumphant entrance we had seen that afternoon. Instead he was just a lone male in the midst of a shouting crowd of females. He was still dressed in his white satin suit and magnificent turban, but because of a thick veil of flowers reaching down to his feet he couldn't see, and stumbled as he felt his way out of the limousine. All this was part of the game. He was not supposed to see anything or anybody until he looked at the face of his bride.

71

She was still in her room, where she was being appraised by the bridegroom's female relatives.

A dozen hands helped the wretched man from the car and guided his feet as he literally groped his way past the assembled crowd of girls to the platform. Instead of martial music and the beating of drums, good-natured jeers and laughter greeted him as he stumbled up to the platform and squatted on the carpet. Six of the bride's friends helped him and arranged his veil so that he couldn't possibly see what was going on.

For the next thirty minutes the bridegroom had to listen while the girls made humorously sarcastic remarks about him and his vaunted manhood. From the roars of laughter that greeted some of the remarks, I gathered that they were anything but ladylike.

Of course the whole thing was done in fun, the object being to let him know that as a man he wasn't such hot stuff as he thought he was. The groom having been thoroughly humbled, it was now time for the bride to make her appearance.

She, too, was completely veiled and had to be guided by six of her friends as she walked and stumbled along. As she neared the platform she had to be practically carried until she, too, was squatting on the carpet beside her husband. Then four of the women held a large cloth over the couple and at a given signal they allowed it to fall and cover the couple completely. The laughter was now louder than ever as the crowd shouted ribald remarks at the covered bride and groom. When I asked what had been said that caused a particularly loud roar of laughter, my companion told me that one of the girls had shouted, "*We* know what you are up to underneath that cloth!"

After at least thirty minutes of this teasing, one of the women raised the cloth slightly and slipped a mirror underneath it so that the bride's face was reflected in it. The bridegroom was then told to look into the mirror and see his bride. Although I have no doubt that modern Pakistanis take good care to see one another at least from a distance before they get married, this was supposed to be his first sight of the woman who was his wife. Courtship as we understand it in the West is not yet the custom in Pakistan. But if they continue to adopt Western habits at the same rapid rate in their marriage customs as in other ways, it won't be long before engaged couples will be permitted to associate more freely.

Having seen his bride, the groom threw back his veil and after receiving the applause of the gathering hurried back to his own stag party while the young bride mingled with her guests.

Not until the last guest had gone did he return to the house and claim his bride.

Unlike the custom of the West, it is the bridegroom who has to provide the dowry for the bride. But in the event of a divorce the dowry must be returned. If there are children, the mother is not bound to support or take care of them. That is the duty of the husband. However, I was informed that divorces are very rare in Pakistan.

Modern Pakistan is a very different country from the one in the days of Rudyard Kipling. There was a time, of course, when the women of Pakistan were kept in strict seclusion, but although some women of the old school still wear the veil in public, as a result of Partition and the birth of a new nation, this custom known as purdah appears to be gradually dying out.

As far as Karachi is concerned, I doubt if I saw more than a dozen veiled women during the time I was there. Yet Barni and I, when securing our pictures, visited all parts of the city, exploring many of the market places and by-lanes.

In a message to the women of Pakistan, the late Mohammed Ali Jinnah said this: "In the great task of building the nation and maintaining its solidarity, women have a most valuable part to play. In the bigger struggle for the building up of Pakistan that now lies ahead, let it not be said that the women of Pakistan lagged behind or failed in their duty."

Inspired by this appeal, the women lost no time in organizing themselves into a real force. Looking over the picturesque crowd at the bride's party, it was difficult to believe that in the morning many of those girls would be practicing with rifles as members of the Women's National Guard or taking special training in the Pakistan Naval Reserve.

But of course not all Pakistani women devote their spare time to military training by any means. There are women artists and poets. There are many women doctors, for although the veil is gradually disappearing, Pakistani women prefer to be treated by women doctors, with whom they are much less reserved than with men. It is not uncommon in the large cities of Pakistan to see a name plate on the same door announcing Dr. Mrs. A., Physician and Surgeon, side by side with another announcing Dr. A., Physician and Surgeon. Often husband and wife run large clinics, the husband attending to the male patients while the wife specializes in women's and children's ailments. Pakistan even has a noted woman industrialist, Mrs. Razia Ghulam Ali, who specializes in the manufacture of concrete pipes. There are women research workers, school principals, accountants, customs officers, receptionists, telephone operators, and even women radio announcers.

Fully conscious of the truth of the saying, "Wise are those

who think of tomorrow," the women of Pakistan are planning for the well-being of their children, the citizens of tomorrow. There are health centers and clinics for invalid children, and of course many parks and playgrounds.

Pakistan has more than seven thousand Girl Guides, who played a notable part in the relief of refugees who poured into the new country after August 14, 1947. They nursed, cooked, made clothing, taught the children, and even looked after such essential matters as sanitation.

Generally speaking, Pakistani women are very busy people. Yet they remain extremely feminine. From head to toe they take elaborate precautions to beautify themselves. In addition to innumerable beautifying devices which have been customary down through the ages, the modern girl of Pakistan increases her resources by using all the complicated devices of the West.

There is hardly any field of national endeavor in which the influence of Pakistani women is not being felt. Among them are some of the finest speakers in the country, who represent their constituencies in Parliament. Lawyers, doctors, professors, journalists, civil servants, and even women in the business world, all are working for the good of their country. With women such as the Begum Liaquat Ali Khan and Miss Fatima Jinnah, sister of the late Quaid-i-Azam, to inspire them, there is little doubt that the day is not far off when the women of Pakistan will take their place alongside the women of the most advanced countries of the world.

CHAPTER FOUR

"No power on earth can prevent Pakistan," said Jinnah in 1940. Said Gandhi in 1944, "Mr. Jinnah is sincere, but I think he is suffering from hallucinations when he imagines that an unnatural division of India could bring either happiness or prosperity to the people concerned."

In his *Autobiography,* which is probably the most widely read book in India, Pandit Nehru had this to say with regard to Jinnah's dream of Pakistan: "Politically the idea is absurd. Economically it is fantastic; it is hardly worth considering."

Nevertheless, on the fourteenth of August 1947, the Dominion of Pakistan was inaugurated, with Jinnah as its first governor general.

And on the occasion of Pakistan's first anniversary, Jinnah said: "Remember that the establishment of Pakistan is a fact of which there is no parallel in the history of the world. It is the largest Moslem state in the world, and it is destined to play its magnificent part year after year as we go on, provided we serve Pakistan honestly, earnestly, and selflessly. Nature has given you everything; you have got unlimited resources. The foundations of your state have been laid, and it is for you to build, and build as quickly and as well as you can. So go ahead and I wish you Godspeed!" Those were his last words to the nation.

Born in 1876 in Karachi of a wealthy merchant family, Mohammed Ali Jinnah at the age of sixteen went to London, where he studied law and was admitted to the Bar. On returning to India, he entered politics and became one of the stanchest members of the Indian National Congress, a political party which became the spearhead for the demand for self-government. Until he reached the age of sixty Jinnah was in favor of a United India. Had he died then, he would be remembered today with Gandhi as a champion of Indian nationalism. Disagreement with Gandhi's extremist policies, especially his non-co-operation movement, in addition to his own conviction that his fellow Moslems would never obtain a fair deal in a United India that was predominantly Hindu, caused Jinnah to reverse his whole life's work and henceforth devote all his energies to the creation of a separate Moslem nation.

Although he was a shrewd politician himself, Jinnah knew only too well that 90 per cent of India's population had little if any political consciousness at all. What they did know was that, as long as they could remember, the British had dispensed justice, collected taxes, and maintained law and order. They also had seen for themselves that British rule was waning, that Hindu members of the Indian Congress party, dressed like Gandhi, sat in government offices, and that the Congress flag with a spinning wheel upon it flew over government buildings. While most Moslem peasants couldn't add two and two, they understood perfectly when some member of Jinnah's Moslem League did the adding for them and explained that the sum total was Hindu domination, that their religion was in danger, and that the man who could lead them to safety was Mohammed Ali Jinnah.

From then on Jinnah the politician became the Quaid-i-Azam, or Great Leader, of the Moslems.

When World War II broke out in 1939, the Indian Congress demanded an immediate grant of full independence for India. This not being forthcoming, Gandhi launched his civil disobedience campaign which resulted in his own arrest and that of Nehru and most of the Congress leaders.

Led by Jinnah, the attitude of the Moslem League toward the British Government was one of limited co-operation, a policy which undoubtedly helped toward the creation of Pakistan.

When the war ended and the Labor party came into power in England, one of its first actions was to order elections in India and to announce that it was the intention of the government to convene a constituent assembly for British India. By capturing all the Moslem seats in the Central Assembly and 446 out of 495 Moslem seats in the provincial assemblies, Jinnah's claim to represent the Moslem population of India was triumphantly vindicated.

The Indian Congress party had a similar victory in the non-Moslem constituencies, so that the division of India into Hindu and Moslem parts became more pronounced than ever. Pending the election of a constituent assembly for the "Union of India," it was decided that an interim government representing the major parties would be formed by the Viceroy to carry on the administration.

The Moslem League agreed to join this interim government, but the Indian Congress refused, with the result that the Viceroy formed a "caretaker government" composed of civil servants.

Regarding this as a breach of a promise on the part of the Viceroy that an interim government would be formed if either party accepted, the Moslem League withdrew its own acceptance and called upon all Moslems to renounce their British titles and start a campaign of "direct action to achieve Pakistan and to get rid of the present slavery under the British and contemplated future of Hindu domination."

This was the signal for the Congress party to withdraw its objection to entering the interim government.

The result was the formation of a Viceroy's council composed entirely of members of the Congress party, with Nehru as its vice-president.

Immediately there was an outbreak of rioting between Moslems and Hindus. According to statistics given by Sir Stafford Cripps in the House of Commons on December 12, 1946, four thousand were killed in Calcutta, five thousand in Bihar, and at least fifty thousand became homeless refugees in East Bengal.

It was under these circumstances that in February 1947 the British Government announced that it would grant full self-government to India by June 1948 at the latest, "whether as a whole to some form of central government for British India or in some areas to the existing provincial governments, or in such other way as may seem most reasonable and in the best interests of the Indian people." In addition it was announced that Viceroy Wavell would be replaced by Lord Mountbatten.

It was Mountbatten who proposed as the only settlement the Partition of India. As the great majority of Moslems lived in the Punjab, Bengal, Sind, the North West Frontier Province, Sylhet, and Baluchistan, it was obvious that Pakistan, when it came into existence, would be in the north of India, and it was there that the wishes of the inhabitants were to be ascertained.

Both Congress and the Moslem League accepted the Mountbatten plan, and when the voting took place, as was expected, Sind, Sylhet, Baluchistan, and the North West Frontier Province voted overwhelmingly to join Pakistan. As for the Punjab and Bengal, it was clear that they would have to be partitioned.

West Punjab and East Bengal voted for Pakistan, while East Punjab and West Bengal voted for India, necessitating the survey of new boundaries across which millions of refugees were to surge in both directions on and after August 14, 1947, when, amidst great rejoicings, the Dominion of Pakistan was inaugurated. But the rejoicings soon turned to tears.

Had such a situation arisen in any other country but India, it is very doubtful if the catastrophe which followed the change of boundaries would have happened. Communal riotings among Hindus, Sikhs, and Moslems involving hundreds and even thousands have been common occurrences even when India was governed by the British, but when the British withdrew and Partition became an accomplished fact, millions of panic-stricken people suddenly pulled up stakes and headed for either Pakistan or India. Those who traveled by road were ambushed and murdered by the thousands. Those who could afford to travel by train were little better off. Many trains were derailed and their occupants cut to pieces.

While accurate figures have never been ascertained because of the insuperable difficulty of taking a census, the Pakistan Government estimates that 6,500,000 Moslem refugees entered Pakistan while 5,500,000 Hindu and Sikh refugees left Pakistan, thus increasing the population of Pakistan by one million.

The number of people who were killed in transit will never be known, but it is believed that 500,000 Moslems alone were slaughtered. As for the number of Hindus and other non-Moslems who met their deaths, no estimate has been given, but in all probability it at least equaled that of the Moslems. In addition to these losses, tens of thousands of women and children were abducted on both sides.

When I was in Karachi in March 1950, there was very little

81

evidence of any refugee problem, and I was informed that about 85 per cent of the 6,500,000 Moslems who had entered Pakistan had been rehabilitated.

Jinnah did not live to see Pakistan as it has developed since those tragic days of 1947. He died on September 11, 1948. During the greatest exodus in human history he organized a government and laid the foundations of the biggest Moslem state and the fifth largest nation in the world. It was an achievement without parallel in the annals of civilization.

If size alone did not justify a study of Pakistan, it has other characteristics of unusual interest. Geographically it comprises two distinct areas separated from one another by a thousand miles of foreign territory. A glance at a map will show that West Pakistan, whose principal seaport is Karachi, adjoins Afghanistan and Iran in the west and the northwest, while the Indian province of East Punjab and the great Indian Desert bound it on the East. To the north lies the disputed state of Kashmir and Jammu, while to the south and southwest the country is washed by the Arabian Sea.

About the size of Texas and Ohio combined, West Pakistan, with an area of 306,860 square miles, has a population of 33,540,000. It is subdivided into four provinces, Baluchistan, Sind, the Punjab, and the North West Frontier Province. There are also a number of formerly independent Indian states of which Bahawalpur is the largest. All of these states acceded to Pakistan.

Running through West Pakistan are five enormous rivers: the main stream of the Indus, the Jhelum, Chenab, Ravi, and Sutlej. Eventually they all join and enter the sea south of Karachi, forming the gigantic delta of the Indus River. The upper reaches of these rivers are in Kashmir, and their sources are in the lofty Himalayas. Were it not for these rivers whose water is used to irrigate the land, West Pakistan would revert to desert. But as a result of the largest system of irrigation canals in the world, West Pakistan has become one of the richest wheat- and cotton-growing areas in the whole of Asia.

The North West Province is known as the "California of Asia" because it is in the same latitude, enjoys a similar climate, and produces every fruit and vegetable that is grown in California, besides others that cannot be grown there, such as bananas. In this part of the world peaches are famous and grapes are so plentiful that in the season they often sell for less than a penny a pound. Just as in California you can see snow-capped peaks, desert, and orange groves all at the same time, so in West Pakistan are there similar variations in the landscape.

Baluchistan is a rugged land of barren, sunburned mountains, rent by huge gorges, with vast deserts and stony plains. But thanks to irrigation, there are many intermittent green-ribboned valleys which produce rich crops and many kinds of delicious fruit.

The seacoast of West Pakistan, being devoid of vegetation, presents a somewhat forbidding appearance. But there is an excellent harbor at Karachi and many fine sandy beaches. Despite the scanty rainfall of only seven inches annually, the gardens of Karachi, especially in the springtime, are ablaze with lovely flowers.

Perhaps the most remarkable phenomenon that has attended the creation of Pakistan is the tranquillity which has replaced the almost constant warfare in the neighborhood of the Khyber

Pass in the North West Frontier Province. The tribesmen who live in this mountainous region of West Pakistan are Pathans, who speak the Pushtu language.

Tall, fair, warlike, yet extremely religious, the Pathans have always been jealous of their liberty. Not even the frequent bombing of their hide-outs and innumerable punitive expeditions of the British ever succeeded in subduing them.

Believing that the real cause behind their constant warring was the presence of an infidel army which menaced their liberty and insulted their religious feelings, Jinnah gave orders for the withdrawal of government troops from the North West Frontier.

Delighted by this friendly and trustful policy, the leaders of the tribesmen greeted Jinnah with enthusiasm when he visited Peshawar in April 1948. Oddly enough, their only complaint was that ever since the withdrawal of the British Army the people had suffered from unemployment. There were no longer any Christians to shoot or odd jobs to be picked up around the British camps.

Jinnah rectified this by promising to continue the subsidies which the British Government had paid them for a minimum of bad behavior and to provide schools, factories, hospitals, and plenty of jobs in their own local administration.

A Pathan is easily recognized, not only by his martial appearance and proud mien, but by his baggy trousers, velvet waistcoat, and bulky turban. At home he is inseparable from his rifle, and he builds his house in the shape of a fort.

East Pakistan, with an area of 53,920 square miles (considerably larger than the state of New York), has a population of 46,720,000. The result is an astonishing density of population. In some districts like Noakhali and Chittagong there are more than twelve hundred people to the square mile, although in general the density of population is 870.

Nearly the whole of East Pakistan is as flat as a pancake, with hardly a hillock visible for miles. Only on the southeastern frontier can a succession of low mountain ranges be seen.

The outstanding feature of East Pakistan is its network of mighty rivers, the Ganges, the Brahmaputra, and their many tributaries. In one area the Ganges is ten miles wide! These rivers not only bring down vast quantities of fertilizing silt which is deposited over the surface of the land, but they contain an inexhaustible supply of fish. The rivers also furnish an admirable and cheap means of transport.

In the south are the famous Sundarbans, dense tropical jungles which abound in big game, including the Bengal tiger, leopard, bear, wild boar, and many other animals.

East Pakistan is served by Chittagong, often called the "Port of Destiny." Until firm and friendly relations are established between Pakistan and India, trade communications between West and East Pakistan are by sea and air. Fortunately for Pakistan, the products of East Pakistan are different from those of West Pakistan, and each part wants what the other produces. Consequently ships that load up with cargoes in Karachi, destined for Chittagong, do not return empty, but loaded to the water line with goods produced in East Pakistan and needed by the people of West Pakistan.

Jute, known as the "golden fiber," is by far the most important product of Pakistan. All of it comes from East Pakistan, which accounts for about 75 per cent of the total jute production of the world. Despite the fact that for many years Americans as well as other people of the Western world have walked on jute, sat on jute, and slept on jute, not many people know that this wonderful fiber comes from Pakistan. Its most obvious use is for making sacks and sackcloth, but jute has a thousand other uses. Carpets are usually woven on a basis of jute; linoleum is built upon a base of jute. Jute might even be called the foundation of the upholstering business.

Like jute in East Pakistan, cotton is the principal non-food crop of West Pakistan, the annual production being about one and a half million bales of four hundred pounds each. About two thirds of Pakistan's cotton is of high-grade, long-staple American varieties.

With regard to food crops, while East Pakistan produces large quantities of rice, sugar, and tea, West Pakistan produces wheat and fruit.

The climates of East and West Pakistan are as different as their principal products. West Pakistan, generally speaking, is cold in winter and hot during the summer, but this extreme climate is bracing and dry, making the inhabitants strong and sturdy.

East Pakistan is warm and humid, with an average rainfall that in many places is at least ten times as great as that in West Pakistan. But there is one feature that is common to both East and West Pakistan. The nights are generally cool, making it easy to sleep.

Strikingly different in products and climate, East and West Pakistan are just as different in the appearance of their inhabitants. West Pakistan is a land of tall men with high cheekbones who often sport large black mustaches and wear turbans, baggy trousers, and speak Urdu, whereas in East Pakistan the men are short, bearded, wear skirts, skullcaps, and speak Bengali.

The camel is the main means of transport in West Pakistan,

while in East Pakistan the people travel from village to village by boat.

But despite all these differences and being separated from one another by a thousand miles of Hindu India, the two areas which together constitute Pakistan are bound together by the strong tie of religion, Islam.

Dacca, the principal city of East Pakistan and once a capital of the Moguls, contains more mosques than any other city in the whole subcontinent.

While it is true that Pakistan, only four years old, is but an infant among the nations of the world, its territory and the people who inhabit it have had a great and glorious past. West Pakistan, lying in the path of all the conquerors of India, was a battleground for invading Aryans, Persians, Greeks, Afghans, and other peoples from Asia and the Middle East. Until recent times it was customary to think of India's civilization beginning with the Aryan invasion which is said to have occurred about 1500 B.C. The savage tribes which still are to be found in different parts of India were supposed to be the remnants of the aboriginal inhabitants of the subcontinent. But excavations which began in the 1920s have dispelled the theories of generations of scholars and revealed that in the Punjab you could have rented a duplex apartment complete with tiled bathroom, kitchen, and a private entrance at least forty-five hundred years ago.

Instead of dressing in skins and painting their bodies blue as the ancient Britons did, those early inhabitants of Pakistan were highly civilized. Judging from the statuary they left behind them, the men wore kilts and the women wore loose-flowing garments with wide girdles. Like their modern sisters, they spent much of their time beautifying themselves. Before mirrors

87

of polished bronze they shaded their eyelids, outlined their eyes and eyebrows, and painted their cheeks with rouge. Skillful jewelers, the men turned out many beautiful objects of gold, silver, bronze, and copper which they decorated with agate, carnelian, turquoise, and other semi-precious stones. The sculptors worked in marble, alabaster, terra cotta, and bronze, while their potters turned out on their wheels many different kinds of objects, some useful, others ornamental, from kitchen utensils to very beautiful eggshell pottery.

They spent their leisure time watching bullfights, cockfights, or dancing to the music of orchestras which used stringed instruments and drums. As for their children, they could play with toys that any youngster today would be delighted with. There were toy carts, toy birds that could whistle, and toy bulls that wagged their heads when their tails were pulled.

The houses these ancient people lived in were built of brick, with plenty of windows, doors, and staircases. They were spacious and faced on wide straight streets that were crowded with well-dressed people, some walking, others riding in chariots. Each house had its own well, which was so expertly constructed that after removing debris the excavators were still able to use them.

Harappa and Mohenjo-Daro are the names of the excavated cities which have already become a Mecca for visitors, but there are signs of many others scattered over the country.

As for the personal appearance of Pakistanis, this varies just as much as it does with Englishmen. Some are dark, others are blond with blue eyes. Some have aquiline features with Roman noses, while many men and women have profiles that are decidedly Grecian.

Politically, Pakistan is a state which was deliberately created, not on an economic, linguistic, or racial basis, but on that of religious unity. This does not mean, however, that religions other than Islam are not tolerated or their adherents persecuted. On the contrary, I saw the churches and temples of many religions, including a Jewish synagogue, a Hindu temple, and the Towers of Silence on the top of which Parsees expose their dead to be devoured by vultures.

It is not generally appreciated that there is a religious bond between Islam and the free nations of the Western world. Moslems worship the same God as they do, and in view of the rapid march of anti-religious and atheistic Communism, Pakistan with her eighty million people constitutes a mighty barrier in its path.

Unfortunately the average American knows very little about Pakistan. This was demonstrated when the wives of three prominent Pakistani diplomats were arrested by the Westchester police, who mistook them for gypsies.

I left Karachi on March 28, 1950, exactly nine days after I had arrived there. Rajput and Barni saw me off at the airport, and as he bade me good-by Rajput handed me a copy of one of his books.

"If you want to do me a favor," he said, "give this book to Mr. Dale Carnegie and ask him to send me an autographed copy of *How to Win Friends and Influence People.* We need his book badly in Pakistan."

Barni's parting present was a fine pair of brown leather sandals "Made in Peshawar." "They will go with your Jinnah hat," he said with a smile.

Sitting beside me in the plane was an eminent Moslem scholar and divine. He had red hair, a red beard, and spoke excellent English. Almost at once he started talking about Communism. "Danger is coming from the north," he said solemnly, using the very same words that an old Malay hadji had in 1939 when I was traveling in the Malay Peninsula.

For the next hour I listened while he told me how Communist agents were at work in Pakistan and India. Finally he said, "The world is divided into two parts: those who believe in God and those who don't."

In Pakistan the danger of Communism was a frequent topic of conversation. The people I met knew what was going on in the Malay Peninsula and Burma. They also were very conscious of the fact that Russia is watchfully waiting on the border of Kashmir. When is America going to use her power and stop the Communists? That was the question that was asked me repeatedly, not only in Pakistan but in every country I visited in 1950.

Another interesting passenger was an Englishman who had boarded the plane at Calcutta.

"I suppose you're going home on leave?" I inquired.

"Not I!" he said sourly. "I'm going home to stay! Calcutta is no place for me," he continued. "Three of my friends were stripped naked by Communist rioters, bound to long poles, and thrust headfirst into a furnace! I'm getting out while the going's good." He then handed me a newspaper in which it was reported that martial law had been proclaimed in Bombay. It seemed to be just as well that I was on my way back to America. Better to wait and see which way the cat was going to jump before heading for Shalimar.

At Basra when I alighted from the plane I ran into John Morley, a neighbor of mine in Brentwood, California, and a member of the Westwood Village Rotary Club. Just time to shake hands and remark on the smallness of the world, then off again for Damascus, where we landed at 8:30 P.M. and had dinner at the airport. At midnight we landed at Constantinople and had boiled camel's tongue and caramel custard. Then off again for Brussels via Yugoslavia.

At 4:30 A.M. we landed. Sleepily I inquired where we were. "Back in Constantinople. Engine trouble. How about breakfast?"

More boiled camel's tongue and caramel custard! And so to bed.

Those few hours' delay in Turkey proved to be a blessing in disguise, for it gave me an opportunity to see what had taken place in Constantinople since my last visit, which had been in 1928. At that time a Turkish guide had said to me, "We have thrown the caliph into the sea forever, and the fez after him." He then explained that derby hats were the correct headdress for men and that the teaching of not only Christianity but of any religion at all was forbidden. As for Turkish women, their veils were off, their hair was bobbed, and those who could afford them wore silk stockings and were not averse to showing their legs. The Mosque of St. Sophia was still being used at that time, its immense floor being covered by what was said to be the largest carpet in the world. But I also remembered that there had been talk of turning the mosque into a dance hall.

"How about some sight-seeing?" I said to a young Indian couple who had also been on the plane. So the three of us hired a car and set out for the Mosque of St. Sophia. On the way they told me that they had boarded the plane at Dum-Dum. "Where the bullets come from?" I inquired. "Yes, Dum-Dum bullets," they answered laughingly.

Upon arrival at the mosque, which had been converted into a museum, I again hired a guide. But I soon discovered that I knew a lot more about the place than he did. Opening his coat, the guide showed me his badge which proclaimed him to be an official guide.

"You tell me! I ask you questions. You teach me be good guide," he said.

"How old are you?" I asked.

"Twenty-one," he answered.

"Then I was in this mosque before you were born."

When I told him that I had seen people worshiping there and that during that same visit I had witnessed the last dance of the whirling dervishes, the guide was astonished. Apparently he was only supposed to tell visitors about the architecture of the building. Or perhaps he had never been told about the frightful tragedy which occurred in Constantinople on May 29, 1453, when the ruler of the Byzantine Empire was Constantine Palaeologus, the last Greek emperor.

On that day Mohammed II, at the head of a Turkish army of 250,000 men and a fleet of 420 vessels, demanded the surrender of Constantinople. To defend the city, Emperor Palaeologus was able to muster only nine thousand men, but he indignantly refused to surrender.

Meanwhile the inhabitants—senators, priests, monks, nuns, husbands, wives, and children—swarmed to the Church of St. Sophia because of a prophecy that an angel from heaven with a flaming sword would destroy the Turks the moment they approached the world's most beautiful church. The Turks followed them and slaughtered thousands. Having broken down the doors of the church, they entered with drawn swords and cut the assembled congregation to pieces. When the massacre was complete, Mohammed entered the church and ordered a mullah to announce that henceforth the world's most famous Christian church would be a mosque.

More than forty thousand Christians were put to the sword and fifty thousand reduced to slavery. All the movable ornaments of the building were destroyed, and the wonderful mosaics were covered with plaster or whitewash.

For the next four hundred and seventy-five years Moslems used it as a mosque until Kemal Atatürk abolished their religion.

When I visited it in 1950 the huge building was so cold and damp that the breath of visitors could be seen just as if it were a winter day. The world's largest carpet was gone.

St. Sophia is the largest church in the world, St. Peter's in Rome is second, and St. Paul's Cathedral in London is third.

For many years American archaeologists have been at work excavating under the floor and removing the paint and whitewash from the ceiling and walls. The result is astonishing, for the Christian mosaics portraying various events and personages in the time of our Lord are as beautiful as ever. I may be wrong, but to my eyes the mosaics that adorn the interior of St. Sophia are the most interesting and beautiful in the world.

It is very improbable that the Turkish Government would permit such a thing, but in view of the aid given to her by the United States to prevent the spread of Communism, I cannot help feeling that Turkey would make a magnificent gesture and contribute much toward world peace if she permitted the Church of St. Sophia to be restored completely and made into a temple again, dedicated to all who believe in God. If that were done, the largest temple of worship in the world would be sacred to Christian, Moslem, and Jew alike.

At present St. Sophia, although a museum, is a monument to

godlessness. As a temple of worship, it would become a monument to the new crusade against atheistic Communism.

That night, after another meal of camel's tongue and caramel custard, we left for London, where we arrived at 5 A.M. the next morning.

"Your bill is ready, sir," said the clerk at the Savoy Hotel. "How did you find Pakistan?"

"Booming," I answered.

"Remarkable the way you Americans get around," chuckled the clerk. "I suppose you'll be in New York tomorrow morning."

I was, and Zetta was there to meet me.

"What about Kashmir?" she asked anxiously.

My face gave her the answer. Shalimar was still just a castle in the air.

CHAPTER FIVE

"If at first you don't succeed, try, try again," said Zetta one day when I was bemoaning the fact that there seemed to be a hoodoo that prevented us from ever going to Kashmir. Long before my unexpected journey to Karachi we had made plans to sail from San Francisco in July 1950 on one of the new boats of the American President Line.

Our first stop was to have been Japan, where we hoped to revisit our old friends, the Hairy Ainus, just to see how they were getting along under democracy. With that in view we had armed ourselves with a personal letter to General MacArthur from our friend Admiral Halsey.

We then planned to proceed to Hong Kong by boat, fly over the Hump to Calcutta, and make our way to Kashmir. But the outbreak of war in Korea knocked all these plans into a cocked hat. The boat we were to have sailed on was pressed into government service. And bothering General MacArthur at such a time, even if we had been able to get to Japan, was out of the question.

Then there was the problem of Kashmir itself. My newly made friends in Pakistan couldn't help me, for the Vale of Kashmir was under the control of India. And when I approached the Indian consulate I found that they, too, were unable to solve the problem.

"We shall be delighted to give you a visa for India," they said, "but Kashmir! Impossible. Only the commander in chief of the Indian Army can give you permission to enter the Vale, and he is in New Delhi."

"It's hopeless," I said. But I could see that Zetta hadn't given up so easily.

95

"I have a brain wave!" she shouted excitedly. "Loy Henderson, our Ambassador to India, is in Washington. The paper says that he is returning to New Delhi this week. We both know him. If anyone can get us into Kashmir, he can. I'm going to Washington."

Zetta was back within twenty-four hours. "It's all fixed," she said happily. "Ambassador Henderson said that he would be glad to see us in New Delhi and that he would arrange for us to meet the commander in chief of the Indian Army, General Cariappa."

"But suppose he won't give us permission to enter Kashmir," I said doubtfully. "All our time and money would be wasted. We mustn't put all our eggs in one basket!"

Zetta put on her thinking cap.

"I have it!" she exclaimed eagerly. "Let's make a survey of world opinion on Communism. Let's travel clear across Europe and Asia, keeping as close as we can to the Iron Curtain. Let's find out what the people in the different countries think about the Marshall Plan and whether they would fight if they were invaded by Russia. Then, if we fail to get into Kashmir, we shall still have material for a new book."

Catching her enthusiasm, I agreed. "We'll start with Scandinavia. We can revisit arctic Lapland. We might even find some lemmings!"

By a stroke of luck we were able to get three passages on the Swedish-American luxury liner *Stockholm*, and on August 9, 1950, we set sail from New York bound for Gothenburg.

The adage, "Two's company, three's not," doesn't apply to an explorer and his wife. Provided the third person is the right kind, three is an ideal number on any expedition.

In this instance our traveling companion was an old friend,

Sam Tatem, whose vocation is Clerk of the House of Parliament, Bermuda, but whose avocation is traveling and photography.

Tall, good-looking, with weather-beaten skin from sailing, Sam can be seen any time in Bermuda when the House is in session, bewigged and sitting in front of the Speaker. Besides being a Rhodes scholar, a talented writer, and a lover of symphonic music, Sam is a good cameraman. Like many other Bermudians, Sam believes that work is the curse of the drinking classes, which is another way of saying that he is a cheerful soul and a wonderful traveling companion.

The last time Zetta and I had sailed from New York for Sweden was in 1932, when we were on our way to Russia. At that time the third member of our party was Harold Sintzenitch, another genial soul and top-notch cameraman. Without "Snitch," it is doubtful if we would ever have got out of Russia alive.

Sir Hubert Wilkins had come down to the boat to see us off on that occasion. By a strange coincidence, this time we were sent on our way by another famous Arctic explorer, Peter Freuchen, the "peg-legged giant," who represented a Danish newspaper.

Eighteen years had passed since our Russian honeymoon. We wondered what changes we would find in Sweden, Norway, and Denmark. But as far as the liner *Stockholm* was concerned, Sweden didn't appear to have changed at all. Spotlessly clean from stem to stern, this lovely vessel, which looked more like a large yacht than an ocean liner, was utterly devoid of that peculiarly unpleasant odor that is usually so noticeable on large ships. At luncheon the illusion of actually being in Sweden was complete when the meal started with *snaps,* smörgåsbord, and Pilsener.

97

Formality is a marked characteristic at all Swedish meals, and I think that a good many of the Swedish passengers were surprised to notice how well Zetta and I "knew the ropes." Sam proved to be an adept at "skoaling." He soon learned to call the five glasses of snaps by their first names, Helan, Halvan, Tersen, Kvarten, and Kvinten. As for quaffing his snaps without moving his Adam's apple, Sam's Bermuda training stood him in good stead.

Only the Swedes know how to live on a long voyage. The routine was as follows: Breakfast at eight-thirty. Walk the deck, rest in deck chairs, and read until 1 P.M., when luncheon was served. Then sleep and get fat until 4 P.M., when tea was served. At four-thirty promptly we had a Swedish bath, a massage, exercise in the gymnasium, followed by a swim in an ice-cold pool. This enabled us to lose the fat we gained during the day and put us in good form to regain the fat at dinner, after which there was an excellent concert and dancing until 11 P.M. On other vessels it would be time for bed, but not on board the *Stockholm*.

At eleven o'clock, led by a bugler and a drummer, all the passengers joined hands and formed a long human snake, winding their way in and out of the different rooms, laughing and shouting, toward a long table upon which had been spread a most elaborate smörgåsbord. Among dozens of other delicacies there were roast pheasant, smoked salmon, pâté de foie gras, caviar, sardines, pickled fish, thinly sliced cucumbers prepared as only the Swedes know how, various kinds of salads, breads, knäckebröd, and heaps of creamy butter. In addition to such gastronomic delights there were always several kinds of meat, fruit, and delicious lingonberries.

All this was just a Swedish snack before going to bed.

The remarkable thing about this routine is that, provided you do as the Swedes do and "sweat it out" regularly, your weight remains stationary.

On the fourth day out, in mid-Atlantic and south of Iceland, we saw a number of Mother Carey's chickens, those wonderful little sea birds that skim the waves within a few inches of the water, regardless of how rough the sea may be. For hundreds of years mariners believed—and some old salts still insist—that the stormy petrel (to give the bird its proper name) never approached land, but that the female laid its one egg at sea and carried it about under its wing until it hatched. However, the petrels of the North Atlantic that are anywhere within reach of the Cape Verde Islands (and "within reach" can mean hundreds of miles) lay their eggs underground on the most desolate place they can find.

There is a legend that no one has ever found a dead petrel, which has given rise to the belief among sailors that they have some secret place to which they fly when death approaches. Believe it or not, the birds do have their own private cemetery on the uninhabited island of Cima. There a plateau covered with the tiny white bones of millions of stormy petrels can be seen. It is Mother Carey's Graveyard.

The night before the *Stockholm* arrived at Gothenburg the ship's orchestra gave a concert of Scottish music while the passengers strained their eyes to see the lights of Scotland.

"There's one," said Sam, who, being a Bermudian is even more thrifty than a Scot. "Not many of them believe in wasting good oil!"

Nevertheless, it was a thrill to see those low-lying islands off the Scottish coast. The last time Zetta and I had passed them

99

we had seen a shepherd with a boatload of sheep which he was ferrying from one island to another.

Most people who see the coast of Sweden for the first time are impressed by the great masses of rounded rock, apparently completely devoid of vegetation, which make the country appear very inhospitable. But a great surprise awaits them once they set foot on shore, for the Swedes love flowers and flowers love Sweden. Not only are Sweden's cities full of them during the spring and summer, but the whole country from Malmö to Lapland is a veritable flower garden, and many walls inside houses are covered with creepers.

By nine o'clock on August 17 the *Stockholm* was tied up alongside her berth in Gothenburg, the largest seaport in Sweden. But Gothenburg is far more than a seaport and center of shipbuilding. This ancient city is also a cultural center of considerable importance. Among other attractions, Gothenburg boasts one of Europe's most modern theaters, a world-famous concert hall, and a magnificent museum of art. There is also a ski jump, snow for which is imported by the trainload from Norway.

It was at Gothenburg that the Vikings outfitted their fleets in which they sailed and rowed extraordinary distances, to Iceland, to the northeast coast of America, and even to Asiatic territory. For centuries before Gustavus Adolphus founded Gothenburg in 1619, the neighborhood had seen several cities rise and fall. Burial vaults have been discovered there five thousand years old.

In the days of Gustavus Adolphus, Sweden was one of the great powers in Europe, and it was a Swede who, in the ninth century, founded the Russian Empire.

We were in the lounge of the *Stockholm,* waiting for the

examination of our passports, when I was airing my knowledge of Swedish history for the benefit of Sam and Zetta. I hadn't noticed that my conversation was being overheard by an elderly Swedish gentleman.

Turning to me, he said, "You are quite right, but if you will permit me, I can tell you even more about our country. The first king of Sweden, named Sven, was the grandson of Noah. It was one of Sven's brothers, named Ubbe, who built the University of Uppsala 246 years *after* the Flood!" Then, seeing my look of incredulity, the enthusiastic gentleman added, "As a matter of fact, Sweden was thickly populated *before* the Flood."

Sam sniffed scornfully. I felt that I had to come to the Swede's defense.

"Now that I come to think about it," I said, "in 1924, when I made my first expedition to Lapland, I was entertained by Sweden's eminent geologist, Baron Gerard de Geer. He told me that it was fifteen thousand years since the great icecap which covered Sweden began to shrink back to the north, and that soon after the ice melted Sweden became inhabited by human beings whose relics have been discovered."

The Swede simply beamed with delight. "Thank you," he said. "Now you know why we Swedes are not so impressed by the antiquity of Egypt as we are by that of our own country."

"This calls for a drink!" laughed Sam.

"Sorry, sir," apologized the bartender. "We are in Sweden now. The bar is closed, and in any case, drinks cannot be served without food. Times have changed!"

We soon discovered the truth of this when we landed and registered at the new Park Avenue Hotel, which is one of the finest in Sweden. Instead of hanging our room key on the door so that anyone who wished might enter, as was the custom in 1932, we were told to be sure and leave our keys at the desk so that no unauthorized person could enter our rooms.

The war has brought about many changes, even in neutral Sweden. But the most striking change of all was the disappearance of the smörgåsbord which always used to grace the side of every hotel dining room, so that guests could line up and help themselves to as much food as they liked and as many helpings as they could eat. Nowadays a waiter hands you a menu from which you can select a miniature smörgåsbord to be served at your table. Once served, you may order snaps. Gentlemen are given a full glass. By law ladies can have only half a glass.

Zetta was furious. "Whether I want it or not," she said, "I believe in equal rights for women."

As the waiter placed three small pieces of butter on the table, she asked him, "Where are those mountains of butter you used to have?"

"Butter is rationed, madam," answered the waiter sheepishly.

All the butter that we saw served in public restaurants was rolled into a small sausage-shaped pat through which there were a number of hollow tubes filled with water. I was told that the machine which makes these standardized water-filled pats of butter costs about one hundred dollars. But it quickly saves its cost.

As for cheese, gone are the days when you could dig into the center of a whole cheese and select a choice piece. Cheese was rationed too; so were sugar and coffee. No longer did we see those bowls of rich cream or large pitchers of creamy milk. Instead, all we got was a tiny jug of half-and-half and a very modest amount of skimmed milk.

The present generation of Swedes apparently do not mind

this comparative austerity at all; in fact, they seemed to think that everything was wonderful. But the older people heave many a sigh when they think of the old days of plenty.

One old-timer told us the following story, which explain why times have changed so sadly:

A Swede died and was greeted at the gates of heaven by St Peter. Before entering, the Swede inquired, "Have you any sugar up here?" "No!" replied St. Peter rather sourly. "Have you any coffee, then?" asked the Swede. "Alas!" moaned Peter. "Not a drop." "What about snaps, butter, cheese?" persisted the famished Swede. Peter looked embarrassed. "I fear that we are extremely short of everything nowadays!"

"Well, if you'll excuse me," said the Swede, "I think that before I decide where I'm going to stay I'll make a few inquiries down below."

On reaching the nether regions, the Swede was greeted by Satan, who smiled affably as he opened wide the door. Taking a peep inside, the Swede saw great mounds of sugar, buckets of butter, sacks of rice, all his favorite brands of coffee, snaps, and, above all, cases of the finest brandy. Astonished, the Swede inquired, "How is it that you have such wonderful things here? I have just been up to heaven and they have nothing like this."

Satan chuckled. "That's quite easy to explain. The Socialists are now managing heaven, so *everything* has gone to hell!"

Of course Socialism is nothing new in Sweden, but it has made many drastic changes since Zetta and I were there in 1932. Whether it will eventually go to the extreme left and embrace Communism remains to be seen, but there is no doubt that the great leveling process is now in full swing.

I asked a wealthy Swedish friend whether he could build a new house if he wished. He said that for all practical purposes it was impossible. Innumerable applications for different kinds of permits have to be filled in, and then they are invariably refused on some pretext or other. Apparently what the Socialist government is trying to do is to force as many people as possible to live in the huge new apartment houses which are springing up like toadstools everywhere.

It is true that they are grandiose projects, with fine playgrounds and day nurseries for children, and of course a community center. The American slogan, "Own Your Own Home," is about the last thing the average young Swede thinks of. He is apparently quite satisfied with a tiny apartment which is exactly like that of his next-door neighbor. It is just his sleeping place. He has the great out-of-doors for play and a beautifully designed and amazingly clean factory to work in. He goes to work on a push bike and often owns a share in a sailboat. In time he may even own his own boat, but the chances of owning his own automobile are remote.

Unlike the United States, where the precincts of a factory are packed with cars, in Sweden they are jammed with bicycles.

To judge from the thousands of pretty window boxes, all the same size and shape, that adorn the exterior of Sweden's giant apartment houses, it might be concluded that this shows the yearning of every Swede to have his own flower garden. However, he can roam through the many beautifully laid out public gardens.

Like all other Swedish towns, Gothenburg has no slums. Just drive to what we would call the "city limits," and you will find that the unspoiled countryside starts abruptly where the residential part of the city ends.

It is said that cleanliness is next to godliness. Generally speaking, most Swedish people are religious and all are extremely clean. As for the Socialists being religious, however, they tell an amusing story of the late King Gustav, who, besides being very democratic, was conservative and deeply religious. His Prime Minister, named Erlander, was never particularly welcome at the palace. This is understandable because not only was Erlander a Social Democrat, but he was not averse to reminding the King of this by appearing before His Majesty dressed in a sweat shirt. King Gustav, for his part, is said to have deliberately mispronounced the Prime Minister's name, invariably calling him "Erlanderson."

One day, being particularly annoyed by the untidy appearance of his Prime Minister, the King said, "Erlanderson, you don't believe in God, do you?"

Taken aback by this unexpected question, Erlander replied with some confusion, "Your Majesty, I must confess that I do not."

"Don't worry," said the King with a sniff. "He doesn't believe in you either!"

That King Gustav was a very democratic sovereign, I can vouch for from my own experience. In 1924, when Dr. Clyde Fisher and I were in Stockholm en route to Lapland, I said, "Clyde, let's go and call on the King!" On arrival at the palace I said to an official who opened the door, "We have come to pay our respects to the King. We are Americans," I added as an afterthought.

After a few minutes' delay the official returned. "His Majesty will be happy to see you at 11 A.M." And at 11 A.M. promptly we met not only King Gustav but also the Crown Prince. Both were dressed alike, in frock coats and top hats. They couldn't have been more gracious as they posed for their photographs.

"Is this the road to Shalimar?" said Sam facetiously as we

jolted and swerved our way to Stockholm on Sweden's fastest electric train.

"Don't ask me, ask Zetta," I growled. "She's the pilot fish on this expedition." I had long since got into the habit of letting Zetta make our plans. Unlike mine, hers had usually materialized. I knew as well as Sam that we were actually bound for Hammerfest, but I also knew that Zetta was making plans to go to Kashmir just the same. Several times in Gothenburg I had noticed her making long-distance calls to Stockholm, but as she didn't volunteer what they were about, I asked no questions.

Except for the traffic, Stockholm looked just as it had in 1932, the loveliest city in Europe and justly called the "Venice of the North." My only regret was that it was so late in the summer. Had we arrived in June instead of August, we would have seen Stockholm by the dreamy half-light of the midnight sun when the city, with its myriad lights reflected in the calm waters of Lake Mälar, looks like fairyland.

"Just look at those bicycles," exclaimed Sam as hundreds and hundreds passed by in one continuous stream, often six abreast. Stopped by a traffic light, their riders dismounted. Then on again and off again, just as automatically as the electric lights which regulated them. "Never saw so many push bikes in my life, and I come from Bermuda!"

When we finally reached the Grand Hotel, the doorman, who has been there for the last forty years, recognized me with a grin.

"Mr. Wells! Back again!"

Outwardly the Grand Hotel hadn't changed a bit. But what a difference inside. Socialism has had a sad effect on hotel service. Instead of waiters, valets, and maids rushing to the sound of every bell, they must run away from it, for we rang until we were exhausted, but nobody came. Help is apparently just as difficult to obtain as in America, and no one dares to offend maids or porters by demanding service, for fear they will quit.

Gone was smörgåsbord, but food, as usual all over Sweden, was excellent. It is a wonderful place to spend your summer and get away from the heat of most American cities. What about cost? I should say that both the rooms and the food are on a par with the Ambassador Hotel in New York, but the service not nearly so good. However, once you leave Stockholm, the prices are very low, the service good, and accommodations are all spotlessly clean. I know of no place where you get so much for your tourist dollar as you do in northern Sweden and northern Norway.

Not all Swedes are Socialists by any means, and it all depends upon a particular Swede's political affiliation what information you are given when sight-seeing. For instance, a Socialist guide told us that the magnificent new apartment houses of which he was so proud, spaced about a hundred yards apart, were so designed for the sake of the health of the occupants. "Plenty of light and fresh air," he said.

But another guide, who hated Socialism like poison, explained that the reason the buildings were so widely spaced and peculiarly constructed was to minimize the effect of bombs. "Whose bombs?" I inquired.

"Russia's, of course," he replied. "They're only minutes away. Haven't you noticed our bomb shelters?"

For the rest of the day he went out of his way to show us that Stockholm was well provided with underground shelters, many of them excavated from solid rock.

Sweden was in the throes of a political election, so that the walls were covered with posters issued by the different parties. Prominent among them was the poster of the Social Democratic party, a very lurid work of art showing the Swedish flag flying side by side with the Red flag. It probably disturbed me far more than necessary, but it gave me a shock to see those two emblems on the same poster, the one so suggestive of forget-me-nots and buttercups, the other of bloody revolution.

One evening we ran into Mr. and Mrs. Hadyn Harris of Virginia and Chicago. Scarcely three weeks had elapsed since we had seen them dining with General Marshall at the Ritz Carlton in New York.

If anyone is a capitalist, Hadyn Harris is, yet when I asked him what brought him to Sweden he told me that he was making a study of Socialism as practiced by Sweden. His eyes had twinkled when he said this, which made me wonder what he was really up to.

He gave us a most sumptuous dinner that night at which the *pièce de résistance* was a large bowl of kräftor, or Swedish crayfish.

The kräftor season starts on August 8 and lasts only a month. During that time all who can afford to devour unbelievable numbers of these miniature fresh-water lobsters. They cost about twenty-five cents apiece, and one person can easily put away twenty at a meal. To a visitor the amount of meat you get and the labor entailed getting it are not worth the expense or trouble, but to mention such an opinion to a Swede would be heresy.

"Give me one Bermuda lobster that provides a meal for four people for one dollar, and you can have all the kräftor in Sweden!" said Zetta. "But as for Swedish prawns, ah, they are so delicious I'd make a trip to Sweden just to feast on them."

In 1932, when I had asked for a bath in the Grand Hotel in
Stockholm, the manager said, "You will have to wait a little
while, sir. The girl who will bathe you is having her breakfast!"

In Sweden bath girls are as different from bathing girls as
black is from white, for the girl who bathed me must have been
at least sixty. But she was as strong as an ox. I must admit that
the prospect of being washed by a female was a little unnerving.
Such a thing hadn't happened to me since my mother sponged
me in a basin. Casting care to the winds, however, I climbed
into the bath, whereupon the bath girl soaped and scrubbed me
violently while I alternately breathed and strangled as I found
myself on my back or face down in the water. Finally the
shriveled Amazon toweled me briskly, and having exclaimed,
"Va so goot!" she curtsied and was gone.

I had told Sam that when we got to Sweden girls would bathe
us, but I had not told him that they were not Lana Turners or
Hedy Lamarrs. I had let him get the idea that they were like
"bathing girls," those beautiful creatures that are shown in color
in magazines to advertise America's bathing beaches in Florida
and California. Sam was eagerly preparing for his bath when I
said, "No luck! Times have changed. They advise me to get our
baths at the public bathhouse."

"This is one time when Socialism has gone too far," said Sam.

But even at the public bathhouse we found that instead of
being bathed by a woman the job was performed, and not
nearly so well, by a man. A new feature was the custom of
buying a large stein of beer for the bath boy. "Too hard work!"
he mumbled as he downed the drink as if he were pouring
water down a sink.

"Nothing so constant as change," said Sam philosophically

as we made our way back to the Grand Hotel. "Did they give you a certificate?"

"That's one thing they didn't do in 1932," I laughed as I read mine, which certified that I had lost four pounds. "Now I can get into my tuxedo for the opera tonight."

August 22 was the opening night of the opera. Zetta was all excited. She was going to wear her prettiest evening dress. What a mistake that was. We were the only people in Stockholm's splendid opera house who were so bourgeois as to "dress for the opera." Everyone else was in ordinary clothing, or should I say extraordinary clothing, for many of the men were wearing sweat shirts. But the *Count of Luxembourg* hadn't changed, and at least we had the experience of being the cynosure of all eyes.

Until I attended the Berkshire Music Festival at Tanglewood a year later I had been inclined to think that Sweden was going to the dogs socially. But I discovered that the fashionable days of Gertrude Robinson Smith, who founded the Festival, had gone forever. No longer was the great shed crammed with beautifully gowned women and opera-hatted gentlemen. There were no jewels, not a scrap of glitter, no shiny limousines with smartly uniformed chauffeurs waiting on the cream of New York society. Instead, Coney Island had come to Tanglewood in busses and jalopies. Long-haired men and short-haired women flopped about the lawn eating ice-cream cones and making love to one another openly to the strains of the Boston Symphony Orchestra, while on the outskirts of the madding crowd were a few old-fashioned music lovers with their radios, selecting programs of their own choice rather than listening to the discordant racket of Prokofieff.

The further away from the great city of Stockholm we

traveled, the more did Sweden resemble the Sweden of my memories. Uppsala, famous for its wonderful Gothic cathedral and ancient university, hadn't changed very much. There was even a good old-fashioned smörgåsbord at the Hotel Gillet.

Hammarby, the home of Linnaeus, the father of botany, was just the same as far as the garden was concerned, but the interior of the house itself had an air of neglect. With autumn approaching fast, many of the flowers had gone to seed and I was able to collect a good quantity of seeds, which I sent to the agricultural station in Bermuda so that a Linnaean garden could be started there for the benefit of garden lovers. Even the large gray snails whose ancestors Linnaeus used to eat were still crawling about the garden, where they are treated with becoming reverence.

Not far from Uppsala is Old Uppsala, where we saw the huge earthen mounds that cover the ships of Viking kings who are buried in them together with their golden treasure. No Swede would dream of disturbing them, but I couldn't help wondering how long those mounds would remain undesecrated if the Russians ever occupy Sweden.

From Uppsala we took the train to Tällberg in Dalecarlia, where we stayed at what is probably the best and most inexpensive hotel in all Sweden. Långbersgården is its name, a charming old-fashioned Swedish mansion owned and operated as a pension by Miss Vilma Långbers. Långbersgården is a little bit of old Sweden that remains unspoiled. The house overlooks Lake Siljan, whose beauty has been an inspiration to Sweden's greatest poets. Here for about three dollars a day on the American plan you can live like a king and enjoy the most beautiful scenery in the whole of Sweden. In fact, the present King sends his little son to stay there, perhaps so that the youngster can know what his country used to be like before the days of Erlander, their Socialist Prime Minister.

Close by are Leksand and Rättvik, where people can still be seen wearing the colorful regional costumes for which the whole of Dalecarlia is still famous.

The hostess of this delightful little hotel is Miss Gertrude Jungbeck, who is even better known in foreign lands than she is in Sweden, because for many years she was the mainspring of Sweden's Tourist Association. Hendrik van Loon dedicated one of his books to her.

Except that her once blond hair was now snow-white, Gertrude had scarcely changed a bit. As she met me at the door she flung her arms around me, saying, "*Dear* Mr. Wells, we meet again after twenty-six years. You and Dr. Clyde Fisher were the very first Americans for whom I ever arranged a tour."

What comfort! What wonderful food! What charming hospitality!

I can forgive the Social Democrats everything, if only they will leave Långbersgården as I found it in 1950.

We wished we could have remained there for months, but Lapland was beckoning and Old Man Winter threatening. So off we went by car for Gävle on the Baltic Coast, where we caught the midnight express for Bjorkliden, an arctic summer paradise.

Once on board the train, it was easy to see that the passengers weren't bound for any such center of sophistication as Stockholm. Men, women, and children all wore heavy clothes and hiking boots. Many carried knapsacks on their backs and guns in their hands. Accompanied by their dogs, which are allowed to travel like humans on all Swedish trains, they were on their way north. Some were to hunt bears, others to shoot the capercaillie, which the Swedes call *tjäder*, that remarkable bird that looks like a giant prairie chicken.

The capercaillie is not only very good eating but is the Don Juan among birds. Not satisfied with his capercaillie mate, he mates with any bird of his own species, such as partridge, hazel hen, and even the ptarmigan, all of which are very much smaller than he. The result is that his variegated offspring are the despair of ornithologists. Never was there such a mixture as the illegitimate children of the capercaillie. So numerous and varied are they that one of Sweden's natural-history museums has set apart a special room for capercaillie and company.

At 11:30 the next morning, with a shrill toot on the whistle, the train slowed down. We were crossing the Arctic Circle. When Fisher and I were there the spot was marked by a rather ramshackle wooden notice board with the word POLCIRKELN painted upon it, and unless you were on the lookout for it you very easily missed what to most people is an experience of a lifetime. Nowadays the line is clearly marked by a sign in three languages and a broad cutting through the forest, in the middle of which runs a long line of white stones. Just a few minutes north of the circle a railway station has been built, and around it a small village called Polcirkeln has sprung up.

Having saluted the Arctic, the train picked up speed and for the next three hours raced through a countryside that might have been mistaken for Minnesota minus any farms. Smaller and smaller became the trees as pines gave way to birches.

Already the tints of autumn prevailed, but the leaves had not yet begun to fall. Under the trees the ground was mottled with patches of gray reindeer moss interspersed with different kinds of berry-bearing bushes whose leaves of gold, red, and brown formed a pattern of rich color. I wished we could have stopped the train and gathered baskets of those delicious berries which Fisher and I had often eaten as we trudged clear across Lapland at this very spot.

It was too late in the year to hear the cuckoos. They had already migrated back to their winter home in Africa, but there were still plenty of butterflies to be seen.

At two-thirty we arrived at Kiruna, the home of Sweden's mountain of iron which supplies the world with the special kind of ore that is required in the manufacture of electrical machinery. Incidentally, it also provides the ore that is used for Gillette razor blades. After years of continuous mining, Kiruna Mountain's shape had changed. When I had seen it in 1924 it had looked like any other mountain, and although trains loaded with silvery ore were continually emerging from its base, there was no outward evidence of mining. Nowadays Kiruna looks like a gigantic stepped pyramid, its natural profile having completely disappeared. But despite the fact that ore trains, each composed of forty-four cars, have been leaving the mountain every thirty minutes, day and night for the last thirty years, it is estimated that the supply of iron ore will last for at least another thousand years.

The city of Kiruna had grown considerably, and the railway station was gay with beautifully laid out flower beds.

On my first visit hardly a handful of people had met the train, among them a family of Lapps whose weather-beaten appearance and boots and leggings of reindeer skin showed that they were on migration but had stopped just long enough to take a look at the train. This time the railway platform was crowded with hunters and hikers. Dogs, knapsacks, guns, and fishing rods were very much in evidence, while dotted about among the crowd were about half a dozen theatrical-looking

Lapps whose brightly colored clothes made them conspicuous targets for the many cameras that were aimed at them by greenhorn tourists.

It was a pity that they were not authentic, at least so far as their costumes were concerned. More Swedish than Lapp, they were tall blondes wearing woolen stockings and rubber-soled shoes. But the Stockholm tourists loved them just the same.

The waterfalls of Lapland had not changed. Thanks to them, everything in this part of the Arctic is run by electricity, including the railroad.

"What happens in the winter? Don't they all freeze up?" asked Sam.

Most people wonder about that. But the fact of the matter is that although the waterfalls and lakes freeze up there is always enough running water under the ice to keep Lapland's power stations operating. Yet the water that runs through the giant turbines is only one quarter of a degree above freezing.

The train reached the shore of Lake Torneträsk, one of the loveliest of Arctic lakes, surrounded by mountains on which large patches of snow could be seen. Had we been able to inspect them, we would have found that the snow was melting and that around the edges of those white patches were many different kinds of arctic flowers.

As we skirted Lake Torneträsk I thought of the time when Fisher and I had nearly lost our lives in it. Caught in one of the sudden storms for which the lake is notorious, our tiny outboard motorboat had been tossed about like a cork. Waves of ice-cold water drenched us, and during one particularly violent gust the tossing boat flung my valuable camera high into the air. By the time the camera came down the boat had moved away, so down went the camera to the bottom of the lake.

It was amazing how the sight of Torneträsk stirred my memory. I spotted the very headland where Fisher and I had photographed an eider duck. There she was, sitting on her eggs, confident that her protective coloration made her invisible. Not until we set up our tripod within three feet of the bird did she show any concern. Then, without hurry, she plucked quite a lot of down from her own breast and, having tucked it underneath her body to protect her eggs, she flew away. Carefully we lifted her thick cover of eider down, and there, warm and cozy, were eight eggs.

It was on this same headland that we had photographed an arctic tern, the bird which nests in Lapland and migrates to the antarctic regions, the longest flight of any bird in the world.

I looked in vain for some of the many birds that had been so much in evidence before, but with the exception of a pair of eagles and numbers of crows, none was to be seen. Autumn and the threat of an early winter had driven them south. Nor could I see any Lapps or herds of reindeer, which had been such a common sight on my expedition with Fisher. Tourists had driven them north.

The train rattled past Abisko without stopping. The lovely chalet which had made Abisko such a mecca for travelers had been destroyed by fire. But a few miles farther along the lake was a brand-new chalet at Bjorkliden.

Here we alighted and, after a stiff uphill walk, arrived at the Hotel Fjallet, where first-class food and lodging were obtained at two dollars a day, which included three meals and afternoon tea. Intended primarily for hunters and hikers, the bedrooms were tiny and were provided with upper and lower bunks, but they were comfortable and clean as could be.

Overlooking Lake Torneträsk, the long dining room of the

116

Bjorkliden chalet has an enormous plate-glass picture window from which a magnificent view of Lap Portal is obtained. This striking gap in the mountains, which must have been scooped out by some prehistoric glacier, is the chief feature of the scenery. Through it the Lapps with their reindeer have migrated for centuries.

Far below and several miles away we could see a tunnel from which the electric ore trains emerged with monotonous regularity every half-hour on their way to Narvik. Time after time we counted the cars, and there were always the same number, forty-four.

The same trains return empty. They always will, until someone can find something Sweden wants from Norway that can be loaded into them for the return journey. I was told that at least eight million tons of iron ore annually pass Bjorkliden en route to Narvik.

There were two things we wanted to do at Bjorkliden: find an encampment of real Lapps and look for lemmings. The first proved to be easy, but when it came to finding any lemmings, I had my doubts as I recited for Zetta's and Sam's benefit that famous poem by England's poet laureate, John Masefield, entitled *The Lemmings*.

"Once in a hundred years the Lemmings come
Westward, in search of food, over the snow,
Westward, until the salt sea drowns them dumb,
Westward, till all are drowned, those Lemmings go.
Once, it is thought, there was a westward land
(Now drowned) where there was food for those starved things,
And memory of the place has burnt its brand
In the little brains of all the Lemming Kings.
Perhaps, long since, there was a land beyond

Westward from death, some city, some calm place,
Where one could taste God's quiet and be fond
With the little beauty of a human face;
But now the land is drowned, yet still we press
Westward, in search, to death, to nothingness."

CHAPTER SIX

"What is the truth about lemmings?" asked Sam that evening as we watched the almost-midnight sun setting over Lake Torneträsk. "I seem to remember some debunking article about them. Was Masefield romancing?"

"That's what I'd like to know too," said Zetta. "I'm sure I must have read the article Sam talks about. It stated that most of the stories that have been written about lemmings are just nonsense."

"Professional jealousy!" I answered laughingly. "Don't you remember the way people scoffed when I came to America from the Malay jungle and told about fish that climbed trees and lizards that broke off their tails when I chased them, and especially my description of the hornbill, the bird that feeds his wife on strychnine?"

"They still disbelieve a good many of your jungle stories. I used to wonder about them, too, until I went with you to the Malay jungle and saw for myself that fish do climb trees. I have never found you to be wrong yet," she added loyally.

"How about your telling us what you know about lemmings?" said Sam. "As we're going lemming hunting tomorrow, we may just as well know something about them."

"Well, in the first place," I began, "John Masefield was using poetic license when he said that lemmings come only once in a hundred years. They may start migrating any old time. It all depends on sunspots!"

"Sunspots!" said Sam incredulously. "Go on. I'm ready to believe anything."

For the rest of the evening I told them of the great lemming

119

migration which Dr. Clyde Fisher and I had witnessed in 1924. We not only saw millions of lemmings, but we photographed them and brought back a family of lemmings which can be seen at the American Museum of Natural History in New York.

A lemming or *Lemmus,* as it is known to zoologists, is a rodent about the size and shape of a small guinea pig. The bones of this mysterious little animal have been found in the caves of prehistoric man. Some historians have claimed that it was a lemming migration of phenomenal size that drove the ancient Norse Vikings from their homes to plunder the coasts of Europe. Strangely enough, in between migrations no one appears to have ever seen a lemming.

"There must be some somewhere," said Zetta, "or how could they breed?"

"Yes. But where?" I laughed. "Probably on the tops of the mountains. That's why we are going to climb Mount Nuolja tomorrow."

"Where do the sunspots come in?" asked Sam.

"According to Julian Huxley, the eminent biologist, who made a study of lemming migrations as far back as there are any records, they invariably correspond with the periods of unusual activity in the sun. Lots of sunspots mean lots of lemmings. And the interval between migrations is not one hundred years, but eighteen to twenty. His theory was that certain rays from the sun stimulate the sexual urge of lemmings. Instead of breeding normally, a pair will produce several litters within a few weeks. Worse than that, the young lemmings mature rapidly, so that they, too, begin to multiply, and so do their offspring. The result is that the mountaintops, which are believed to be the normal home of lemmings, quickly become overcrowded. Having eaten all the food in sight, the animals begin to starve. Then it is that they descend from the mountains in millions, searching for food and breeding while they are on the march."

"I suppose," said Zetta, "that is why the Lapps say that the lemmings come from heaven."

"Not only the Lapps, but other people too. I once saw an ancient Swedish woodcut that showed lemmings falling out of the sky and being devoured by wolves."

"Enough of these theories," said Sam. "Tell us just what happened when you saw that migration in 1924."

Here is the story:

Dr. Clyde Fisher and I were traveling with a family of Lapps who were following their reindeer across Lapland, heading toward the high mountains of Norway, where they hoped to find pasture. The father of the family was named Tuolja. He believed in magic supplemented by a fine pair of Zeiss field glasses for keeping watch over his herd.

One day I saw ahead of me, perched on a pinnacle of rock, a large white bird. Fisher saw it at the same time. "Look!" he shouted excitedly. "A snowy owl! I wonder what he's doing up here in Lapland."

When I used my field glasses to look at the owl I noticed that the whole countryside ahead of us was dotted with snowy owls, about a quarter of a mile apart, just like sentinels. I counted fifty and then gave up counting, for they were scattered as far as the horizon.

"They have been here for about a month," said Tuolja. "Very wise birds! They are waiting for the lemmings."

"Do you mean to tell me that those birds are expecting a migration?" asked Fisher incredulously.

"Yes," answered Tuolja, "and so are those hawks," indicating about a dozen large birds which were wheeling high up in the sky. "And there are plenty of wolves and other animals waiting for them too," he added.

"Well, well!" said Fisher, who rarely gave vent to his feelings with any stronger remark. "Those hawks must be *Buteo lagopus.*" He always talked Latin when discussing animals and plants.

A few minutes afterward I saw my first lemming. Evidently I was poaching on its preserve, because the little animal reared on its hind legs, showing its teeth and chattering with rage. When I stood and watched it, the lemming sprang at my legs and then retreated a few feet, only to return to the attack more savagely than ever. It was a pretty little animal with rich golden fur. In its efforts to frighten me away it jumped as high as my knees, barking, snapping its jaws, and snarling ferociously.

"Let's catch him and take him home to America!"

After one or two attempts I managed to make the lemming land in my hat, whence I transferred him to Fisher's leather camera case. When we camped for the night I filled the case with grass and reindeer moss. "That ought to satisfy him!"

But when morning came all the moss had disappeared and so had the lemming. He had chewed his way through the leather case.

I hated to lose him. But I needn't have worried.

Before noon that day we were walking through country that was swarming with lemmings, millions of them. Instead of advancing in a closely packed horde, as I had always imagined a migration, the animals were usually spaced about ten feet apart, each lemming in the middle of its own little plot of ground, motionless except for the champing of its jaws while eating.

Occasionally we came across two lemmings fighting until one

of them scampered away. Evidently the lemmings have a highly developed sense of proprietorship. Trespassing is strictly forbidden. At close quarters the animals did not appear to be traveling in any particular direction, but when I scanned the country with my field glasses there was no doubt that they were slowly moving westward, just as Masefield had described, "Westward, in search, to death, to nothingness."

Obviously nothing seemed to stop them, not even Fisher's leather camera case, which was ruined beyond repair.

We saw them swimming streams. Thousands of drowned lemmings floated past while others scrambled madly across. At one spot they were jumping off a cliff which they could easily have avoided. But once a lemming starts to migrate, he travels in a straight line, overcoming all obstacles. Thousands of dead lemmings at the base of the cliff provided a springy mattress for others to land on safely. Tuolja told us that not even a fire could stop them. Sooner or later, by sheer numbers, they extinguish the flames.

Although we didn't see any wolves, we did see the owls and the hawks carrying off the lemmings in their talons.

"Yes," said Tuolja, "even the fish have a feast. They gobble up lemmings as they swim the fjords into the sea. Look at my dogs," he said.

Two of Tuolja's dogs were rushing about, catching lemmings and shaking them until their heads flew off, which were promptly eaten.

"Reindeer eat lemmings too," said Tuolja. "They hate them. They stamp on them and eat their heads."

"I'll believe that when I see it!" remarked Fisher incredulously.

"You would eat lemmings yourself if there was nothing else to eat," I said.

For twenty miles we walked through lemmings, killing hundreds with our sticks. Fisher dissected one of them.

"Well, well," he said in astonishment. "Its reproductive organs occupy nearly one quarter of its body. Its penis has a bone in it."

"Blame it on sunspots!" I chuckled.

Then, just as suddenly as we had come upon them, the lemmings were gone. The horde was about twenty miles wide, traveling almost due west, and we were walking nearly north.

"Why on earth didn't you follow them and see what happened when they reached the sea?" asked Zetta.

"Because at the rate they were moving it would have taken them about two years to get there," I explained. "But Tuolja told us what would happen when they arrived. The lemmings would collect in an immense swarm, closely packed together, fighting and dying by thousands from sheer excitement, until suddenly a leader appeared. Braver than the rest, the leader would plunge boldly into the sea and start to swim. The rest would follow until there wasn't a live lemming left on land."

"Where do they think they're going?" asked Zetta.

"The theory is that they are looking for the lost continent of Atlantis, the place to which their ancestors used to go in search of food when overpopulation caused a famine. It is supposed to be a case of inherited instinct," I explained.

"But are lemmings aquatic animals?" objected Sam.

"No, they certainly are not," I said. "They have claws and there is no sign of webbed feet. In fact, unlike most animals, lemmings have hair on the soles of their feet. But they can swim just the same. Dr. Wilfred Grenfell once told me that he had followed a migration of lemmings for ten miles in a rowboat, and when he gave up they were still swimming strongly. Yet according to Grenfell, lemmings aren't such good swimmers as might be expected. He found that a splash of his oar would cause several of the little animals to drown, while a breaking wave would destroy hundreds."

Sam looked thoughtful.

"What happens to all those owls and hawks and other animals that feast on the lemmings during a migration?"

"Presumably they make their way back sadly and somewhat biliously to their distant homes. Not in their lifetime will living ever be so easy again." I laughed. "But I can tell you this. After that 1924 migration, large numbers of snowy owls were observed flying across Canada, but where they were going I cannot say."

"Wouldn't it be wonderful if we were to find a lemming tomorrow?" said Zetta as we went to bed. "There must be some left to carry on."

However, when tomorrow came and we climbed to the summit of Mount Nuolja, all we found was the cairn of rocks which Fisher and I had built in 1924, on top of which we had planted the Explorers Club flag. On the way down we met several parties of hikers who had been mountain climbing farther inland. To each we put the same question, "Have you seen any lemmings?" But the answer was always "No! They are never seen between migrations."

"What beats me," said Zetta, who has a business mind, "is why somebody doesn't watch for a migration and then make a fortune in fur!"

"What is the use of a lemming, anyway?" asked Sam.

The only time I ever discovered anyone who had ever made use of a lemming was in Minnesota, where I once met an old Swedish farmer to whom I put the same question.

"Sure lemmings are useful," he said. "I have a scarf made of lemming fur." Then with a grin he added, "Lemming fur makes a fine bag to keep your most valuable possession warm in the wintertime. And I don't mean money!"

The late President Theodore Roosevelt used to take his sons Theodore and Kermit on "lemming walks" in order to train them to overcome all obstacles once they had embarked on any line of endeavor.

One day the French Ambassador arrived at the White House to pay a call just when the President and his sons were setting out for a lemming walk. This consisted of driving out into the country and then, having set their course by means of a compass, walking for two hours in that direction, regardless of all obstacles. Over hill and down dale they would go, climbing fences, scrambling over haystacks, letting nothing deflect them from their chosen path.

Needless to say, the President and his boys were dressed in their roughest hiking togs. But the French Ambassador wore formal dress with patent-leather shoes, spats, top hat, doeskin gloves, and a walking stick.

"Won't you join us?" invited Mr. Roosevelt with a twinkle in his eye.

"Delighted!" replied the somewhat mystified Ambassador as he piled into the waiting automobile.

Having arrived at a deserted spot in the Virginia countryside, the President discharged the car. "This is where we start!"

"How about walking due south?" said Theodore as he set a course with his compass.

More mystified than ever and probably thinking to himself, "These Americans are strange people," the Frenchman started walking.

Soon his shoes were covered with mud and his spats ruined. But the Ambassador was a good sport. It all seemed crazy, but it was fine exercise and, after all, he was in distinguished company.

Over hedges, across muddy farmyards, through swamps and even a cow barn that due-south course led them. Lemmings meant nothing to the Frenchman. He had never heard of them. But when the President of the United States assured him that this was how he trained his sons to overcome all obstacles, the Ambassador entered into the spirit of the occasion and even set the pace himself, top hat and all.

Soon they came to a river. Was this the end? he thought.

Evidently it was not, for, having undressed themselves completely, the Roosevelt family, with their clothing in bundles on their heads, started to wade the river. Undaunted, the Frenchman followed suit.

They were halfway across the river when Mr. Roosevelt looked back.

"Mr. Ambassador," he said in a serious voice, "I see that you are still wearing your gloves."

"Of course," said the Ambassador just as seriously. "Suppose we meet some ladies!"

At Bjorkliden people hike, hunt, eat, and sleep, and nothing else seems to matter. So long as those iron-ore trains keep running night and day, the people of Bjorkliden know that all is well and prosperous in the rest of Sweden.

We left Bjorkliden by train at eight-twenty that night, bound for Narvik.

Crossing the border into Norway was extremely simple. First Swedish inspectors came through the train examining passports and inquiring how much money we were taking out of the country. Then the Norwegians boarded the train and did the same thing. There was no customs inspection. At eleven o'clock we arrived at Narvik, a pretty little town built on the sides of the hills which overlook the harbor and the fjord which was the scene of one of the great naval battles between the British and the Germans during World War II.

More than thirty wrecks still clutter up the bottom of Narvik Harbor, often making anchoring a hazardous and expensive operation. Many a ship has lost an anchor at Narvik. But the most conspicuous thing about this arctic seaport is the equipment for loading iron ore into the ships which come from all quarters of the globe to get it.

It was now clear why the trains had forty-four cars. That was the number which fit the chutes down which the ore tumbled from train to steamer. Unloading such a train is only a matter of a few minutes. Just time to run onto the wharf, unload, and shunt off again before the next train arrives and repeats the process. Not a second is lost, and as fast as a ship is loaded another is waiting to take its place. Narvik is a noisy place, for the roar of the tumbling ore never ceases.

Narvik is also a tragic place, for the faces of the people are lined with sadness and suffering. The Nazi occupation was a time of horror for the inhabitants, many of whom were executed on the slightest provocation. But Narvik was a veritable Gethsemane for the thousands of Russian prisoners of war whom the Nazis kept in concentration camps with little more than the barbed wire to keep them warm in the freezing cold. Forced to do hard labor on empty stomachs, hundreds of them died. Starving, they would beg the Norwegians for food, but feeding a Russian meant death before the firing squad. Unable to stand the sight of such awful suffering, many a Narvik resident would hide some sandwiches or throw out garbage where some starving Russian would find it, only to be shot for his mercy. Narvik's cemetery contains many such good samaritans.

Yet when I visited the war cemetery I noticed that the graves of the hundreds of Nazis were just as carefully tended by the Norwegians as those of their Allies.

Although it meant risking their lives, a good many of Narvik's people succeeded in making friends with the Russians, who showered them with blessings and promises to repay their kindness if ever they got home to Russia. Poor devils. Little did they dream that the fate that awaited them in their own country would be far worse than anything they were suffering at the hands of the Germans.

The Norwegians who told me these prisoner stories did so with tears running down their cheeks. When I asked them to tell me about their own sufferings they either broke down completely or they said, "Please don't ask. It is too awful. I cannot talk about it."

When the Germans were eventually driven out of Narvik it wasn't very long until Russian ships arrived to take the prisoners back to Russia. With unspeakable cruelty and deceit the officers allowed the wretched prisoners to load themselves down with presents. Food, clothing, and many kinds of gifts, from soap to wrist watches, were showered upon them by the generous people of Narvik. Addresses were exchanged and many a Russian took with him a photograph of his benefactor. Before the ships sailed, the Norwegians even gave a banquet in honor of the Russian "liberators," who made many speeches of thanks for the kindness which had been shown to the prisoners.

Finally the ships sailed, and had it not been for the presence on board one of the ships of a Norwegian doctor who had been permitted to accompany those who were seriously ill, the fate of the prisoners might never have been known. Why the Russians permitted that doctor to return to Narvik and reveal the pitiful tale can only be attributed to a mistake on the part of some official who has probably long since been liquidated for his stupidity.

Upon arrival at Murmansk, the joyful but unsuspecting Russians landed with cheers. But their joy was short-lived. Instead of being placed in trains for transport to their homes or a hospital, as would have been the case in the United States, the men were herded into cattle cars, their clothes and presents taken away, and off they went to some remote part of arctic Russia to die or be worked to death in labor camps. They had tasted the forbidden fruit of Norwegian freedom. Their infection was dangerous to others, especially to their relatives, according to the Communist creed. Had even one per cent of them carried out their promises to write and thank their Norwegian benefactors, the other 99 per cent might have been thought guilty of base ingratitude. But not one of those Russian prisoners has ever communicated with Narvik. The Norwegians say quite frankly that they must have been liquidated.

Months afterward a Russian ship arrived at Narvik with a cargo of building material for the erection of a large monument to those prisoners who had died in camp. But no news was forthcoming as to the whereabouts of the men who had left Narvik so joyfully.

Having erected this monument on Norwegian soil, the Russians now have an excuse to return at all too frequent intervals, ostensibly to inspect the monument. But according to the Norwegians, their real purpose is to spy and make charts and take soundings of the approaches to Narvik Harbor.

"What will you people do if Russia invades Norway? Will you fight?" I asked numbers of people.

"Yes! Of course we'll fight," they answered, "but it won't do much good. We know that the Russians are coming. Who's going to stop them?"

We left Narvik, crossing the fjord by ferry and then motoring to Tromsö. It was a magnificent drive, for not only did we have incomparable mountain and fjord scenery, but the whole countryside was gorgeous with the golden colors of autumn.

At Tromsö a representative of the Scandinavian Airlines contacted us. He explained that Miss Astri Tonberg was waiting anxiously for our arrival in Finnmark. She had managed to persuade several families of Lapps to postpone their departure, but as this had meant persuading about five hundred reindeer to postpone theirs, too, she was experiencing quite a lot of difficulty. The deer were impatient, and if we didn't hurry, they would be gone.

It should be explained that Laplanders do not drive their herds of reindeer as cow hands drive cattle. They follow the reindeer. The idea that reindeer are as domesticated as cattle is quite wrong. Twice annually the herds migrate: once to their winter feeding grounds and once to their summer ones. Generally speaking, they follow the same route as their ancestors did. The deer graze as they travel, but they do not ask the Lapps' permission when to go or where to settle down for a feed. Sometimes they will stay around one locality for several weeks. At another time, if conditions are not to their liking, the deer start off at a gallop to another camp site.

The extreme importance the Lapp attaches to his reindeer is

indicated by the fact that there are in his language more than three hundred words relating to the animal. Whether the Lapps live on reindeer or the reindeer live on Lapps is hard to say. In trying to explain the matter, a Lapp once told me, "I cannot tell you where we come from, but I know this, that we Lapps have always been scared away by the approach of other people. If this had not happened, perhaps we would not have become nomads. We might have taken to building houses and living like other folk. But we fled before strangers just as the wild reindeer did. The Lapps and the reindeer ran away together and became dependent upon one another. We have been companions in adversity and have lived together ever since."

When a reindeer is slaughtered, not an atom of it is wasted. Most of the blood is collected in a barrel and fed to the dogs. Some of the blood is placed in the dead animal's stomach, where it solidifies and keeps indefinitely. Mixed with hot water, this solidified blood makes a nutritious drink. All the meat is preserved by being smoked and dried. It is eaten uncooked, being cut into thin shavings with a very sharp knife. But the most prized part of a reindeer is the bone marrow. In fact, the barter of well-cured marrow bones is the only commercial transaction among Lapps. Well-aged marrow is as prized a delicacy to a Lapp as Limburger cheese was to Mark Twain. Other bones and the antlers (which are shed annually and are found on both sexes of reindeer) are made into various kinds of implements and curios for sale to tourists.

The sinews of the animal are carefully preserved for converting into sewing thread. This is accomplished by the women, who spend hours pulling the sinews through their teeth until they are as fine as silk. A woman will take a handful of sinew fiber in one hand and a spinner in the other. Hour after hour she spins the fiber into thread by rubbing the fiber on her cheek. The result is that most of the elderly Lapp women have a very shiny left cheek.

The hide of the deer is used for boots and winter clothing or rugs.

Fortunately for the Lapps, the deer during migration rarely leave the beaten track. As they have been doing this for centuries, camp sites with fireplaces and often a sod house are always ready. At least they were before World War II. But one of the mischievous acts of the retreating Germans was to destroy many of these camp sites and break up the stone fireplaces which were often more than a hundred years old. Consequently many of the present-day Lapps are forced to carry iron stoves with them and to live in tents. But a much sadder thing than an uprooted camp has befallen many of the Lapp families.

In order to save their children from dying because of the Nazi brutalities, some of the Lapps left their babies with Norwegians. But when the war was over and the Lapps reclaimed their children, they soon discovered that the softer life in well-heated homes had unfitted them for the rigors of nomadic life. The children fell sick and many of them died. To save the rest, many Lapps gave their children back to their foster parents. Not only was this a cause of great grief, but it weakened the family as a unit.

I could just picture those Lapps who were waiting for us. I could imagine the Lapp dogs racing round and round the reindeer herd trying to keep the animals from breaking away. No wonder Miss Tonberg was anxious. So after a night's rest in Tromsö we boarded a seaplane and started north to Alta.

"There's the German battleship *Von Tirpitz!*" shouted our pilot as he obligingly descended and flew completely around the ship that had given the allies such anxiety when she escaped into the North Sea. Half submerged and upside down, the huge vessel was lying close to the shore of the fjord near Tromsö. In her bottom was a huge hole through which men were still removing her valuable machinery. It must be a gruesome job for the salvagers, for when the ship capsized after a direct hit with a British blockbuster she had more than a thousand sailors on board. Since we were there, I have heard that the Norwegians have constructed a tearoom on the *Von Tirpitz* bottom for the benefit of sight-seers!

It took only two hours to fly from Tromsö to Alta, but it was an unforgettable experience to see Norway's glorious fjords, snow-capped mountains, and glistening glaciers at close quarters through the window of an airplane.

Miss Tonberg was waiting at the dock for our arrival. Young and pretty, this remarkable Norwegian girl is the government administrator in charge of building what she calls "mountain huts" all over Finnmark, an area bigger than Denmark.

Why they are called "huts" I cannot imagine, for they are anything but huts. On the contrary, they are charmingly designed resthouses, very comfortably furnished and spotlessly clean. Each place has a housekeeper, who looks after any traveler who may happen along. One section of the house is reserved for Lapps and the other for hikers or tourists. The prices charged are absurdly cheap, as far as I remember, varying from one dollar and fifty cents to two dollars per day, meals included. The food is excellent though plain, if you call freshly caught lake trout plain!

"I'm so delighted you have arrived at last," said Miss Tonberg. "We must hurry. Hop into the car. There is a fifty-mile drive ahead of us. The Lapps were there when I left, but the reindeer were getting restless!"

As we motored through the countryside, glorious with the rich colors of autumn, we asked Astri to tell us something of the kind of life she leads. "Summer is lovely except for the mosquitoes. You're fortunate to miss them." She smiled.

"What about the winter?" asked Zetta.

"Sometimes I travel on skis or snowshoes, but more often I have to drive very long distances by sleigh, and as it is perpetual night most of the winter, I have to watch out for wolves. They are very numerous." From the casual way she spoke of wolves following the sleigh, you would have thought that they were no more dangerous than dogs; but, like a soldier who has just come back from war, she didn't want to talk about the dangers of her solitary occupation.

"I love the Lapps," she said enthusiastically. "They are my friends. And I think they love me too. I speak their language."

"So do I," said Sam. *"Pooris pooris! Pooris pooris!"*

"That's wonderful!" laughed Astri. "If only more people who come to Finnmark could say 'Greetings' in the Lapp language, they would have a much more interesting time."

Mile after mile we motored through the rolling hills of Finnmark which are so reminiscent of Dartmoor or the north of Scotland, but minus the heather.

"There's lots of game and plenty of trout," said Astri gaily, "but when the hunters and hikers begin to swarm here, as they are sure to do when they know about my comfortable 'huts,' I'm afraid the Lapps will go still farther inland. They prefer loneliness."

Suddenly the car slowed down. Astri was listening.

"D'you hear the dogs barking?" she said excitedly. "The Lapps are over that rise. We'll have to walk."

The car had stopped in the middle of a wind-swept plateau, treeless but beautiful as a Persian carpet.

"Not much shelter up here," remarked Sam, who was shivering.

Soon we were knee-deep in springy moss and berrybushes. Astri picked a handful of grayish-green lichen. "This is the principal food of the reindeer," she said. "Reindeer moss."

"What happens when the moss is covered with snow?" inquired Sam.

"The deer just scrape the snow away," replied Astri, "and if the snow is really deep, three or four feet, they have to dig holes in it, and then all you can see of the animals are their tails wagging on the surface. Now can you see the Lapps? Look!"

But for the life of us, all we could see was the beautiful patchwork of color against a background of rolling hills which were violet and patched here and there with snow fields.

Astri laughed. "They tell me that you cannot see the Grand Canyon until you stand suddenly at its very edge. Look again."

Only then did we see a small lake at the bottom of a saucer-shaped depression. Beside the lake was a large patch of gray.

"You're looking at more than five hundred reindeer. They have been resting there for two days, waiting for you people to arrive."

But only when the deer, having seen us first, began to move and stand up did we notice the herd. "There are the Lapps," cried Astri as she started shouting to them in their queer-sounding language.

In a few moments we were surrounded by about a dozen people—men, women, and children. All were dressed in dark blue material beautifully embroidered on the edges with narrow strips of red, yellow, and green military cloth. On their heads the men wore peaked caps surmounted by a large scarlet pompon as big as a grapefruit. The women and girls wore closely fitting red bonnets with red-and-white embroidered handkerchiefs draped over their shoulders. On their feet all wore Lapp boots made of reindeer skin.

The reason we hadn't seen them was that they had all been sitting on the ground, and as the vegetation came up to their shoulders, only their red hats were visible and they blended with the prevailing red and golden brown of the leaves.

About a hundred yards from the lake were two Lapp tents, or *kotas,* looking very much like Indian tepees except that the tent poles did not interlock at the top. The reason for this was clear when we inspected the construction of a kota.

"I wonder where the Lapps learned mathematics," said Sam as he pointed out that the framework of the kota consisted of two parabolas erected vertically and kept about three feet apart by means of two wooden bars. Against these parabolas rested twenty tent poles forming a cone-shaped framework which was covered with cloth. For convenience in moving the kota, the two parabolic frames were hinged at the top so that they could be folded easily. They and the tent poles were shiny with age.

About fifty feet from the kotas was another structure, consisting of a small wooden platform raised on piles about eight feet from the ground. "That's the larder," explained Astri. "They have to keep their food away from the animals."

While we were examining the houses the Lapps crowded around us, laughing and chattering. "Pooris pooris!" was all we could say, but even that slight knowledge of their language obviously delighted them.

"They look like Santa Claus!" laughed Sam.

"Finnmark is the summer home of Santa Claus," said Astri.

"Come, let's call on Mrs. Santa Claus," I said.

My knowledge of Lapp etiquette came in useful. Instead of knocking, I lifted up the flap of the door and sat down just inside the threshold. A woman was sitting beside an iron stove which was in the center of the kota, directly beneath the opening in the roof through which the smoke escaped.

"Pooris pooris," I said.

"Pooris pooris," she replied, beckoning me to a more comfortable place beside the stove. The stove and the cheap enamelware saucepan that was upon it were evidence that the Nazis had destroyed the original stone fireplace and the birchwood cooking utensils which all Lapps used before the occupation. Otherwise the interior of the kota was just as I had remembered. Birch branches covered the ground, and upon them were reindeer skins, making a springy and fairly comfortable floor.

Sitting beside the woman was a little girl, about two years old, whose cheeks were as rosy as apples. Beside the child was a fierce-looking dog which growled at me menacingly. It was her guardian.

When a Lapp girl is born the father gives her two presents: first a female reindeer, to start a herd for her dowry, and second a female dog. No one except her parents dare touch the baby, although a Lapp dog is so intelligent that it knows when to bite and when not.

The dog knew that I was an invited guest, so when I reached to shake hands with the baby, it took hold of my hand gently but firmly and drew me away from the child.

The kind of life that a Lapp dog leads can hardly be called a "dog's life," because Lapps regard their dogs as honored members of the household, and the dogs know it. Four dogs lived in this particular house, and by the time I had entered they, too, had taken their places, where they sat and eyed me solemnly.

Twice a day the dogs are fed on reindeer blood mixed with hot water. No dogs are so well behaved as Lapp dogs. At meal-times they watch patiently while their food is being prepared and poured into a large pan. Then at a word from the master the oldest dog walks very slowly toward the food and drinks his share. Then dog number two walks forward and takes his, and so on down the line. There is no barking or fighting.

Lapps will explain that all dogs are very sensitive. For small offenses a dog must only be scolded. For a serious offense a dog may be whipped, but no matter how badly a dog behaves, it must never be whipped and scolded at the same time. Such treatment breaks a dog's spirit.

"Where do the people sleep?" asked Sam.

"On reindeer skins under mosquito nets in the summer, but without nets in the winter," I answered, for I remembered how Fisher and I had lived when we were traveling with Tuolja.

"What about the dogs?" asked Zetta.

"They sleep with the different members of the family," I said, "and they act as hot-water bottles too! The dog snuggles into the small of your back, and when you turn over, the dog turns too."

Incidentally, when a Lapp has a stomach-ache he makes a dog go to sleep on his stomach. Very soon, according to Tuolja, the dog gets the stomach-ache, having drawn it out of the man.

"Some Lapp medicine is more drastic than that," laughed Astri. "A Lapp once told me that the best way to cure tooth-ache was to fill the cavity with tinder and ignite it!"

"Didn't you tell me that the Lapps were magicians?" asked Sam.

"They certainly used to be in the days of Linnaeus," I answered. "They were very successful in locating their lost reindeer by means of a magic drum. But nowadays they have even better luck with field glasses."

Astri looked interested. I hadn't told her that I had once stayed with Johann Turi, Lapland's most celebrated philosopher, or that I had lived with a Lapp family on migration for three months. I could see that she was wondering where I got my information.

Lapp divining drums were always used by the ancestors of present-day Lapps, and not so many years ago either. The drums were somewhat oval, about eighteen inches at the larger diameter and twelve inches at the smaller. Imagine an egg as big as that. Cut it in half lengthwise, stretch a skin over the top, and you have a Lapp drum. On the drumskin was drawn a map of the locality in which the Lapps were camped. To locate a lost reindeer, the Lapp held the drum in his left hand with the drumskin level. On the map he placed a small iron ring about one inch in diameter. He then tapped the side of the drum with a small hammer made of reindeer antler. The blows caused the drumskin to vibrate, and this in turn made the ring dance about from place to place.

Sooner or later, as the vibrations diminished or ceased, the ring would come to rest on the very spot where the missing reindeer was to be sought. If it were not found there, the deer was assumed to have wandered to some other place. The drum was then consulted again and again until by perseverance the lost animal was usually located.

Nowadays, however, reindeer which may have strayed

hundreds of miles from their herds are easily located with field glasses, a piece of birchbark, and a notice board.

"Sounds intriguing," remarked Sam. "How do they do it?"

Leading the way outside the tent, I pointed to one of the Lapps who was peering intently at the reindeer herd through his field glasses.

"He's examining the shapes of their ears," I said.

"They all look alike to me," said Sam after looking intently at the herd.

Just as he spoke, the Lapp put away his glasses and walked into the herd with his lasso. At his first attempt he lassoed a deer, which he hauled in as if it were a fish.

"See?" I said. "He's making a pattern of its ear. He's cutting a piece of birchbark to match the notches on it. That's because the shape of the deer's ear is different from the rest. It's a stray."

Having placed the pattern of the deer's ear in his pocket, the Lapp released the animal, which promptly rejoined the herd.

"There's honesty for you," I said. "The next time the inspector of nomads comes along he will be given that pattern. It will then be pinned on a notice board where Lapps who have lost reindeer are accustomed to look. Attached will be full information where the owner can find his lost animal. The shapes of all deer's ears are registered."

"Ah!" said Sam. "It is debatable which is best after all—the drum or the field glass. With the old-fashioned drum a Lapp could find his own deer. With field glasses he can only find someone else's. Give me the drum!"

"It's about time we returned to Alta," said Astri. "Now, Mr. Tatem, can you say 'good-by' in Lappish?"

"*Hivasti, hivasti,*" said Sam. "Hivasti, hivasti," replied the Lapps. Never before were two words of a foreign language put to such good purpose as Sam's "Pooris" and "Hivasti." He never did let Astri know that those were the only words of Lappish he knew, or that I had taught them to him only that morning.

By the time we reached our car the Lapps had broken camp; the reindeer, their hind hoofs clicking like castanets, were moving rapidly away with the Lapps trudging stolidly behind them.

"What a life!" said Sam. I agreed with him. What a life!

So far as scenery is concerned, the drive from Alta to Hammerfest was a magnificent experience, but it will take many years to efface the scars of the Nazi occupation and their scorched-earth policy during retreat. Ugly black patches were all that remained of villages whose inhabitants had not yet returned to rebuild them. Mile after mile of telephone poles had been chopped down or burned, but beside the stumps new poles had been erected. Even the snow fences, so necessary in Finnmark, had been burned, and it will take many years to replace them in this part of Norway, where large trees are conspicuous by their absence.

We were almost afraid to look at Hammerfest, which, when we had last seen the town in 1932, had been such a picturesque sight. Astri had warned us that the whole place had been razed by the Germans.

However, it is an ill wind that blows no one any good. Old Hammerfest had been like Topsy: it had just grown haphazardly. But new Hammerfest, which, phoenix-like, has risen from its ashes, has been well planned. Still picturesque, its new wooden houses are equipped with baths and toilets, so that for the first time in their lives many of the inhabitants are enjoy-

142

ing the luxuries of life which we in America take so much for granted.

Before the Nazi occupation Hammerfest's leading citizen was Mr. Hagen, who owned the town's one and only bookstore and lived in a fine house. Although the Nazis burned his store and house, they failed to crush the spirit of this fine old gentleman, who, with the help of his charming wife, has reopened his store and is carrying on bravely. In readiness for our arrival they had prepared an elaborate luncheon, complete with aquavit, smörgåsbord, and wines.

A letter was awaiting Zetta, and as she read it she shouted, "It's all arranged! Our tickets for India are waiting for us in Oslo. We can fly from here. Just imagine, only three days from arctic Hammerfest to Calcutta!"

"This calls for a toast to the Scandinavian Airlines," laughed Sam as he raised his fifth glass of aquavit. "Skoal!"

But it was not so easy as we had expected. The last plane had already left Hammerfest, and there wouldn't be another for nine months. If we were to catch our plane for India there wasn't a moment to lose.

"The mail steamer leaves in an hour," said Mr. Hagen. "You can go by her to Tromsö, and there you can catch your plane to Oslo."

I can still see that sturdy old Norwegian with Astri by his side waving us good-by as the little vessel set sail. It was strange to realize that Hammerfest would soon be enveloped by the long arctic night while we, if all went well, would be gliding over Dal Lake in the Vale of Kashmir.

By midnight we were safely in bed at Tromsö, and at seven in the morning we boarded a flying boat for Trondheim and Oslo.

143

When we had left New York, Shalimar had been just a castle in the air, but by the time we reached Oslo's Grand Hotel the dream of a lifetime began to materialize.

"You certainly know the art of pulling strings," said Sam to Zetta as she showed us the pile of letters that awaited us.

Plane reservations to India had seemed impossible to secure when I tried. But here were three tickets to Calcutta with a most cordial letter from the president of Scandinavian Airlines, telling us that a representative of the line would meet us at every stopping place en route, which meant Copenhagen, Frankfurt, Zurich, Rome, Lydda, Karachi, and Calcutta.

Oslo, which was celebrating its nine hundredth anniversary, is a city of the greatest interest to explorers, for it is here that one can see several ships of the Vikings which have been preserved complete, including masts and oars, and housed in an immense building specially built to receive them. But even more interesting to us was Nansen's famous ship *Fram*, which is also housed in an enormous building high enough to cover her completely, despite the fact that she is fully rigged except for her topmasts. This wonderful old ship still holds the record for having sailed farther north and farther south than any other ship in the world. Although it is now a museum of arctic and antarctic exploration, the vessel is in such excellent condition that it could very easily be refloated and used again.

Close by and housed in its own shed was the famous raft *Kon Tiki*, on which a group of explorers so recently floated from South America to the South Sea Islands. By a strange coincidence, hanging on the wall of the building was a photograph of the two men who saw us off on our own expedition, chief of the Clan Fhearghuis and Peter Freuchen.

But to the average visitor, the most interesting sight in Oslo is the Sculpture Park, which has caused so much controversy in the world of art. This beautifully laid out park is jam-packed with the works of a Norwegian sculptor who, by arrangement with the government, exchanged his whole life's output of statues for a house, a studio, and all his living expenses. The sculptor's heart now rests in the tower of his house, which has been turned into a national museum. Months could be spent in this one park just looking at the hundreds and hundreds of statues which Adolf Gustav Vigeland chiseled from solid stone during the span of his prodigious life.

His masterpiece, known as the *Monolith,* chiseled out of a solid block of stone, stands nearly sixty feet high. This one sculpture took the artist forty years to complete.

The last lap of our Scandinavian odyssey landed us in Copenhagen, the city of towers and a metropolis of a million Danes who are just as enthusiastic about their diminutive country as Texans are about Texas.

"It makes me think of London," said Zetta as we watched the traffic from our window of the Hôtel d'Angleterre.

Although their country is only one sixteenth the size of Texas, Danes have the same sly sense of humor as Texans. For instance, they tell you that Denmark, although hardly noticeable on a map of the world, consists of five hundred islands, most of which are kept apart by bridges. Low-lying, from approximately four feet below sea level to 570 feet above it, Denmark resembles a contented red cow in an enormous green field. It has one waterfall, which is four feet high. But it also has broad streams and blue lakes, idyllic fjords, white sandy beaches, and unexpected cliffs. Dotted about this little land are thousands of gardens surrounding thousands of small white farms which produce incredible numbers of pigs of identical size, length, shape, and fatness. Yet if you ask for Danish bacon in your hotel the waiter will tell you that such a luxury can be had only in England. The same applies to Danish butter, Danish cheeses, and Danish eggs, every one of which is identical in size and so marked that the consumer may see which hen laid it and when.

But besides farms, Denmark has numerous ancient parks surrounding even more ancient castles that are haunted by gray and white ladies who look down from the mullioned windows upon real white swans on the green waters of the moat. Most of the castles are for rent, for, like Sweden, Denmark is very democratic and castles are no longer in fashion.

Denmark has Socialism, but none of the Danes we met seemed to worry much about it. Nobody looks down on a millionaire. Everyone knows that the taxation system will soon make him one of them. Class distinctions exist, but the Danes haven't yet discovered where to put the distinction. They told us that out of the four million inhabitants of Denmark there were only two people who could neither read nor write. On the other hand, they claimed that there were still two thousand Danes who had never written a book or a play or painted a picture, but this figure was steadily diminishing.

Denmark's very high standard of education brings professors and ditchdiggers to the same cultural level on which they can and do converse. The main difference between those classes is that the ditchdigger earns far more money than the professor, and there are many more ditchdiggers than professors.

Danish women are completely emancipated. While they do not yet smoke cigars on the street, they smoke them everywhere else, and cheroots too. Otherwise they are just as attractive as most Scandinavians. It is not unusual for ladies to stand up when they are being introduced to men. Nor is it unknown for a man to remain seated when a lady enters the room. From which it will be seen that Danes are not quite so formal as Swedes. But their hearts are in the right place just the same. They think nothing of driving a visitor miles into the country to see some famous place such as Kronborg Castle, the traditional site of Shakespeare's *Hamlet*.

Our time was far too short in hospitable Denmark, whose national drink is beer and whose national weakness is another beer. But Kashmir was calling, so with a last wave to the land of cherry brandy we boarded a DC-6 of the Scandinavian Airlines bound for Calcutta.

CHAPTER SEVEN

We arrived at Calcutta at 3:40 A.M. on the dot, just as the S.A.S. timetable said we would. Scarcely thirty-six hours had passed since our DC-6 had taken off from Copenhagen. During that time we had had afternoon tea in Frankfurt, dinner in Switzerland, and supper in Rome. During the night we had flown over the Aegean Sea to the Holy Land, where we arrived in time for breakfast at Lydda. There, having been screened by a young lady who told us with a Brooklyn accent that we were not in "Palestine" but in Israel, we were offered a breakfast which was not very appetizing.

For the next twelve hours we flew above the clouds, enjoying the almost unbelievable hospitality of the Scandinavian Airlines. Delicious food, fresh fruit, chocolates, assorted wines or soft drinks, cigarettes and cosmetics, all were on the house and served by a blond stewardess who could have won a beauty contest almost anywhere.

While the plane refueled at Karachi we enjoyed a good dinner in the airport restaurant, and by ten-thirty we were in the air again, crossing the thousand miles of India which separate West Pakistan from East Pakistan.

The keynote of the flight, as far as the airplane itself was concerned, was perfect service and spotless cleanliness. Yet the moment the plane rolled to a stop at Calcutta, in walked a far from clean porter who fumigated us and all our belongings with DDT.

"What's the big idea?" I said querulously.

"You stopped at Lydda," grunted the porter as he pumped

149

more vigorously than ever on his DDT fumigator. Evidently Lydda wasn't popular in Calcutta.

"I wonder what'll happen when they find that Sam is traveling on a British passport," whispered Zetta as we prepared to pass through customs. We had been warned by a good many people that the Indians hated the British and despised Americans; that newly independent India was feeling her oats and that her minor officials often went out of their way to provoke foreigners so that they could find some excuse to arrest them. How false this malicious propaganda was we soon found out.

"Mr. Tatem!" shouted the immigration officer.

Sam produced his passport nervously.

"British! And from Bermuda!" exclaimed the officer. "First Bermudian I have ever met! Okay, no questions. Welcome to India."

Sam grinned all over his face. His British passport evidently worked wonders. It was now our turn.

"Mr. and Mrs. Carveth Wells!" shouted the same official. "Americans, I see. Kindly step aside."

My heart almost failed me when a police officer took us in tow and conducted us to another desk, at which sat a smartly uniformed young Indian. Taking from a drawer a large sheet of paper that must have measured at least eighteen inches wide and two feet long, divided into squares like a checkerboard, he said:

"I must ask you to fill in this questionnaire carefully."

"But it will take us hours!" I exclaimed with exasperation.

"What business brings you to India?" he said sternly.

"Pleasure, I hope. I'm just another tourist," I answered.

"Tourists!" The man's face changed from frowns to smiles. "I beg your pardon," he said cordially. "I shall have much pleasure in filling out the forms myself. Just sign your names here. I'll fill in the little squares!" Then, handing each of us a small card, he said, "Carry this with you. You may go wherever you wish. Welcome to India!"

"How about Kashmir?" inquired Zetta.

"Sorry, madam," said the official politely. "Kashmir requires a special permit from the War Department. That may be difficult."

"What a relief that was!" laughed Sam. "These present-day Indians aren't so bad as they have been painted. Not by a long shot!"

In less than ten minutes, with our baggage piled in one taxi and ourselves in another, we were on our way into town.

"Queer-looking ducks, these taxi drivers. And two for each taxi, I notice," said Sam as he eyed the two fierce-looking huskies who could only just manage to squeeze into the front seat.

"They're Sikhs," I explained. "Good fighters despite the fact that they wrap their beards around their ears and wear their long hair in a topknot under their turbans."

The reason why all Calcutta taxis carry two men in the front seat was explained to us later. One's job is to drive. The other's is to prevent passengers from murdering the driver and stealing the cab.

Exciting place, Calcutta!

Dawn was breaking when we drove from the Dum-Dum airport into the great city, which, with a population of about three million, claims to be the second largest city in the British Commonwealth.

For two hours we crept along in the wake of dozens of creaking bullock carts loaded with produce for market, occasionally spurting past a string of them, only to take our place once more behind another caravan. On both sides of the road were long lines of women carrying incredible burdens on their heads, followed by children, many of whom were carrying infants straddle-legged on their hips. How many times a week they made that long trip into Calcutta I cannot say, but from the look of most of them, I marveled how they could possibly make even one. They were nothing but skin and bones covered by filthy rags.

Honking their horns impatiently, our taxi drivers drove many of them into the ditch in order that we might proceed.

All the world knows that India is poverty-stricken, but it takes a trip to Calcutta to realize what a gigantic problem Nehru has to cope with. Sam, who had never traveled in Asia before, was filled with horror.

"Now I can believe what John Gunther said in his *Inside Asia*," said Sam grimly. "Disease, squalor, and degradation of the human being to the level of animals are rampant as men live in stinking filth."

"This is nothing!" I remarked. "Wait till you see the city itself."

The road leading to the Great Eastern Hotel passes through one of the worst sections of Calcutta, and there we saw what a calamity has befallen as a result of the influx of refugees from East Pakistan.

Bear in mind that the hour was about 5:30 A.M. and that it was scarcely daylight. At first the sidewalks, broader than those of Fifth Avenue, were completely covered with sleeping people. A few were practically naked, lying flat on their backs with outspread arms. But most were covered with filthy gray cloth which later in the day would serve as clothing. Here and there were bodies, obviously dead, which had been wrapped around with rags. They would be picked up by the "dead cart" when it made its morning rounds. Sitting on the housetops, watching hungrily, were vultures and kites.

Just before six o'clock the sleepers began to stir. We watched them stepping over their neighbors, who were either still sleeping or dead, and make their way painfully to the edge of the sidewalk, where they squatted over the gutter.

"The city is yours. Keep it clean. Curb your dog," I said, remembering the signs on New York's lampposts.

"Good lord! Look at that!" whispered Sam as we stopped close to the sidewalk.

A woman was building a fire under a small brass pot which presumably contained rice. Her fuel was a small round pat of brown substance that she had peeled off the wall against which she was leaning.

I knew what it was, but Sam didn't. "Cow dung!" I said. "They slap it on the walls of buildings, where it dries in the sun."

Sam couldn't believe his eyes. "D'you mean to say that the whole side of that house is plastered with it? I thought they were tiles. They are so neatly arranged and they even have a pattern on them," he marveled.

"The pattern is the mark of the hand and fingers that slapped it on when it was wet," I explained.

I don't think Sam would have believed me had it not been for our seeing the process from start to finish. A few yards farther on we saw on the sidewalk a large pile of freshly gathered dung that was slowly spreading out under its own weight. Several people were shaping it into balls about the size of tennis balls, while others were slapping the balls against the wall.

153

"Quite an artistic job," Sam remarked sourly.

As he spoke, a large gray cow walked across the street and, after conveniently dropping a contribution near the pile, inconveniently lay down in the middle of the street, right in front of our taxi. There it remained, contentedly chewing its cud.

"Doesn't anybody own the animal?" asked Sam. "Where does it get its food?"

An Indian who approached us provided the answer. On his arm he carried a large wicker basket in which numbers of small bundles of fresh green grass were neatly arranged.

Noticing our interest, our driver gave the man a small copper coin in return for which he received a bunch of grass, which he promptly gave to the cow.

"Quite an interesting cycle," muttered Sam, who was far removed from laughing. "Man cuts grass and sells it to another man who gives it to the cow who provides fuel for the masses!"

An Indian friend later explained that the owner of the cow had taken a vow that for the rest of its life the sacred animal should live a life of ease and luxury. To fulfill his vow the man had to stop being a farmer, cut grass, bring it and the cow into town, and sell the grass to good Hindus. Both the man and his patrons thereby gained merit, while the cow had the time of its life.

"That fellow has another way of gaining merit," I said, pointing to a bearded individual who was slowly rolling over and over, trance-like, in the middle of the street. "Holy man!" said our driver.

Nobody appeared to be taking any notice of the man except the drivers of cars and busses, who carefully went around him. At the rate he was progressing, he covered about fifty yards an hour. We saw him again later on in the day, and he was still rolling.

Worn out from lack of sleep, we finally drew up in front of Calcutta's celebrated Great Eastern Hotel, which in the days before Partition had the reputation of being one of the most luxurious in the East. Practically fighting our way through the mob of beggars and onlookers who wanted to carry our baggage, we entered the lobby, where a sleepy-eyed clerk assigned us our rooms. Those who are familiar with the Great Eastern will remember the seemingly endless passages through which it is necessary to walk in order to reach the bedrooms.

Dozens of sleeping forms almost covered the floor, leaving barely enough room for us to walk without stepping on them. The same situation prevailed upstairs. To enter our rooms it was necessary to step over the huddled forms which lined the balcony on which the bedrooms opened.

Large and lofty, our rooms nevertheless were as hot as Hades, for the windows were shuttered and barred. After turning on the switch, a large electric fan suspended from the ceiling began slowly to stir up the fetid air.

Sam flung open the windows which opened on to a narrow side street. "That's a cheerful sight!" he exclaimed as he noticed a vulture perched on a ledge within a few feet of the window.

Apparently the bird made a habit of perching in the same spot. Startled by the sudden opening of the window, it flapped heavily away. But in a few minutes it returned with a large chunk of putrid meat which it proceeded to tear apart and devour viciously.

"No fear of starving to death around here," said Zetta. "They don't have to go to the Towers of Silence for a meal. They can get one in Calcutta anywhere and at any time."

Zetta had never forgotten the Towers of Silence which she had seen in Bombay in 1939, nor the flocks of vultures carrying off various parts of Parsee anatomy just at sundown. During the rest of the day the birds have to wait with patience but confidence, for only late in the afternoon do the Parsees expose their dead on the top of those celebrated towers.

"Thank heaven there's a decent bathroom," I said, "and a shower too!"

But bathing is a dangerous occupation in Calcutta. About the only favorable thing that can be said about the water is that it was wet. Brown and smelly, the water doubtless contained plenty of germs.

"Better keep your mouth shut," I shouted to Zetta, who had lost no time in getting under the shower. "Beware of dysentery, not to mention cholera."

Never were halazone tablets put to better use than they were by us in Calcutta, for although a notice informed us that all drinking water was boiled, that was no guarantee that the receptacle that held the water had been sterilized.

Refreshed, Zetta was preparing to lie down on her bed when she gave a shout. "Just look at this pillow. Someone has been using it."

I looked. "Did you say someone? More like dozens!"

On both sides of the pillow were telltale brown patches where dirty heads had rested. And this is the best hotel in Calcutta. But I doubt very much if the management knew anything about it, for when I pointed out the dirty linen to the bearer, he soon brought us all the clean sheets and pillowcases we asked for.

Presumably the works that make the wheels go round in the

156

PAKISTAN. Carveth Wells shows Explorers Club flag to Liaquat Ali Khan and his wife.

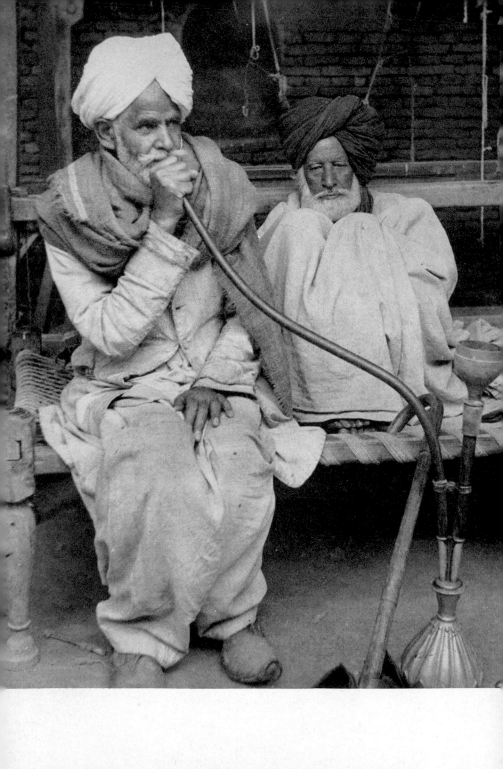

PAKISTAN. *Left:* The "hookah," or "hubble-bubble," is the favorite pipe of Moslems. *Below:* Women's National Guard stand at attention during inspection by their colonel, Begum Liaquat Ali Khan. *Below bottom:* A greater variety of fruit is produced in Pakistan than in California.

PAKISTAN. *Above:* This professional letter writer
will handle your business correspondence, write your
love letters, or sell you a love potion. *Right:* Historic
Khyber Pass is now Pakistan's responsibility.

SWEDEN. *Left:* Socialist Sweden takes great pride in her co-operative apartment houses and discourages the building of private homes. LAPLAND. *Above:* Bjorkliden chalet, overlooking lovely Lake Torneträsk, with Lap Portal in the distance and Mount Nuolja in the right foreground.

FINNMARK. *Left:* Laplanders in summer dress in arctic Finnmark. *Below:* Zetta asked to taste some reindeer milk. NORWAY. *Bottom:* Hammerfest today, the most northerly town in Europe.

INDIA. *Above:* Famous Indian dancer performing a *Bharat Natyam,* in which the emphasis is on the movement of the hands. *Right:* I took this photograph of Zetta and Sam in front of the Taj Mahal at sunrise.

KASHMIR. *Above:* The third bridge, with Hari Parbat in background. The pagoda-like building with wooden steeple is one of the most sacred mosques in Kashmir. *Left:* One of Srinagar's numerous canals.

KASHMIR. *Right:* When we were in Kashmir, the maharajah's palace was minus the maharajah. *Left:* Dundoo, captain and owner of *H.M.S. Pinafore.* *Above: H.M.S. Pinafore,* our houseboat home on Dal Lake.

KASHMIR. *Above:* Reflections on Dal Lake. *Right:* Sam's parliamentary problems were soon forgotten as he glided over placid Dal Lake to Shalimar. *Below:* A Kashmir house is a ramshackle affair.

Great Eastern Hotel had slowed down. Cleanliness was apparently classed among the nonessentials.

"But it's better than Russia," said Zetta sleepily. "At least we don't have to stay up all night swatting bedbugs."

The only disadvantage of flying to India from Scandinavia is that the change from immaculate cleanliness to filth is too sudden.

"It's all a matter of education," remarked Sam at breakfast, after he had carefully wiped off the crockery and cutlery on his handkerchief (the serviette was dirtier than the tablecloth). "You can't tell me that the educated Indians are any dirtier than we are. I'll bet Nehru is as clean as a whistle, and his food as well. There are just too many Indians for Nehru to cope with!"

I agreed with him. "Liaquat Ali Khan, with only eighty-five million to handle, has a simple job compared with Nehru's three hundred million," I said. "Besides, he hasn't fifty million 'untouchables' to contend with."

"I thought that caste had been done away with in India," said Zetta.

"Legally it has," I answered. "You can lead a horse to water, but you cannot make him drink! The only way India will ever rid herself of caste is through education, and it's going to take generations to educate the masses of India. And before an Indian can be made to take an interest in the three Rs, he has got to be given a full stomach."

"I feel like emptying mine," said Sam mournfully as he toyed with a plate of slippery bacon and eggs. "From now on it's going to be dry toast and tea."

The palatial dining room of the Great Eastern looked most inviting, especially in the evening, when dinner was served to the music of quite a good orchestra. I didn't count the number of tables, but there must have been at least a hundred. And as there appeared to be as many waiters as tables, the room always looked full. But it wasn't. Rarely did we count as many as fifty people there. The reasons were obvious: unappetizing food, dirty linen, and dirty waiters. Conditions were quite different before Partition. In those days of Indian "enslavement" the linen was clean, the silver glittered from constant polishing, and the waiters were dressed in spotless white uniforms with scarlet-and-gold turbans and sashes. When we were at the Great Eastern, the waiters' uniforms looked as if they hadn't been washed for years. Asking for a menu was quite unnecessary. All you had to do in order to know what there was to eat was to look at the cloth or the napkin.

"Scandinavia has spoiled you people," laughed the representative of the Scandinavian Airlines when we told him our troubles. "There are two sides to the picture, and you've only seen the black side. Dine with me tonight at Firpos and I'll promise you as good a tenderloin steak as you can get anywhere." He was right, of course, for it is hardly fair to judge a city from impressions gained in the small hours of the morning.

By nine o'clock most of the refugees had scattered over the city to beg or find some shady retreat where they could lie down and die. The sidewalks which had been covered with sleepers were now crowded with people, mostly men, hurrying to work. The streets were filled with traffic of all kinds, except camel carts, yet even in the busiest thoroughfares Brahman cattle wandered aimlessly about in all directions, regardless of traffic cops. It was quite a common sight to see a cow standing on the sidewalk in front of a market, helping itself to anything that suited its taste.

"Are they holy too?" asked Sam as a herd of buffalo passed by.

"No. They're probably on the way to some hotel with the day's supply of milk." I chuckled. "That was buffalo milk you had in your tea this morning."

Just then a man passed by wearing a gauze mask over his mouth.

"He looks as if he's afraid of catching influenza," remarked Zetta.

"Not at all," I corrected. "He's a Jain. Jainism forbids the taking of life in any form. He's afraid he might inadvertently swallow a gnat."

Hailing a taxi, we drove to the Jain Temple, one of the most interesting sights of Calcutta. There we saw quite a number of people wearing the same protective strip of gauze over their mouths.

A reformed sect of Hinduism, Jainism teaches that all living things have souls. Altogether there are less than two million Jains in India, but they form a very wealthy community, concentrating their efforts on commerce and banking. Thanks to the Jains, there are many fine hospitals for animals and endowments for the care of birds in different parts of India.

To pass from the confines of the Jain Temple to the Howrah railway station provided another one of those extraordinary contrasts which are so common in India. The temple, with its gorgeous decorations and beautiful lake, supported by people who go to great extremes to save the life of an insect; the huge railway station crowded with people who took not the slightest notice of the starving hundreds who had taken refuge there from the blistering heat of the sidewalks.

"It is even worse than this morning," said Zetta as we picked our way gingerly among the groups of people who were squatting about everywhere. "Why don't the Jains save some of these lives?"

Wandering about from one group of people to another were half a dozen cows, eating their garbage. Propped against a post was a woman, dreadfully emaciated yet trying to nurse a tiny baby which tugged at her empty breasts. Beside her, straight and stiff, was the corpse of a man, probably her husband, for she had covered his face with a rag. Within arm's length was a cow from whose distended udder milk was dripping.

"Why doesn't she milk the cow and feed her baby?" exclaimed Zetta, horror-stricken. "Why doesn't somebody help her?"

Finding that she had nothing to give her, the cow, after nudging about among the woman's pitiful belongings, moved away to another group, leaving a trail of milk on the dirty platform.

"Where's Sam?"

Sam had moved away. He was vomiting.

Yet within a stone's throw of this scene of squalor and misery hundreds of well-dressed people were laughing and jostling one another as they crowded onto an excursion train which was about to leave Calcutta for the country.

"Macaulay called Calcutta 'the city of palaces,'" said Sam as we walked away. "I wonder what he would call it if he could see what we have seen."

Calcutta's chief glory is the Maidan, an extensive public park dominated at one end by the Indian memorial to Queen Victoria, who still sits on her throne in front of a magnificent white marble building.

We had been told that the Indians had destroyed the numerous statues of England's empire builders, but this is not the case. They are still there, dotted about the Maidan, among them being equestrian statues of Lord Roberts and Lord Lansdowne which face one another on each side of the Red Road where Calcutta's elite take their evening drive. Several herds of buffalo grazed on the Maidan, but I didn't notice any holy cows. They evidently prefer the more varied diet afforded them in the streets and alleys of the city. Facing the Maidan for a couple of miles is the Chowringhee, one of the most famous streets in the world, formerly a row of palatial residences but now given up almost entirely to hotels, clubs, and shops.

In fairness to India it must be said that the government has spent huge sums trying to solve the refugee problem. It has done a great deal, but the problem is such a gigantic one that the effort to solve it is like a mouse nibbling at a fifty-pound cheese.

One of the difficulties has been to persuade the refugees to live in the new three-storied tenement houses that were built for them. Unaccustomed to living in apartment houses, the destitute people prefer to live in the street, as we had seen them, or wander off into the country and build the same kind of unsanitary huts they occupied when the disasters following Partition drove them out.

Numbers of modern housing projects were built for them, but as they remained unoccupied they had to be filled with persons of limited means, such as poor students and artisans. As an experiment many small detached houses were also built, but they have never been used by the people for whom they were intended. Whole townsites have been laid out beyond the city limits, but so far the resettlement of the homeless seems to be a problem that is growing rather than diminishing.

"That vulture is still perched outside my bedroom window," said Sam as we started out for dinner at Firpos. "It's the only well-fed resident of Calcutta I've seen yet."

"How do they get away with serving beefsteak?" I asked our host.

"Buffalo!" he replied. "It isn't holy, but it tastes good just the same. And talking about killing buffalo, there will be quite a massacre of them tomorrow in the Moslem quarter—it's called Bakr-Id."

The annual festival of Bakr-Id commemorates Abraham's intended sacrifice of his son, whose name, according to the Moslems, was Ismail and not Isaac.

"Could we see it?" I asked.

"If you want to take a chance," answered our host, "but be sure you have a Moslem chauffeur."

Had we known what we were going to see or the real danger that we were running into, we would have remained at home. But fools rush in where angels fear to tread.

After experiencing some difficulty in getting a Moslem driver, we started out. Soon the streets became narrower and narrower as we drove into the Moslem quarter. Although it was not yet nine o'clock in the morning, the streets were packed with holiday makers dressed in their brightest clothes.

"Better lock the doors and close the windows," I advised when a man whose face was smeared with blood poked his head into the car. He shouted something to the driver, whose reply must have been satisfactory, for the man withdrew his head and joined the throng.

"He wanted to know whether you were Hindus," explained the driver, his dark face beginning to turn a sickly green.

"Look!" whispered Zetta. "Blood is running down the gutters!"

From a side street blood was simply pouring down the slight incline to where we were.

"They're killing a goat," said the driver as a crowd of young men came running toward us with blood all over their clothes.

"We must get out of here quickly," said Zetta as she urged the driver to step on the gas.

"What fools we were to come here!" muttered Sam as the excited people began to follow us, some of them actually hanging onto the rear bumper. Meanwhile our driver was shaking his head vigorously and shouting, "Americans! Americans!"

It was easy to see how communal riots take place in India. All that was needed to have started one that day would have been to spread the rumor that the Moslems were killing a holy cow instead of a goat. Then all Hades would have broken loose.

"Thank God we're safely out of that!" I exclaimed as we emerged into a broad thoroughfare and made our way back to the Great Eastern.

It was hard to believe that within such a short distance the streets were running with blood.

What could happen in Calcutta and other Indian cities, should India and Pakistan go to war, was easy to imagine. Instead of goats' blood running down the gutters, it would be the blood of human beings, for Hindus and Moslems would start murdering one another.

"I just can't wait to get out of here," said Zetta the next morning as we boarded a twin-engined Viking of the Indian National Airways bound for New Delhi.

With regard to the festival of Bakr-Id, it is not suggested that all Moslems celebrate their holy day in such a gruesome manner, but, to say the least, the celebrants we saw in Calcutta were a bit untidy about it.

When I mentioned our experience to a well-educated Moslem he remarked sourly, "Anything can happen in Calcutta!"

CHAPTER EIGHT

"Would you care to see these newspapers?" said an Indian gentleman cordially. "I see that you are Americans." As the plane was flying too high to make window gazing interesting, we spent the time reading some of the most sensational news imaginable. With three papers among us, we took turns reading the headlines.

TRUMAN RESIGNS. TELLS CABINET HE INTENDS TO RETIRE FROM PUBLIC LIFE ALTOGETHER

UNCLE SHAM GETS IT FROM ALL SIDES

GENERAL DOUGLAS MACARTHUR HAS BITTEN OFF MORE THAN HE CAN CHEW IN KOREA

WHILE ASIA'S MILLIONS STARVE UNCLE SHAM MAKES A BONFIRE OF SURPLUS CORN, WHEAT, AND POTATOES

TRUMAN, MACARTHUR, AND COMPANY WOULD DO WELL TO RECALL THE FATE OF HITLER AND MUSSOLINI

RULERS OF AMERICA HAVE OUTHITLERED HITLER

ZERO HOUR FAST APPROACHING IN KASHMIR

"Surely you don't believe all this rubbish," I said impatiently. "That's what we read in our papers," replied the Indian. "What are we to believe?"

For the next hour I did my best to undo some of the harm which had been done, but I could see from the man's air of skepticism that I hadn't made very much of an impression.

"Nehru doesn't seem to be very popular either," said Sam as he handed me the front page of *Blitz*, which described itself as "Asia's Foremost Newsmagazine." A large cartoon showed a map of East Asia, giving prominence to India, Korea, and Russia. Nehru was shown standing upside down with his head in the sand of India, surrounded by four ostriches which also had buried their heads. In Korea, John Bull and Uncle Sam were shown bayoneting men, women, and children, while over Russia atomic bombs were being dropped from American airplanes. Inset was a note signed "Editor": "Pandit Nehru at his usual yoga exercise. Any resemblance between the Prime Minister and the ostriches around him is purely a coincidence."

Accompanying the cartoon was an article in which Nehru was asked the following questions:

"We want to know whether we have struck any bargain favorable to India on issues such as Kashmir and South Africa involving our very deepest honor. We want to know whether, like Britain, France, Italy, Greece, Chiang's China, the Philippines, and Burma, we also have gained any material advantages in the form of Marshall aid or dollars or doles in return for sacrificing our independence. We want to know whether we are even getting the two million tons of wheat which were dangled before Nehru's eyes last year and withdrawn because the Prime Minister was not ready at that time to sacrifice his conscience to any such devil's deal. The people of India await your answer, Mr. Prime Minister. Yes, we want facts and not the customary claptrap about Gandhiism and all such nonsense with which our people have been humbugged far too long."

"I take it that you aren't one of Mr. Nehru's supporters," I said, handing the papers back to the Indian. "Do you agree with what this paper says about humbugging the people with claptrap about Gandhiism?"

The Indian smiled as he answered, "Was it not your Abraham Lincoln who said, 'You can fool some of the people all of the time, and all of the people some of the time, but you cannot fool all of the people all the time'? Nehru thinks differently."

The plane landed at the New Delhi airport before our Indian friend had time to tell us what he really thought of Gandhi.

"Don't tell me that the American Government doesn't take care of its citizens," said Zetta as we emerged from the airport to find an embassy car awaiting us.

"Welcome to New Delhi. Ambassador Henderson is expecting you," said two good-looking Americans. "We're from the State Department."

"How about Kashmir?" I asked anxiously. "I see from the paper that the zero hour is fast approaching there!"

"That's news to us," said our new-found friends. "You must have got hold of the wrong paper. Colonel Sutherland can fix you up. I understand that he has arranged for you to meet the commander in chief of the Indian Army. Delightful fellow, General Cariappa."

New Delhi might be called the Washington of India. Until 1911 the capital of India was Calcutta, but on December 12 of that year it was announced at the Delhi Durbar that the capital was to be transferred to Delhi. Three days later the foundation stone of the new capital was laid by the King-Emperor George V.

Just as Pierre l'Enfant laid out Washington with mathematical accuracy, so did England's famous architect, Sir Edwin

Lutyens, design New Delhi, his aim being "to express, within the limit of the medium and the powers of its users, the ideal and the fact of British rule in India, of which New Delhi must ever be the monument." With that in view, the inspiration of the designs is obviously Western and not oriental. It took twenty years to build the capital, which was inaugurated with elaborate ceremony in February 1931.

Queen Victoria surveys the Maidan in Calcutta, but it is George V, on a lofty pedestal, who looks over the large park in which New Delhi's magnificent government buildings have been built. A drive around New Delhi soon took the taste of Calcutta out of our mouths.

Five miles from New Delhi is Old Delhi, the ancient capital of the Mogul Empire, while one hundred and twenty-five miles south is the ancient city of Agra, site of the Taj Mahal. The two cities owe much of their importance in both historical and modern times to the advantage of being located on the banks of the river Jumna.

"You certainly should take time to see both of these historic cities if you're on your way to Shalimar," advised Colonel Sutherland, United States military attaché in New Delhi. "All are closely connected with the Mogul Emperor Shah Jehan. It will take a couple of days to get your military passes for Kashmir, anyway," he added.

So having made our headquarters at the Cecil Hotel in Old Delhi and having hired a car and driver for ten dollars a day, we proceeded to follow the colonel's advice. We didn't regret it.

Though the remains of earlier cities are scattered around Old Delhi over an area estimated to cover about forty-five square miles, the present city dates only from the middle of the seventeenth century, when Shah Jehan rebuilt it, adding the title Shah-jehanabad from his own name. Locally Old Delhi is still called Shahjehanabad. The city is surrounded by a great wall built by Shah Jehan but greatly strengthened by the British after they captured Delhi in 1803. At the time of the Indian Mutiny the strength of this wall was turned against the British.

Nowadays there is a constant stream of traffic through the Kashmir Gate, the storming of which was one of the epics of the Mutiny.

The shattered wall over the gateway still bears the scars of the British cannonade of September 1857. Close by is the ancient imperial palace, now known as the Fort, over which the flag of India was flying. In front of the entrance to the Fort a cricket match was in progress, cricket being just as popular in India as it is in England. Within the Fort are located numerous buildings, among which are several exquisite examples of oriental architecture.

"One of them is the place where the Peacock Throne was kept," remarked Sam, who knew far more about Indian history than he admitted. "It was known as the Diwan-i-Am."

Sam was right. The Peacock Throne, valued at thirty million dollars, used to stand in a recess at the back of the hall. Tavernier, the French jeweler and world traveler, who visited Delhi in 1665, described the throne as of the shape of a bed, six feet long and four feet wide, supported by four golden feet about twenty inches high. Above the throne rose a canopy supported by twelve columns. The bars of the canopy were decorated with crosses of rubies, emeralds, diamonds, and pearls. He counted one hundred and eight large rubies and one hundred and sixteen large emeralds in the throne.

"What happened to it?" inquired Zetta.

Sam again came to the rescue. "It was carried away by the Persian invader, Nadir Shah, in 1739 and is rumored to exist still in the Treasure House of the Shah."

Another celebrated building that we saw inside the Fort was the Diwan-i-Khas. Here can be seen in Persian characters the famous inscription, "If a paradise be on the face of the earth, it is this, it is this, it is this." At the time of the Delhi Durbar in 1903 to celebrate the proclamation of Edward VII as Emperor of India, this exquisite building was used as a supper room.

"This is the Chandni Chauk [Silver Street]," said our driver as we passed along Delhi's main street. "It is the richest street in the world."

"Used to be," corrected Sam. "It was sacked at least four times and most of its riches carried away."

Nowadays it is the abode of the jewelers and ivory workers of Delhi.

Ten miles south of Delhi, amid the ruins of another ancient Delhi, stands the Kutb Minar, which is said to be the most perfect tower in the world and one of the seven architectural wonders of India. Built of marble and sandstone which is dark red at the base, pink in the middle, and orange on the top story, this remarkable structure, 238 feet high, looks almost brand new, yet it was built in A.D. 1200.

Close by is another Indian wonder, the Iron Pillar, dating from A.D. 400. A remarkable tribute to Hindu knowledge of metallurgy and engineering, this pillar, some sixteen inches in diameter and twenty-three feet eight inches in height, is made of pure rustless malleable iron and is estimated to weigh more than six tons.

Overlooking both the Fort and the city, and approached by a magnificent flight of stone steps, is the Great Mosque, also erected by Emperor Shah Jehan. It has three domes of white marble, two tall minarets, and a front court measuring 450 feet square, paved with granite and inlaid with marble.

"Sight-seeing in Delhi is as tiring as doing the Mediterranean," I remarked as we finally came to rest in the Cecil Hotel.

"No rest for the wicked!" laughed Sam. "We leave for Agra in the morning. I wonder whether the Taj Mahal will come up to my expectations."

The drive from Old Delhi to Agra proved to be one of the most interesting experiences of our travels, for not only did we pass through several Indian villages, but we encountered numbers of monkeys.

Dedicated to the god Hanuman, Indian monkeys are neither tame nor wild. They just seem to drift up and down the subcontinent as they please, sometimes enjoying a spell of jungle life but usually preferring to live in villages or even large cities, where they often become quite embarrassing to the human population. Rigidly protected from any kind of violence at the hand of man, the monkeys not only appreciate their privilege but they heartily abuse it. Strangely enough, the influx of monkeys by the thousand to some of India's largest cities is difficult to deal with not only because more than two hundred million Hindus revere them, but also because millions of Moslems think twice before they try any monkey business with the sacred monkeys for fear of causing a riot.

India has many problems to solve, but it is only recently that her monkey problem has received much publicity. In the New York *Times* of August 21, 1951, there was an Associated Press dispatch from New Delhi which stated: "India has 100,000,000 unwanted monkeys. The National Government today approved a Madras State plan to export as many monkeys as possible because they were destroying food crops. In the Hindu religion, monkeys are sacred and cannot be killed or harmed."

Some of the exploits of India's monkeys are almost unbelievable. These privileged simians think nothing of raiding a food store and carrying off all the contents. In some places the monkeys go around in gangs and, encouraged by some monkey agitator, they have been known to invade a train and hold up the passengers.

Several times in the past, Hindus, debarred by religious scruples from taking any personal action against them, had appealed to the British Government for help, just as they are now appealing to their own government.

The British used to run special one-way excursion trains "for monkeys only" to the jungle, where the festive animals were offloaded for a grand picnic. But those city slickers, having lost the art of living the simple life, provided a grand picnic for leopards and tigers. No return tickets are necessary.

In all probability, when the British left India, the monkeys were just as delighted as the Indians. But their freedom has apparently been short-lived. The plan now is to export them by the shipload to foreign countries, where they will supply the large demand of zoos, circuses, and medical research workers.

"Monkeys is the kwaziest people," shouted Zetta as a large brown monkey dropped out of a tree and with outstretched hand approached our car. "In America the slogan is 'Spare a dime, lady,' but over here it is 'Spare a peanut.'"

The moment Zetta threw the monkey some food, dozens more began to converge upon us from all directions. We stepped on the gas to avoid them.

"They're just a bunch of Reds," Sam said facetiously as the retiring monkeys showed their scarlet buttocks.

"I wonder why the Indians regard them as sacred," asked Zetta.

It was now my turn to show off my knowledge of folklore.

"According to legend, they are direct descendants of Hanuman, the famous monkey god of southern India, who is supposed to have aided Rama in the conquest of Ceylon by building the bridge of rocks between the island and the mainland of India."

Late that afternoon as we were approaching Agra we saw several flying foxes, the largest of the bat family. Four feet wide from wing to wing, these huge bats roost by day and feast on fruit by night. Our driver told us that he had often seen them in their roosts, hanging upside down and fanning themselves, first with one wing and then with the other, trying to keep cool.

Talking of bats, India is the home of the painted bat, whose vermilion and black wings are said to make it the most brilliantly colored mammal in the world.

Another remarkable Indian bat is the false vampire (*Megaderma*). It is false for two reasons. It has never been known to "suck" anybody's blood, and it has two pairs of teats, one for milk and another for the convenience of its baby, who clings to them.

"Falsies!" laughed Zetta. "There's nothing new under the sun!"

It was nine-thirty at night when we arrived at Agra and registered at the Hotel Laurie.

"Full moon tonight," said the room clerk. "Just the time to see the Taj in all its loveliness."

173

As we started out to see the world's most beautiful building Zetta whispered, "You've always wanted to see Shalimar, darling, but I'll admit that the one thing I have wanted to see more than any other in the world is the Taj Mahal."

Lord Roberts in his *Forty-one Years in India* says: "Neither words nor pencil could give to the most imaginative reader the slightest idea of the all-satisfying beauty and purity of this glorious conception. To those who have not seen it, I would say, 'Go to India. The Taj alone is well worth the journey.'"

In his history of architecture Fergusson says of it: "This building is an early example of that system of inlaying with precious stones which became the great characteristic of the style of the Moguls after the death of Akbar. All the spandrels of the Taj, all the angles and more important architectural details are heightened by being inlaid with precious stones such as agates, bloodstones, jaspers, and the like. These are combined in wreaths, scrolls, and frets, as exquisite in design as they are beautiful in color, and relieved by the pure-white marble in which they are inlaid, they form the most beautiful and precious style of ornament ever adopted in architecture."

In his *From Sea to Sea*, Rudyard Kipling says: "It was the Ivory Gate through which all dreams come true; it was the realization of 'the gleaming halls of dawn' that Tennyson sings of; it was veritably the 'aspiration fixed,' the 'sigh made stone' of a lesser poet; and over and above concrete comparisons, it seemed the embodiment of all things pure, all things holy, and all things unhappy. That was the mystery of the building. . . . To the one who watched and wondered that November morning the thing seemed full of sorrow—the sorrow of the man who built it for the woman he loved, and the sorrow of the workmen who died in the building—used up like cattle. And in the face of this sorrow the Taj flushed in the sunlight and was beautiful, after the beauty of a woman who has done no wrong."

Tavernier, who witnessed the commencement of the Taj and its completion in 1648, states that twenty-two years were spent on the work, during which twenty thousand men were employed day and night. "It is said," adds Tavernier, "that the scaffoldings alone cost more than the entire work because, from want of wood, they had all to be made of brick, as well as the support of the arches."

With regard to the materials for the building, the white Makrana marble was brought from Jaipur, the red sandstone that was used for the entrance gate to the Taj gardens came from Fatehpur Sikri, the diamonds that once adorned the actual tomb but have since been plundered came from Panna. Turquoise was brought from Tibet, lapis lazuli from Ceylon, jasper from Cambay, malachite from Russia, carnelian from Baghdad, chrysolite from Egypt, and various other precious and semi-precious stones from many different parts of the world.

The garden of the Taj, 1860 feet by 1000 feet, is surrounded by a high wall of red sandstone. From the entrance gate to the base of the platform on which the Taj is built there is a reflecting pool with a long row of fountains. Avenues of cypress trees parallel the reflecting pool on either side.

The mausoleum stands in the center of a double platform, the first one of red sandstone four feet high, in the center of which stands the second platform about eighteen feet higher than the first, paved with alternate squares of white and black marble. At each corner of this huge square platform stands a lofty marble minaret 162 feet high.

Inside the mausoleum a flight of narrow stairs descends to an underground vaulted chamber in which lie the remains of

Mumtaz and her husband, Shah Jehan. Above this chamber are the cenotaphs of the Queen and her consort. Surrounding the two cenotaphs is a very delicately carved screen of marble, octagonal in shape. On the Queen's cenotaph are inscribed her name, the year of her death, and the ninety-nine beautiful names of God together with passages from the Koran.

Mumtaz Mahal, after whom the Taj is named, was married to Emperor Shah Jehan when she had just passed her nineteenth year in 1612. For eighteen years, during which she bore eight sons and six daughters, Mumtaz was the Emperor's devoted lover, comrade, and counselor. It was she who inspired him to acts of charity and filled his heart with mercy for the weak and the needy. Mumtaz could not bear a moment's separation from her husband, whom she accompanied even on the most dangerous of his military expeditions. But her greatest joy was to go with him to Kashmir and wander through the lovely garden of Shalimar, which was Shah Jehan's favorite pleasure resort.

She died in childbirth. Before she closed her eyes she asked the Emperor to grant her two boons; namely, that he would not marry again and that he would build such a memorial over her grave as would be the wonder of the world. Both her wishes were literally fulfilled.

We reached the entrance of the Taj at about ten o'clock. It was bright moonlight. Sitting on the ground outside the entrance were groups of people selling alabaster models of the Taj and picture postcards.

"That's the first thing I'd do away with if I had anything to do with it," said Zetta, who had prepared herself for an atmosphere of peace and reverence. "It's a shame to commercialize the place. It makes me think of Niagara Falls."

176

"Don't be impatient. It will be different inside," I assured her.

Not a glimpse of the Taj Mahal itself can be had until you are actually standing under the arch of the entrance to the garden.

"Look!" said an ancient attendant with a long white beard as he pointed through the archway.

We looked and were speechless. None of us said, "How lovely," or "Isn't it wonderful?" We were unable to say anything. But I knew what was passing through Zetta's mind when she squeezed my hand.

In one respect at least, the Taj Mahal is like the Grand Canyon. It silences every person who sees it for the first time, and it is constantly changing color. If I had had the time and the proper equipment I would have remained there for a full twenty-four hours, taking motion pictures of the mausoleum as its color changes with the changing light.

For a full five minutes we just stood there in silence. Then in a whisper Sam said, "How clever it was of the architect to make it of white marble."

By moonlight the Taj was pale green, yet even that color varied as the moon rose. On moonless nights, with just the stars for illumination, the white marble assumes a dark violet color.

We walked into the garden and stood on the marble bridge so that we could look directly at the Taj along the center line of the reflecting pool. Again we were speechless with awe.

Suddenly the stillness of the night was broken by a woman's shriek, followed by a burst of raucous laughter. The spell was broken. A party of young Indians, probably students, were having a picnic on the marble platform of the Taj. We walked toward them and discovered several more picnic parties on the terrace behind the Taj, overlooking the river. One of the men had a flute which he was playing.

"That spoils everything," remarked Zetta sadly. "There's no more reverence here than at Coney Island. Let's go back to the hotel."

"I propose we leave an early call and return to the Taj before sunrise. The merrymakers will have gone to bed by then."

And that is what we did. Dawn was just breaking when we again stood at the end of the reflecting pool and watched the Taj. The dome looked like a great pink balloon and the four minarets like giant sticks of pink candy. The picnickers had gone home, and except for the old man with the beard, we were alone.

For the next hour we just sat and watched the changing colors of the Taj as the sun rose.

"I'm satisfied," said Sam quietly. "It exceeds my greatest expectation."

We raced back to the hotel for breakfast, then back again to the Taj, which had now assumed a beautiful golden yellow. Already sight-seers were arriving, and the hawkers with their baskets of souvenirs. There was no object in keeping quiet any more, for the whole garden of the Taj resounded with voices and laughter.

By noon the Taj was dazzling white. The hawkers were doing a roaring business.

"Shah Jehan must be squirming in his grave," said Zetta sadly. "The memorial to his beloved Mumtaz has become just another attraction."

Whether this was so before Partition I cannot say, but it seems a great pity that the Indian Government doesn't request silence from the multitudes who must annually visit this glorious Moslem monument.

As a tourist attraction, it brings thousands to India. But it would bring many more if the garden were properly maintained and vandals were prevented from scratching their names here, there, and everywhere. We saw one man using a walking stick to write his initials on the bottom of the reflecting pool, where long neglect has allowed some fungus to cover the marble. As we walked the full length of the pool we counted thousands of such disfiguring initials, dates, and drawings.

Not even the mausoleum walls were safe from such vandalism. Many precious stones had been pried loose and stolen. As for the pall of pearls which once covered the tomb of Mumtaz, that disappeared long ago together with the mausoleum doors of solid silver. But out of reach of man, the gorgeous inlaid work is as good as it was three hundred years ago.

"Well, darling, are you satisfied?" I said to Zetta as we started back to New Delhi.

"Perfectly," she replied. "It's the Taj Mahal I wanted to see. The neglected garden and the slimy reflecting pool can soon be restored, and I'm sure they will be."

Awaiting us at the Cecil Hotel was a letter from Colonel Sutherland. "Our military passes for Kashmir!" shouted Zetta. "They're here. Blessings on General Cariappa. We can leave for Srinagar in the morning."

"It won't be long now!" I chuckled the next morning as I strapped myself into the seat of a twin-engined plane of the Indian National Airways bound for Srinagar, capital of Kashmir. "My mother's prophecy is coming true."

"I'm so happy for you, darling," said Zetta with an affectionate gleam in her eyes. "I promised you that we would go to

179

Kashmir this summer or bust." Then as she looked around her, comparing this small Indian plane with the magnificent DC-6 of the Scandinavian Airlines in which we had flown from Copenhagen to Calcutta, she added, "I hope we don't bust!"

As a matter of fact, the planes of the Indian Airways are just as safe as any other, but it did give us a queer feeling to see the pilots. Both the captain and his co-pilot were Sikhs wearing large white turbans. Like all Sikhs, they were unshaven and wore their beards braided and wrapped around their ears. Instead of a stewardess, the plane carried an Indian steward, who immediately started passing round small pieces of candy to suck. We were the only Europeans on board, the rest of the passengers being Indians of various faiths and dress.

"Shall we see Mount Everest?" inquired Zetta eagerly as she scanned the horizon to the north.

"Not in that direction," I replied. "Everest is hundreds of miles to the east. We're already north of Everest and even north of Lhasa."

Without looking at a map, it comes as a surprise to many people to hear that Kashmir is far north of Tibet. Nevertheless, it is surrounded by the lofty Himalayas, with several peaks rising well over twenty-five thousand feet.

Only Nepal, with Everest towering to twenty-nine thousand feet on its boundary, can claim higher peaks than Kashmir. Mount K2, which is twenty-eight thousand two hundred and fifty feet above sea level, is Kashmir's mighty landmark, located about one hundred and fifty miles northeast of Srinagar, while about seventy miles north of the city is another mighty peak, Nanga Parbat, twenty-six thousand six hundred and sixty feet.

"Thank heaven we're flying fairly low," remarked Sam, who

had his face jammed to the window, looking at the extraordinary sights.

Below us was the great plain of India which stretches in a curve from the Arabian Sea to the Bay of Bengal. More than two thousand miles from end to end, and with an average width of about two hundred miles, the plain is almost as flat as a table. Made up of deep fertile soil washed down for thousands of years by mighty rivers, this northern plain is the home of two thirds of India's population, most of whom live in small villages built of sun-dried mud bricks and usually surrounded by a wall. India is said to have at least seven hundred thousand of these villages. Usually I could count at least thirty of them, spaced several miles apart, but not once did I spy an individual farm.

"No wonder India is threatened by a famine," said Sam. "The land seems to be flooded everywhere. Look at those wretched cattle."

Here and there, stranded on some slight elevation, were groups of cattle waiting forlornly for the water to recede. Several carcasses were floating near them, and it looked as if it wouldn't be long before the whole lot would be swept away by the swirling flood.

Nor did the villages appear to be very much better off, for water could be seen between the houses. Generally speaking, the whole landscape presented a scene of utter desolation.

"Terrible, isn't it?" remarked an Indian. "But our government is now doing what the British should have done. It is building bunds to control the rivers. Soon floods will be a thing of the past."

I didn't want to get into an argument as to what the British had done for India, but I couldn't help saying, "We have just as bad floods in America, and our government has been building bunds for generations."

"But your villages are built of stone; your people have electric light. Those people down there don't even have kerosene; the only light they have is from a taper floating in mustard oil. They have no roads; they are lucky if they earn a dollar a month," objected the Indian. "It's the fault of the British."

"Ask him what the people do in their villages," whispered Zetta.

"Nearly all of them are farmers," said the Indian, "but they're always in debt to the moneylender. He lends them money on their crops in advance. Then he gets his money back by keeping the only shop in the village at which they can buy their necessities."

"What do the others do who aren't farmers?" I inquired.

"Each village has its carpenter, potter, washerman, barber, weaver, and winnower," he explained. "The only person who has an easy time is the village minstrel, who plays at weddings. The minstrel is quite a genius. He has to learn by heart the genealogical trees of the leading families. He is also the courier, conveying news of births and deaths to relatives in distant villages as well as invitations to marriages." Then with a smile he added, "Such magic as the telephone he has never heard of."

"Is it true that a Hindu may have as many wives as he likes?" asked Zetta.

"Technically, yes," answered our friend, "but practically, very few Hindus ever have more than one wife; they find it too expensive. It also destroys harmony in the home. Moslems may also practice polygamy," he added. "They may have four wives at once, but the husband is expected to deal equally and equitably with each."

Suddenly Zetta shouted, "Look, darling! We're flying over Amritsar. I can see the Golden Temple you have been telling us about."

Almost echoing her words, the pilot walked back from the cockpit and said proudly, "Look, we're flying over the Golden Temple of the Sikhs."

As founders of a sect and makers of history, the Sikhs rank high among India's numerous peoples. The actual founder of the Sikh brotherhood was a man named Baba Nanak. One day, after he had been missing from home for three days and given up for lost, he returned in a daze, saying, "There is no Hindu and no Mohammedan!" Those seemingly senseless words expressed the main idea of Sikhism. Baba Nanak wandered far and wide, preaching as he went. He went as far south as Ceylon, north to Kashmir, and as far west as Medina, where an Arab discovered him sleeping with his feet toward the holy city of Mecca. When the Arab reproached him for pointing his feet toward the House of God, Nanak replied, "Show me where the House of God is not."

Nanak's sole purpose in life was to reform and restore the Hindu religion to its ancient purity. He forbade the burning of widows, the killing of girl children, and the element of sacrifice in worship. He required truth and the utmost simplicity in worship, without ritual of any kind.

Wherever he preached, men followed him. These he named "Sikhs," or "disciples," from the word *sikhna*, which means "to learn." In turn the Sikhs called their leader "Guru," which means "teacher." Nanak was the first of ten Gurus.

In the days of the Moguls, Sikhism flourished unmolested; in fact, it was the Mogul Emperor Akbar the Great who gave to the fourth Guru the tract of land where the holy man dug the now famous pool at Amritsar, a name meaning the "Pool of Immortality." Here the Sikhs eventually built the Golden Temple as a shrine for their Bible, the Adigranth. This book opens with an exposition of the Sikh faith which every orthodox Sikh must learn by heart and repeat every morning. In the Golden Temple it is read aloud daily, and a copy of this Bible is always carried at the head of every Sikh regiment.

Purposely flying low so that we could all get a good view, the captain pointed out the Golden Temple, which was on a small island in the middle of the sacred pool. Surrounding the pool was a very wide marble pavement, and leading from it to the Temple was a causeway across which people were walking. Others were bathing in the pool.

In the days of the Great Moguls the Sikhs were anything but warlike, as was shown by the reply made by Guru Nanak to the Moslem governor of the Punjab, who had asked him to state the principles of the Sikh religion. "Make love thy mosque, sincerity thy prayer carpet, justice thy Koran, courtesy thy Kaaba, charity thy creed, and the will of God thy rosary." Guru Nanak died as he had lived, a man of peace.

To the Sikhs the Golden Temple is just as holy as the Kaaba in Mecca is to Moslems, or the Church of the Holy Sepulchre to Christians.

Had they been left alone to practice their religion, the Sikhs might never have developed into the great fighters they are today. But trouble began for them when the Mogul Emperor Jehangir, father of Shah Jehan, came into power. Noticing the rapid spread of Sikhism in the Punjab, Jehangir started to persecute the sect. Their fifth Guru was thrown into prison, where he died under torture, but not before he had told his son and successor to defend the brotherhood by force.

184

Thus it came about that the sixth Guru, Har Govind, developed into a soldier rather than a saint. So fired were the Sikhs by his military enthusiasm that they quickly became a menace to the Moslems. Alarmed, Emperor Jehangir imprisoned the Guru, who managed to escape but died. For the next thirty years the Moslems persecuted the Sikhs with the usual result. Sikhism increased in power, and it was the ruthless cruelty of the last Mogul Emperor that welded the Sikhs into the great warrior clan that was and still is implacably hostile to Moslem power.

An extraordinary thing occurred when the ninth Guru was discovered gazing intently from the window of his prison cell. Accused by the Mogul Emperor of looking in the direction of the royal harem, the holy man replied with this prophecy, "Emperor, I am not gazing at thy royal apartments. I am looking across the sea toward the men, fair-skinned and wearing helmets, who shall come from the West to avenge my death, to tear down thy purdahs and destroy thine empire."

This prophecy, which is authentic, was so firmly believed in by the Sikhs that they used it as a battle cry during the Indian Mutiny, when they fought on the side of the British against the last of the Moguls at Delhi. The Guru who made that prophecy was named Tegh Bahadur. He was executed, but his son, who was the tenth and last Guru, fled to the hills. There, having brooded on his followers' wrongs for twenty years, he finally emerged as a great military leader as well as Guru, resolved to overthrow the Moslem power and to set up his own Sikhs as an independent nation. Thousands flocked to join him, and at a great assembly he announced his mission, binding his followers more closely than ever by a ceremony of baptism at which every Sikh received the name "Singh," meaning "lion."

To this day all Sikhs are Singhs, but as a Hindu friend recently told me, not all Singhs are Sikhs.

In addition to the name Singh, all Sikhs have five distinctive items of dress known as the five *kakas*, all of which begin with the letter *k* and by means of which all orthodox Sikhs can be recognized. *Kirpan* is a knife, which denotes readiness for battle; *kara* is an iron bangle denoting fidelity; *khanga* is a comb; *kes* is the uncut hair on which the comb is used, and *karchh* are knee-length shorts denoting manhood. All Sikh women wear long trousers.

Henceforth the Sikh fellowship was to be known as *khalsa*, meaning the "elect" or the "pure."

It was the tenth and last of the Gurus, named Govind Singh, who taught the Sikhs to die in the defense of their faith. For this reason Sikhs are just as fanatical as Moslems.

When Govind Singh died in 1708 he left no successor, but he told the Sikhs that henceforth their spirits would dwell in their Bible.

During the eighteenth century the Punjab was the scene of ceaseless turmoil between Sikhs and Moslems, and on January 7, 1761, at the battle of Panipat, the Sikhs were defeated. On their homeward march the victorious Moslems destroyed the holy city of Amritsar, blew up the Golden Temple with gunpowder, filled the sacred pool with mud, and purposely defiled the holy place by slaughtering a lot of holy cows within the temple enclosure.

Although this happened in 1761, the Sikhs have neither forgotten nor forgiven it. When the Partition of India took place and Pakistan came into being, the dividing line passed between Amritsar and Lahore, leaving many thousands of Sikhs and Moslems on the wrong side of the line. In the scramble to get out of India and into Pakistan, great numbers of Moslems were killed by Sikhs. On the other hand, the Moslems who were already in Pakistan avenged themselves by slaughtering thousands of Sikhs who were trying to escape into India.

How true it is I cannot say, but I was told that there isn't one Sikh left in Pakistan. In India they number about six million.

Soon after leaving Amritsar the character of the country changed. The great plain of India was left behind as the ground rose steeply toward the mountains ahead of us. After stopping for a few minutes at Jammu we headed toward what appeared to be a solid wall of huge peaks.

"This makes me think of the time we flew from Mexico City over the top of Popocatepetl," said Zetta as the level of the plane showed that it was climbing steeply. "Surely we aren't going to try to fly over those mountains."

Overhearing her remark as he walked toward the cockpit, the captain reassured her. "No, madam. We are headed for the Banihal Pass, which is only about ten thousand feet high. The mountains themselves are far higher than that."

The captain's comforting words were undone when one of the Indian passengers leaned over and said, "The Banihal Pass is where a United Nations plane crashed the other day. Everyone was killed."

As our plane was not pressurized and the elevation of the Pass through which we were to fly was ten thousand feet, I understood why we were flying only about two thousand feet above the ground.

"We must be entering the Pass now," said Sam as the mountains began to close in upon us on both sides. "I'd hate to fly through here in a fog."

Higher and higher we climbed, but the ground beneath us

187

looked just as close, for we were flying parallel to it. Closer and closer came those rugged walls, until it seemed as if the slightest swerve on the part of the pilot would dash us against them.

My ears popped as the plane leveled off at twelve thousand feet. That we were through the Pass was soon obvious, for although the plane was now flying on a level keel, the ground beneath us was rapidly receding.

I have seen the Rockies, the Alps, the Pyrenees, the Caucasus, the Mountains of the Moon, and many other of the world's most famous peaks, but none can compare with the magnificent panorama of the mighty Himalayas that slowly unfolded as we emerged from the Banihal Pass and entered the Vale of Kashmir. We were spellbound. No matter in what direction we looked, north, south, east, or west, snow-covered mountains in apparently unbroken chains met our gaze, while nestling at their feet was the vividly green valley of the Jhelum River with its chain of crystal lakes.

The Mogul emperors Akbar, Jehangir, and Shah Jehan, enamored of its intoxicating loveliness, likened it to "an emerald set with pearls," and there they built their wondrous gardens, among them Shalimar, "The Abode of Love."

"It's been a long way round, but we've made it!" I laughed as we landed at Srinagar's airport. "I feel as if I were walking on air!"

"You very nearly are," said Sam. "The captain tells me that the elevation here is six thousand feet. It's only 68 degrees."

"No wonder I'm cold," said Zetta as she wrapped her fur jacket around her shoulders. "I'm shivering. I hope it won't be as cold as this on Dal Lake."

"Don't worry," I said. "The lake is one thousand feet lower

than this, and besides, they have real fireplaces on the house-boats if you want a fire."

Little did we dream that within a few days we would actually be sitting around a blazing log fire roasting Kashmir chestnuts.

CHAPTER NINE

"You're right, darling," said Zetta as we drove up to Nedou's Hotel, "it's much warmer down here." Instead of the cold wind which had been blowing across the airport straight from the surrounding snow-capped mountains, a warm gentle breeze now caressed our cheeks like velvet.

"Makes me think of Bermuda," said Sam. "I feel like going to sleep under a tree and letting the rest of the world go by."

Among us, including cameras, tripods, and other paraphernalia, we had twenty-seven pieces of baggage, all of which was piled on the veranda of the hotel while we walked into the huge entrance lounge to look things over.

It was luncheon time. Through the screened doorway we could see that the dining room was crowded.

"How about tidying up?" said Sam as he and I went in one direction and Zetta in the other. Usually Zetta takes quite a time to powder her nose, so we were surprised to find her waiting for us when we emerged, laughing.

"Did you see what I saw?" asked Zetta with a sad smile.

"You mean the six little thunder mugs sitting in a row?"

Zetta nodded. "Quite a difference from the powder room at the Ambassador! I tink I live houseboat!"

Nedou's is the largest hotel in the world without plumbing. It's by far the most conservative hotel on earth. Not so long ago it had burned down but was rebuilt just as it had been in the days of Sir Francis Younghusband, who was British Resident in 1908. But it is by far the best hotel in Srinagar, and when you get used to its old-fashioned atmosphere, which includes the Victorian-era courtliness of its charming proprietor, and after you have sat around a blazing open fire in a bedroom as big as a barn, and enjoyed early-morning tea on your own veranda to the music of the bulbul, Kashmir's most famous songster, you soon forget about the disadvantages of commodes and what my mother used to call a "chamber."

Mr. Nedou himself placed us at a table and with a clap of his hands summoned a waiter. While the luncheon served was nothing to boast about, it was at least clean and the service excellent.

Sitting at a table next to us was an elderly Englishman who looked like what he turned out to be, a retired army officer. I had noticed him eying us with interest, and as he didn't seem to be one of those unapproachable types who require a formal introduction before a stranger may speak to them, I decided to get into conversation with him and find out about houseboats.

"Who are the people in uniform?" I asked, indicating several tables at which about twenty men were eating.

"United Nations observers," he replied, not very enthusiastically. "There are about fifty of them altogether. They spend much of their time here. It's more comfortable than on the cease-fire line! Their uniforms are quite interesting."

"What do they observe?" I inquired.

"Heaven only knows. Not one of them can speak Kashmiri. How can they be expected to find out what the people want?" he said hopelessly.

"What *do* the Kashmiris want?" I persisted.

"That all depends," answered the Englishman. "Most of them have about as much political consciousness as my foot. But if you ask the man in the street here in Srinagar what he wants, he'll tell you, 'Thomas Cook and the American Express Company.'"

"That would mean a return to the good old days of tourists and prosperity," I said.

"Precisely. If you had lived in Kashmir as long as I have," he continued, "you'd know that the average man would rather lose his eyesight making shawls and doing embroidery work with a needle that most women can hardly see, still less thread, than be bothered with this political squabble between India and Pakistan."

"Then you've lived here a good many years?" remarked Zetta.

"Almost as long as old Nedou himself, and he's been here at least sixty years, you know." The Englishman stood up. "How about joining me in a cup of tea? It's quite pleasant out there on the veranda."

"Now is our chance," whispered Zetta as we followed him out of the dining room. "He ought to have all the answers."

"How do you go about getting a houseboat?" she inquired eagerly. "We're awfully anxious to spend a few weeks on Dal Lake."

The old-timer smiled. "You Americans are queer people. Pardon me, I should say wonderful people," with a bow to Zetta. "You travel halfway around the world to Kashmir, stay a few weeks, and then rush back to write a book about it!"

Zetta bristled and gave me a look that I knew meant to come to her rescue.

"General," I said.

"Colonel," corrected the Englishman with a pleased smile.

"You've forgotten your Kipling," I said. "Concerning the globe-trotter, he wrote, 'The man who does kingdoms in days and writes books upon them in weeks . . . is worthy of a book.

Given absolute freedom for a month, the mind contents itself with following in old and well-beaten ways paths that we in India have no time to tread.'"

Zetta, supporting me loyally, then added, "When Clare Luce, one of our congresswomen, returned from India and wrote about it, one of the critics scoffed at her presumption in writing about such a vast continent after having been there only three weeks. As far as I can remember he said something like this: 'To write about India, you should have lived there thirty years, not three weeks!' To which Clare Luce replied caustically, 'If I lived in India thirty years, I wouldn't be able to write about anything.' Besides," she continued, "although this is my husband's first visit to Kashmir, he has been in India many times. Few Americans know Hindus and Moslems as well as he does. He had hundreds of them working for him for six years when he constructed the railroad from Singapore to Bangkok."

Warming to her subject she added: "Carveth was their sahib, doctor, lawyer, banker, mediator, and father-confessor. They often came to him when they had trouble with their various wives. Next to Jesus, I believe that Carveth has had more Moslem babies named after him in that area than anyone else. He even celebrated their religious festivals with them, Moslems, Hindus, and Christians."

"Quite understandable," remarked Sam dryly. "Carveth was on government pay!"

"My dear Mrs. Wells," said the colonel humbly, "I had no idea your husband was an author or that he had been in India before. Accept my apologies. How about another cup of tea?"

"Knighthood is still in flower!" laughed Zetta. "Sorry I had to let off steam! We really are most fortunate to have met you.

Do tell us how you happen to have lived in Kashmir all these years."

"Most refreshing!" said the colonel genially. "I can tell you in a very few words. When I retired from the Army I bought a houseboat for a song, and my wife and I have lived on Dal Lake ever since. I hope I die here. The Vale is my Shangri-La."

"How extraordinary that you should have mentioned Shangri-La," said Zetta. "That's exactly what my husband says the Vale of Kashmir is."

The colonel gave a sigh. "Not now," he said wistfully. "Things have changed a lot since they let this fellow Abdullah out of jail. Perfectly astonishing, that chap's career. Old friend of Nehru's, you know. Starts mixing in politics. The maharajah claps him in jail for high treason. Nehru comes here and he gets shoved into jail too. Now they're both out. The maharajah has skedaddled, Abdullah is the ruler of Kashmir, and Nehru is the Prime Minister of India. Meanwhile Kashmir's gone to pot. The people are starving to death, and if this trouble with Pakistan continues much longer, I'll be starving too." He gave another sigh.

"Excuse my outburst, Mrs. Wells. You asked me how to hire a houseboat. See those people waiting outside the railings over there? They're all waiting to rent you one, but if you take my advice, you'll go and see the Kashmir Express Company. You'll find their office on the Bund. Better hire a tonga."

"Tonga?" I said inquiringly.

"One of those two-wheeled pony carts. Cheap as dirt. A couple of them will take you and your luggage to the Bund for less than the cost of a decent cigar."

Thanking him for his kindness, we engaged three tongas, and with a crowd of at least twenty people running behind, plus one man who rode on a bicycle, off we rattled to the Bund.

"Take no notice of these people," shouted the man on the bicycle as he rode alongside Zetta's tonga. "They're all rascals. I have the finest houseboat on Dal Lake. Stop, you'll be sorry if you go to the Kashmir Express Company."

"Go home to your wife!" laughed Zetta.

"Let's ask him to watch our tongas while we go to the Bund," I said. "He's at least clean and looks quite prosperous."

"Yes, yes!" agreed the man on the bicycle as he handed Zetta a printed card. "I will watch your luggage. No charge. You'll rent my houseboat. You see! It's the most beautiful one on Dal Lake. It is called the *Flower Garden*."

By this time our tongas had arrived at the foot of a flight of steps leading to the top of the Bund. There was no alternative; we couldn't drive up the steps. The drivers didn't mind. The longer they waited, the more money we would have to pay them. So placing our cycling friend on guard, we walked up half a dozen steps and found ourselves on the top of the Bund. Moored to the bank were hundreds of boats, while along the Bund itself were rows of shops whose signs alone repaid us for our visit. I wish I had written them all down, but the ones I can remember were "Subhana the Worst," "Cheap John," and "Suffering Moses."

Soon we found a sign with an arrow pointing to a flight of very rickety stairs: "The Kashmir Express Co., Ltd., Agents for Thomas Cook and Son."

The news of our arrival in Srinagar had gone before us, for waiting in his office was a stoutish Hindu, and beside him stood a fine-looking Kashmiri. Had he not clipped his beard short he would have looked like a patriarch. On his head he wore a large white turban, and on his feet leather sandals. A pair of very baggy white trousers and a striped jacket which some European must have given him completed his attire.

"You desire a houseboat?" inquired the Hindu. "Yes," he said, answering his own question. "I have arranged for the best boat on Dal Lake, *H.M.S. Pinafore*. Here is the captain; his name is Dundoo."

Dundoo smiled and bowed politely, murmuring, "Sahib."

"I represent Thomas Cook," said the Hindu. "You may trust my company. Your boat is ready. Here's the contract. Please read it carefully before you sign." Whereupon he placed before us a single sheet of paper. "Houseboats engaged on the contract system," read the top line.

"Part 1 includes items in the price quoted," said the agent. "Part 2 is regarded as extras."

Zetta and Sam looked over my shoulder as I read the contract. "Part 1 is what interests me," I said. "That's what we get for our money."

Here is what Part 1 included:

1. Houseboat, cook boat, and small boat for going aboard and coming ashore

2. Servants: cook, general servant, waterman, and sweeper

3. All "bazaar" food (including fruit for cooking and dairy produce)

4. Stores in daily use, such as porridge, tea, coffee, jams, marmalade, salt, pepper, etc., etc.

5. Small cakes and scones for tea

6. Firewood for kitchen, baths, etc.

7. Tins for bath water, sweeper's utensils, jars for storage of drinking and other water

8. Electric light

"That all sounds wonderful," said Zetta, "but it doesn't say anything about the size of the boat or what it's all going to cost."

With a pained look the Hindu explained: "The boat will be completely furnished with carpets, furniture, linens, silver, cushions, and ornaments. It will be one hundred and ten feet long, twelve feet wide with a fine living room twenty-four feet long, dining room fifteen feet long, serving pantry seven feet long."

"How many bedrooms?" inquired Zetta.

"Three with baths," said the agent. "I presume you have your own bedding."

On hearing that we didn't carry blankets and sheets around with us, Dundoo, who could speak fairly good English, remarked, "Do not be disturbed, mem-sahib, there will be plenty of bedding. No charge. Just some baksheesh when Mem-sahib goes back to America."

I began to get nervous. What was all this going to cost? I had visions of what such things would cost in America. One dollar an hour for a cleaning woman. Our contract called for five servants. The cheapest rooms in America, even in a tourist camp, were anywhere from three to eight dollars a day, and there were three of us. And what about the food for three people and five servants? Then there were the three boats, and from the agent's description our houseboat was a regular floating palace.

"Darling," I whispered to Zetta, "I believe Shangri-La is going to bankrupt us."

"How much is all this going to cost?" asked Zetta again.

The agent looked more pained than ever. "Madam, I assure you that our charges are reasonable."

"Then tell us how much it's going to cost. I wouldn't even enter heaven without asking St. Peter the same question."

Dundoo and the agent went into a huddle. Zetta had forgotten how Orientals love to bargain and haggle. She wanted a fixed price and she was going to get it.

"Hold on," said Sam, "here it comes!"

"Mem-sahib," said the agent apologetically, "I have discussed the price with Dundoo. He says he's a poor man with many children. Would two dollars a day for each of you be too much?"

"I'll think it over," said Zetta while I squirmed. I have always hated to ask the cost of anything.

Thrifty Sam was different, but even he was overjoyed at the price. However, he couldn't resist being facetious.

"Two dollars a day each!" he exclaimed with mock horror. "Surely you must mean two dollars a day for all three of us!"

"I see that Sahib has a sense of humor," remarked the agent.

Poor Dundoo took Sam seriously. "Sahib forgets," he said with tears in his eyes, "I must pay the agent his commission. I must buy many chickens. I must pay the servants their wages. I must pay the government for the electric light."

Incidentally, when I say that Dundoo had tears in his eyes, I do not exaggerate. Kashmiri men have a way of bursting into tears at the least provocation.

"Put him out of his misery, darling," I pleaded.

"Okay!" said Zetta with apparent resignation. "Two dollars a day on the American plan it is." Whereupon I signed on the dotted line.

"Now let's take a look at this list of extras."

Part 2 of the contract was headed: "Items normally considered 'extras.'"

1. Laundry

2. Large cakes and "bazaar" confectionery for teas, etc.

3. Table fruit (usually bought from hawkers)

4. Bacon, cheese, tinned biscuits

5. Tinned stores coming under the head of "luxury." Stores such as sardines, tinned fruit, pickles, tinned asparagus, etc.

6. Mineral and soda water

7. Coolies for moving houseboat after tenant has embarked

8. Firewood for stoves in inclement weather

9. Mooring charges payable to owner of land (Kashmir government or private landowner) to which houseboat is moored. These range from eight rupees to thirty-five rupees a month, according to position.

10. Taxi shikaras (water taxi)

ADDITIONAL PERSONS: In the event of additional persons joining up with those already on the houseboat, a new contract is necessary.

By this time it was four o'clock. Our tongas had been waiting for us an hour, but the man on the bicycle was still on the job. When he saw us coming with Dundoo his face fell.

"My houseboat is the best one on Dal Lake, Dundoo's is a *dunga*."

A dunga is a boat whose superstructure is hung with mats of woven reeds. A large part of the population of Srinagar are born, live, and die on dungas.

Dundoo was furious. Anyone but a Kashmiri would have punched the other fellow in the nose for such impudence. All Dundoo did was to let out such a string of bad language that his cyclist competitor just slunk away like a cur with its tail between its legs.

There was just one little detail that the Hindu agent had

failed to mention. The whole of the Vale was in the throes of a record flood. More than ten feet above its normal level, the water of Dal Lake had spread over the road that winds along its shore, even covering the stone retaining wall.

"Lucky thing we didn't try to get here in a taxi," said Sam as our ponies waded along the road with the water up to their bellies and sometimes splashing through the floor boards. For nearly two hours they stumbled along, covering the four miles from Srinagar to the spot opposite which our houseboat was moored. It was almost dark.

The horses stopped. "Now what?" said Zetta as Dundoo pointed to the *H.M.S. Pinafore* moored to an island about half a mile away.

Standing in his tonga, Dundoo, with his hands cupped to his mouth, gave a prolonged "Halloooooo!"

Suddenly we saw a light in the boat. Then a small boat called a shikara, very much like a gondola, shot out from the side of the big boat and headed swiftly toward us. On reaching the flooded retaining wall, the boat stopped. There wasn't quite enough depth for it to go over the wall and reach us. So the tongas moved to the wall, and with Dundoo and the drivers standing up to their ankles in water on top of the wall, our baggage and lastly ourselves were lifted safely into the boat.

Painted on a board on the roof of the shikara was its name:

HAPPY BEST NEW SUNLIGHT
Best Spring Seats
If you come once
you will come again!

"Look at the shape of the paddles!" exclaimed Zetta. "They are perfect hearts! That's a good omen."

"Well, darling, I'm gliding over the Lake of Cashmere with my loved one by my side," I said, "but I never thought it would be quite like this. Twenty-seven pieces of baggage and not a lotus in sight."

"This doesn't count," laughed Zetta happily. "The flood can't last forever. I'm dying to get on board that houseboat and know the worst!"

Ten minutes' paddling and we slid alongside our new home, the *H.M.S. Pinafore.*

"Looks like a battleship," said Sam. "It's enormous. When do we eat?"

"Dinner at eight, sahib!" said Dundoo as he helped us aboard and, having opened a pair of full-sized french doors, ushered us into our living room.

"I just can't believe my eyes!" exclaimed Zetta as her gaze roamed over the room. "Hand-carved paneled ceiling and walls! Heavy brocade curtains over the windows! Richly colored oriental rugs! Three overstuffed armchairs! A writing desk and even a love seat! Look, darling, there's a large silver elephant on the mantelpiece. It's your trade-mark."

Pleased as Punch, Dundoo led the way into the dining room, where a manservant was already laying the table for three.

"Walnut from Shalimar!" said Dundoo proudly as he tapped the table and the beautifully carved chairs.

"And here's the bar!" shouted Sam as he walked past us into the serving pantry. "What, no ice? No beer? Dundoo, you're slipping."

"Tomorrow, sahib. Plenty of ice and beer. Whatever you want. You give me money. I buy."

"Now let's look at the bedrooms," said Zetta. "Dare we look at the bathrooms?"

"Just as good as Nedou's," I said, noticing the commode and old-fashioned thunder mugs. "You can sit in that tin bath or you can take a shower. It's just like they have at Raffles Hotel in Singapore, big brown jar, tin dipper and all!"

"I wonder how they look after the bathrooms," queried Zetta.

Dundoo drew back the curtains. Running alongside the boat was a kind of catwalk. Evidently the water boy entered the bathroom from outside.

"Keep your bedroom door locked and you're all right," I said.

Every inch of the boat, bathrooms included, was paneled; all the doors slid into the walls à la Japan. There were cupboards galore and a small table with a reading lamp beside each bed.

"The beds aren't so bad, either," said Zetta as she tried to bounce. "And the sheets are clean, thank heaven!"

Just then Dundoo arrived carrying a kerosene lamp.

"What's the idea? Oil lamps! I thought we were supposed to have electric light," I complained.

"The flood, sahib," moaned Dundoo. "It has swept away my light pole. The wires are in the water."

"Cut it off the bill," said Sam. "No electric light, no payment."

"Now you've made the poor man cry," said Zetta reproachfully. "Of course we'll pay for the light, Dundoo."

Dundoo cheered up immediately. He saw a chance to make a few cents' profit.

"Mem-sahib, I buy kerosene. Much more expensive than electric light. I have many lamps. Sahib will allow me buy large can oil, then we have bright light again."

"Light her up like a Christmas tree, Dundoo," I said cheerfully.

"Dinner is served, mem-sahib," announced our butler.

"Chicken soup. Breasts of chicken, French-fried potatoes, green beans. Stewed fresh peaches for dessert! What more could you want?" said Sam genially. "And look at those walnuts! Dundoo, where do these come from?"

"Shalimar, sahib. Always plenty walnuts."

Even the coffee was passable, but when Zetta produced a bottle of Courvoisier brandy, our delight was complete.

"Just a mouthful for me," said Sam. "It'll be a long time before we get any more of that!"

After dinner we climbed the stairs to the upper deck and just sat silent in the moonlight. Every few seconds we could hear a voice shouting, followed by another voice from far away across the lake. "That's the Dal Lake telephone service," I said. "Someone's stranded by the flood and he's calling to his wife to come and get him. Isn't that right, Dundoo?"

"Yes, sahib. Man can call his wife several miles."

Sam smoked one of his precious Corona Coronas while Dundoo squatted on the deck smoking his hubble-bubble. It had been a wonderful day.

"Some people just don't know how to live," said Zetta. "Just imagine, dinner at eight without fear of the cook leaving, service with a smile instead of a frown, no housekeeping worries, ordering our lives to suit ourselves, no traffic noises, no filthy smog, no dust; why, I could go on like this for ages. And all for two dollars a day, food and everything."

"And don't forget that we can move our house whenever we want a change of scenery," said Sam.

"What amazes me," I said, "is the solidity of this houseboat. It might as well be set in a bed of concrete. It doesn't roll, it doesn't pitch, it doesn't even tilt the slightest bit when all three of us sit on the same side of the living room."

"The catch is getting here," said Zetta. "If it didn't cost a small fortune to fly to Kashmir, I think Bermuda would be deserted in a week. The funny thing is that Kashmir and Bermuda are both in the same latitude too."

"The grass is always greener in the other fellow's yard," I said. "Nevertheless, I defy anyone to find a place where you can live as cheaply as in the Vale of Kashmir and at the same time enjoy a better climate or such sublime scenery."

"I'm going below and turn in," said nautical Sam. "Mind you don't break your necks on the companionway. My cabin's aft on the poop deck!"

The next morning we found Sam warming his coattails in front of a fire in the living room.

"We've been swindled," he growled. "Dundoo says that firewood is an extra. I'm positive it was included in Part 1 of our contract. Let's look at it. . . . by Jove, the old boy's right! Firewood's only free for the kitchen and baths."

Strangely enough, although Kashmir is blessed with many wonderful trees, firewood is so expensive that it is weighed stick by stick.

It was just seven-thirty. We had ordered breakfast for eight-thirty, so we had an hour to enjoy the early-morning beauty of the lake. Evidently we were being watched, for no sooner had we gone to the top deck and hoisted the Explorers Club flag than a boat put out from shore. As it came nearer we saw that it was loaded from stem to stern with flowers. Paddling it was a typical Kashmiri with long baggy trousers, voluminous shirt that came to his knees, a kind of waistcoat, and a tightly fitting skullcap. Had his clothes been clean they would have been white. Actually they were gray. But the drabness of his costume was more than made up for by the brightness of his smile. His face was brown, his eyes were like those of a woman, and his eyelashes curled like a movie star's. In between the strokes of his heart-shaped paddle he saluted us.

"This makes me think of Xochimilco," said Zetta, who would rather spend her time arranging flowers than anything else. "Just look at those zinnias and asters. They are even larger than the ones in our Bermuda garden."

"Flower seller!" said Dundoo.

Zetta chose a bunch. "How much?" she asked.

The flower seller held up a small copper coin about the size of a penny. "Flowers very cheap," said Dundoo.

It didn't require very much mental arithmetic to discover that twenty cents would buy the whole boatload.

"I'll buy the lot!" said Zetta.

The flower seller looked confused, but when Dundoo explained that we were buying his whole cargo and that we would repeat the process every morning, he was delighted at such good fortune.

It seemed a terrible waste to throw away flowers that were only a day old, but at twenty cents a boatload it seemed silly not to convert *H.M.S. Pinafore* into a flower garden. I had always thought that the cheapest place to buy flowers was Mexico, but the prices charged by Xochimilco's flower sellers, cheap as they are, are exorbitant compared with those of the Vale of Kashmir.

Gardening in Kashmir is not the problem that it is in Bermuda, where water is so scarce, but while Bermuda has flowers all the year round, Kashmir has them for only eight months. When we were there in September, asters, zinnias, salvia, cannas, fuchsias, and geraniums were at the height of their beauty, but the sun was already losing its strength and the night temperature dropped to 52. All through October, Kashmir's chrysanthemums are in full bloom, and while many of the gardens begin to lose their beauty, then is the time for the trees to change from green to the gorgeous colors of autumn, and by the first of November the Virginia creeper has turned to a rich hue of red and purple. Then winter comes and the temperature drops to freezing. Leaves fall from the trees, flowers die, and the lovely green lawns, touched by the first frost, turn brown. By mid-December the temperature may drop to 25, and even at midday it is cold enough to see one's breath. But although the Vale of Kashmir is snow-covered, the temperature is never severe, averaging about 40 degrees Fahrenheit through January and February.

Early in March the gardens begin to wake from winter sleep, and although the grass is brown and the trees leafless, Srinagar's gardens are gay with masses of violets, pansies, wallflowers, narcissus, crocuses, and daisies. Willow buds show signs of bursting, and the apricot trees are almost ready to blossom. But even in March the night temperature often drops a degree below freezing, while at midday the shade temperature reaches only 55. By the beginning of April the English primroses which were introduced by Sir Francis Younghusband are in full bloom, together with daffodils and hyacinths, while the apricot and peach trees form little clouds of delicate pink-and-white blossoms.

Tulips and irises are blooming by the middle of April, closely followed by poppies and peonies. By the first of May the rambler roses are out and the shade temperature at midday has risen to 80. May is the time for lilacs, roses, and columbines, and by the middle of the month the strawberries are ripe. By the end of the month the gardens are glorious with geraniums, delphiniums, poppies, and sweet peas. June brings the gladioli, Canterbury bells, pinks, carnations, sweet williams, and foxgloves, and by the middle of the month the fuchsias and hollyhocks are at the height of their glory. Yet the night temperature still stays around 54. The hottest month of the year is usually July, when the shade temperature reaches 97 and the sun 142, but even in that month the night temperature is only 62, so that it is never difficult to get a sound night's sleep in Kashmir, especially if you're living on a houseboat.

And so we're back again at August and September, when people's thoughts turn to fall and eyes watch the surrounding mountains for the first dazzling fall of winter's snow.

Zetta spent the whole morning arranging flowers, while Sam and I overhauled our cameras. Shalimar Garden was less than an hour's journey away, but I was determined not to spoil my dream by gliding over Dal Lake when its waters were muddy and covered with debris brought down by the flood.

"Here comes the vegetable man," cried Sam, "and he's brought his garden with him."

Sure enough, a floating island was coming our way, steered by a Kashmiri with a long pole. Half the size of a tennis court, the garden came neatly alongside the kitchen boat, where it was anchored by thrusting the pole through the island and into the lake bottom.

Growing on it were tomatoes and brinjals, a kind of small-sized eggplant. Having sold his produce to Dundoo, the man pulled up his pole and off he drifted downstream.

"The trouble about real estate that floats," I remarked with a laugh, "is that someone might steal your lot during the night."

This is by no means an unusual occurrence in Kashmir.

But floating islands have uses other than raising vegetables.

208

Dundoo had one of his own, anchored about ten feet from his kitchen boat. On it was an old hen and her chicks. For their shelter at night Dundoo had built them a little chicken house.

There was no need to ask where he kept his other chickens. They were all over the house, inside, outside, and on top of the roof, but evidently they had been trained never to trespass on the big houseboat, for they never bothered us except occasionally at night when the rooster crowed the dawn.

About fifty yards downstream was our nearest houseboat, called *The New Golden Hind,* but according to Dundoo, it hadn't been occupied since Partition. He told us that except for permanent residents like the English army officer, no European visitors had lived in a houseboat for months. The tourist business was kaputt.

News that there was a houseboat with a flag upon it spread rapidly. Long before lunch, boats were converging upon *H.M.S. Pinafore* from all directions. Flower sellers, fruit vendors, tailors, jewelers, rug sellers, and peddlers of all descriptions surrounded our boat, shouting and holding up their stock in trade for our inspection. But I noticed that they kept their distance and did not actually come alongside.

I afterward learned that this was because some of the old residents kept powerful water pistols in their houseboats, ready to shoo away anyone whose persistence became a nuisance.

Thanks to Dundoo, who told them in no uncertain terms that when they were wanted we would give him word and he in turn would tip them off, many of the peddlers moved away, but there was rarely a day when at least one or two could not be seen floating idly about, hoping that our curiosity would get the better of us and that we would invite them aboard.

Once or twice when we had nothing better to do we did

allow a hawker to tempt us. Usually he had a companion whose job was to unwrap and display the articles for sale, and then wrap them up again. Time and trouble mean nothing to these Kashmiri salesmen. They have the patience of Job and the tenacity of a bulldog. Their manners are invariably charming, but they are masters of every dishonest trick of the trade it is possible to imagine and many that you wouldn't dream of. Nowhere in the Orient is it so important to bargain as it is in Kashmir. Divide the asking price by four with a view to getting eventually what you want for half is a good rule. Then, having beaten the seller down to half and paid for your treasure, you suddenly realize that the real value is almost sure to be much less or he wouldn't have closed the bargain.

"Only looking, not buying, mem-sahib," is the almost universal line adopted by these charming tricksters.

One day Zetta noticed a piece of Tibetan jewelry that intrigued her. It was a heart-shaped pendant made of native gold and encrusted with twenty-nine stones. Among them were three star sapphires, three star rubies, three polished emeralds, and a large carved emerald in the center the size of her thumbnail around which were a number of small rubies and turquoises. On the back were the characters and engravings which showed its origin. It was obviously old and well worn.

"Make me an offer," said the merchant.

Zetta did, whereupon the man, without saying another word, packed up all his belongings, which had taken at least an hour to display, returned to his boat, and was paddled away.

Two days later the jeweler returned.

"I have had no sleep, mem-sahib. You mocked me, but I know that you will never be happy if you leave Kashmir without that pendant. I felt that I must come back and tell Mem-sahib that I am an honest man and that even if I sell it at a loss I shall give her happiness."

Then, having unwrapped the jewel and caressed it, he thrust it into Zetta's hand.

"Take it," he said in a broken voice, but mentioning six times as much as Zetta had offered him.

Zetta weakened. She doubled her original offer, and before she could change her mind the jeweler had taken her money and the pendant was hers.

Several months later Zetta had her treasure appraised, to find that the carved emerald was genuine and was worth far more than the price she had paid for the whole pendant.

Even in its flooded state Dal Lake and its surroundings were so lovely that we just hated to leave the boat. North, south, east, and west were snow-capped mountains, and only several miles away to the west was Hari Parbat, a pyramid-shaped hill five or six hundred feet high and crowned by an ancient fort which rises abruptly from the floor of the valley, making it the principal landmark of Srinagar. Sir Francis Younghusband, who has seen both, says that Hari Parbat bears some resemblance to the Potala at Lhasa. Both the fort on the summit and the wall around the base of the Hari Parbat were built by the Mogul Emperor, Akbar the Great, who visited Kashmir three times.

One afternoon as we were sunning ourselves on the top deck while drinking in the exquisite scenery that surrounded us, we saw a very snappy-looking shikara headed our way. As it came nearer I could read the name, *Buckingham Palace, Full Spring Seats.*

Dundoo had also seen the boat coming, for he suddenly appeared on deck and announced, "Sahib Colonel is coming."

Sahib Colonel turned out to be the same retired English

officer whom we had met at Nedou's Hotel the day we arrived.

"Just in time for tea!" said Zetta. "You're the very person my husband wanted to see. He wants to ask you about the animals."

"I must apologize for not bringing my wife," said the colonel, "but she's gone to New Delhi to do some shopping. However, here's her card and here are a couple of mine."

"Have some dragon's blood," said Sam as he poured a cup of Lipton's best. "We like ours strong."

"I say!" said the colonel with surprise. "I didn't know you Americans knew how to make tea. Thanks, a couple of lumps and a little milk, please."

"Notice he said 'milk' and not 'cream,' " I teased Zetta.

The colonel glanced around the room approvingly. "Charming place you have here. First time I've been aboard the *Pinafore*, but I've passed her many a time in my shikara."

"I notice you've called your boat *Buckingham Palace*," said Zetta. "I suppose you must get a little homesick sometimes, don't you?"

"Ah yes! Buckingham Palace, of course. The King, God bless him. Homesick, did you say?" The colonel's face clouded. "There was a time when I would have given my right arm for a stroll down Bond Street and along Piccadilly, but from what I read in the London papers, England is no place for a retired man of my age, or any age, for that matter. I'd land in the workhouse! No indeed. As I told you, Mrs. Wells, Kashmir is my Shangri-La even though my mansion is only a houseboat."

"Don't these boats ever leak? Wouldn't it be better to have a house on land?" inquired Zetta.

"No foreigner may own real estate in Kashmir, unfortunately. That's the reason we all live on houseboats," explained the colonel. "Of course they leak if you don't take care of them, but given proper care and maintenance, one of these houseboats will last a century." Then with a chuckle he continued, "Besides, if I have undesirable neighbors I can move my home. It used to happen occasionally when Kashmir was full of people from all over the world. But nowadays visitors are as scarce as hens' teeth."

"How's the hunting up here?" I inquired.

"Unfortunately we don't have any. No hunters. No hounds. Plenty of red foxes. They have the time of their lives."

"You see, darling," I said to Zetta, "you have to be specific when you talk to an Englishman. Colonel," I said, "my wife and I have been married nearly twenty years, but we still have arguments about the English language. English and American are very different. What I call a dish she calls a platter. If she wants me to wash the dishes, she means all the china used at the table. When an American talks of hunting, he means shooting."

"Good God, man! Surely you Americans don't shoot foxes!" said the colonel in a horrified tone.

"I give up!" laughed Zetta. "Carveth and I are always having these arguments about English, but thank heaven he's as good an American as I am." Then, turning to me, she said, "Try again, darling."

"Colonel, what do you shoot up here?"

"Ducks, snipe, partridge, pheasant. There's all kinds of game."

"Any deer shooting?" I inquired.

Zetta gave a giggle. "You're forgetting your English, darling. You don't shoot deer, you 'stalk' them."

"Quite right, my dear," said the colonel. "We have a number of deer in Kashmir, but our most famous is the stag, similar animal to your American wapiti."

"Wapiti means elk, darling. They call a moose an elk in England."

"One of our most valuable animals in Kashmir is the ibex," continued the colonel. "Extraordinary horns. They curl back and almost touch the middle of its back. The Kashmiris hunt them for their soft woolly underfur, which they use for lining shawls and making stockings and gloves. From the long hairs of the ibex's coat, blankets and ropes are made. And the skin of the animals provides the best leather for the soft socklike boots that the natives wear in the mountains."

"Better ask the colonel about those ermine skins the fellow tried to sell you this morning."

"*Caveat emptor*," said the colonel. "Beware of buying any furs here unless you know the business. We get many different kinds in Srinagar. The caravans bring them in from central Asia, but they are often improperly cured and the fur soon wears off. Ermine are quite plentiful here. Nature has endowed them with wonderful protective coloration, brown in the summer and pure white in the winter except the tip of the tail."

"They tell me you have flying squirrels in Kashmir."

"Plenty of them," said the colonel. "Pretty little animals. Brown on top and white underneath. They come out at night and sleep in the daytime. Our Kashmir flying squirrel rolls himself up in a ball when he sleeps, but his Indian cousin sleeps on his back with his legs and parachute outspread to keep cool."

The colonel looked at his watch.

"By Jove! It'll soon be dark. D'you hear the shouting? People calling for a boat to pick them up and take them home to dinner. Extraordinary how the sound travels on Dal Lake. Good-by. Delightful time. Thanks for the tea. You must come up and see me sometime! Extraordinary woman. We have a shikara named after her, *Mae West* on full spring seats. Ha-ha! Ha-ha!"

The colonel was gone.

CHAPTER TEN

"Were you cold last night?" asked Zetta as Sam and I forgathered in her bedroom for early-morning tea. "I simply froze!"

It was seven o'clock, but instead of sunlight streaming through the window to warm us up, the kerosene lamps which we brought with us from our bedrooms had to suffice.

With a knock at the door Dundoo entered bearing a tray of hot tea and the usual diminutive bananas. Something about his appearance was unusual. He seemed to have suddenly grown fat and portly.

Pointing at Dundoo's stomach, Sam exclaimed, "Going to have a baby?"

Dundoo seemed flabbergasted. He looked down at his unusual protuberance and after lifting up his shirt pointed to a small wicker basket which he had slung around his waist. "Kangra!" he said. "Must keep karm. Very cold day!"

A kangra consists of a basket lined with earthenware and filled with glowing charcoal. When winter comes a Kashmiri carries it with him wherever he goes and would no more be without it than the average American girl would be without her lipstick. Both men and women carry them. When they squat down, indoors or out, they arrange their long cloaks around them and bask in the warmth of their kangras. Occasionally, overcome by the fumes of carbon monoxide, they have been known to fall asleep and burn themselves severely.

We simply roared with laughter at Dundoo's portable radiator.

"There's nothing new under the sun," I remarked. "I remember my father carrying a little metal kangra in his overcoat pocket. And when we used to come out of the theater late at night in London, there was usually the 'hot-potato man' with his portable oven, selling large baked potatoes. I've often bought one and carried it to keep my hands warm."

All the lamps were lit and a large fire was blazing cheerfully in the living room by the time we had finished breakfast. From the upper deck Sam and I surveyed the prospects of a day's photography.

Heavy clouds filled the sky; the mountains were invisible. We couldn't even see Hari Parbat for the mist that covered Dal Lake like a shroud. The level of the lake was falling rapidly. Already we could see the retaining wall, but the road still had water over it.

An army truck filled with soldiers passed by, sending clouds of spray over the wall into the lake.

"We arrived here too late," I said bitterly. "We should have left the Taj Mahal until later. Let's go below and warm up."

"What are you two moaning and groaning about?" said Zetta as she walked into the room, dressed in her raincoat and plastic rubbers.

"No hope of color pictures today," I said gloomily. "Look at the weather."

"Let's sit around the fire and eat Shalimar walnuts," suggested Sam. "We can wash 'em down with brandy. That should keep us all in good spirits."

"Brandy in the middle of the day, without as much as a tummy-ache as an excuse!" replied Zetta. "Besides," she added, "I'm a sundowner. I never touch the dreadful stuff until the sun is sinking below the horizon. As for walnuts, I'll admit they're delicious, but for me they're hip food, and I'm certainly not going to add to my 124 pounds by sitting around the fire all day munching them.

"Listen, darling, why don't you make that Carveth Wells political poll à la Gallup? Let's spend the day asking as many Kashmiris as we can find what they think of Partition. Then our cloudy day won't be wasted.

"I'll be real good to you two boys," she continued. "I'll say a little prayer for sunshine tomorrow so that we can visit Shalimar. My prayers are usually answered, you know."

"How about it, Sam?" I said, reacting to Zetta's cheerfulness.

"Okay with me," replied Sam with resignation. "But you'd better be discreet or you'll be making us unpopular. This fellow Abdullah may slap us all into jail as spies."

"Don't be silly, Sam," said Zetta. "Besides, we can wear the United Nations badges that we got in San Francisco. For all they know, we might be special observers. Come on, let's go."

The badges that Zetta referred to were red and white enameled disks, one inch in diameter, with a map of the world on them, and in gold printing the words: "San Francisco 1945. The United Nations Conference on International Organization." We had been given them by the State Department as representatives of press and radio when we reported the conference for station KFI, Los Angeles. They had worked wonders then and they worked wonders in Srinagar. Few of the official United Nations observers had seen them before, so to them we were pioneers, and for all they knew, we were on some special mission.

As a result of those badges we were all three invited to several social functions given by different foreign observers.

"Better bring the cameras," I advised. "The sun may still put in a belated appearance."

"How about lunch?" asked Sam, who rarely neglected the inner man.

"That's all fixed too," answered Zetta. "D'you remember that man who sold me those embroideries? He's got a factory in Srinagar, and he's anxious for us to have lunch with him at any time. I have his card somewhere."

Zetta fished around for at least three minutes in her handbag. "Here it is," she shouted triumphantly. "'M. Sadak Ali & Bros. 3rd Bridge. Srinagar. Kashmir. Manufacturers of Papier-Mâché & Wood Carving. Fine display of Embroideries, Shawls, Carpets, Tapestries & Rugs.'"

Dundoo was delighted. It meant a trip to town, and besides, the food that he had expected to serve us for lunch could now be used for dinner. All was grist that came to Dundoo's mill.

"What are you going to do with your kangra?" I inquired.

"I take kangra with me," answered Dundoo. "Soon all Kashmiris will have kangras."

The sun was trying gallantly to break through the clouds as we set out for Srinagar in our shikara, *Happy Best New Sunlight.*

"These certainly are comfortable," remarked Sam as the three of us settled down on the "full spring seats."

Dundoo squatted down in the bow, puffing contentedly on his hubble-bubble, while we occupied the roofed-in section of the shikara amidships. Behind us, perched on the very tip of the stern, was our boatman, using his heart-shaped paddle as a rudder. There was no need to do much paddling, as the current of the Jhelum River carried us swiftly downstream toward the city.

The blight that had fallen on the Vale of Kashmir as a result of the dispute between Pakistan and India was evident as we passed the hundreds of vacant houseboats, many of them listing badly and some completely submerged except for the roof. It was indeed a depressing sight to compare their names with their present situation. *Cherry Stones, Golden Apple, Henley, New Tiger, Maid of the Mountains, Tit-Willow, Dulce Domum, Highland Queen, Duke of Windsor, Unfaithful Collette, Hot Jazz,* and so on. I got tired of taking down all their names.

At one place we passed two very large houseboats which were anchored alongside the retaining wall, where they were surrounded by hundreds of dugouts packed with women and children. Except for the large red flag that floated over one of the houseboats, there wasn't one speck of color in the crowd. Anyone who has seen the coolies loading coal into ocean liners at Port Said or Aden, their filthy clothes and the entire absence of color, will have an idea of what that crowd of Kashmiris looked like. It is true that they weren't covered with coal dust, but they might just as well have been, for their faces and hands were almost as dirty as their once-white clothing. The bottoms of their long skirts dragged in the stinking water of the bilge, in which little children were dabbling their hands and splashing their feet.

"What's it all about?" I asked Dundoo.

"No food," he answered. "Gardens washed away by the flood. Government give them rice. Many people starving. Too much war. No tourists. No jobs. Dundoo very poor man too."

Whether there was any particular significance in the red flag I cannot say, but it seemed unfortunate that the relief of suffering thousands of Kashmiris should be associated with the bloody flag of Communism. I have since wondered whether any of the rice that India received from the United States ever found its way to Kashmir, and if so, whether those houseboats flew the Stars and Stripes instead of the red flag.

"Let's get closer and see if we can get some pictures of the people," suggested Zetta.

Scarcely any men were to be seen, but as a rule there were three women and as many as half a dozen children in each boat. I could imagine those people, given a good scrubbing with soap and hot water, almost as white as we were. Occasionally I saw a pretty girl, but not often. Yet with few exceptions the women had fine features, beautiful eyes, and good teeth. All were loaded down with silver jewelry, especially necklaces and very large pendant earrings which are better described as ear ornaments, for they were so large and heavy that their weight was carried by a string that passed over their heads. In many instances these earrings touched the shoulder.

Here and there we saw women with a pronounced Jewish cast. I recalled reading that some of the Kashmiris belong to the lost tribes of Israel. In fact, there exists today in Srinagar the tomb of the man who founded the sect of Quadiani, whose theory is that a certain saint named Yus Asaf, who preached in many of the same parables as Christ, was indeed Jesus himself.

Sir Francis Younghusband, in his *Kashmir*, writes: "When the people are in appearance of such a decided Jewish cast, it is curious that such a theory should exist; and certainly there are real biblical types to be seen everywhere in Kashmir, and especially among the upland villages. Here the Israelitish shepherd tending his flocks and herds may any day be seen."

"Better get out of here," shouted Sam. "Look what's coming down the river!"

Almost completely blocking the channel of the Jhelum was an immense raft of logs. In America or Sweden a raft of such a size would have had half a dozen lumberjacks to keep it under control. But not in Kashmir. The frantic efforts of one man and a little boy sufficed. Evidently they had come a long way, for they had built a house on the raft. How they kept that raft from sweeping away the relief barges was miraculous, but they did.

The raft was almost at its journey's end, for its progress through the city of Srinagar was barred by seven bridges. Numbers of merchants were waiting for the raft to arrive, for no sooner had it been moored to the retaining wall than bargaining started. None of the logs was very long, but they were from one to three feet in diameter and about eight feet in length. Despite their weight, they were hauled one by one over the wall and deposited in the street, where some were carted away to be sawed into beams and planks, while the smaller ones were split into firewood and sold by weight to a crowd of householders. From the way they haggled over the weight, it was easy to see that firewood was an expensive commodity in Srinagar.

As we approached the outskirts of the city we saw to our left Srinagar's most conspicuous object, a little Hindu temple perched on the very top of a thousand-foot hill known as the Takht-i-Suliman, the Throne of Solomon. Built one thousand years before the time of Christ, according to some authorities, the temple is still in use and at night its light can be seen for miles.

Gradually the Jhelum River narrows, and houses and temples appear on both banks. Except for the first bridge, which is a modern stone structure over which the main road from Rawalpindi runs into the city, Srinagar's bridges are ancient ramshackle-looking affairs that look as if they might collapse at any moment. But they are very much stronger than they look. Built on foundations of old boats which are filled with stone

223

and then sunk, the piers are strengthened with piles. These piers, which are square, hollow, and filled with large boulders, certainly obstruct the river, but they have withstood hundreds of floods. From them, by means of cantilever construction, the wooden arches which support the roadway have been built.

"So this is the 'City of the Sun,' the 'Venice of India,'" remarked Sam as we started to pass through the very center of Srinagar. "Looks as if it had been shaken by an earthquake," he added facetiously.

Now that I think of it, Sam's observation was quite apt. Not one of the unpainted wooden houses was vertical, and many of them, on the point of collapse, had been propped up by logs. Several stories in height, nearly all the houses had balconies with carved verandas conveniently overhanging the river. No two were the same height or shape, but many of them had grass growing on their gently sloping roofs. This covering of sod keeps the houses warm in the winter and cool in the summer.

Late in September when we were there the grass was brown, but in the spring the same roofs would be gay with tulips, irises, and other flowers. Some of the roofs were very colorful when we saw them, being covered with scarlet chilies drying in the sun.

When we came to the second bridge the current looked so swift and dangerous that we decided to land with our cameras, while Dundoo and the boatman shot under the bridge, which only just missed the roof of the shikara.

Intending to take a picture of the river, I started climbing up the bank toward the Bund. It was steep going, but I persevered until, to my horror, I found myself completely surrounded by human excrement. How I had failed to notice it before is beyond my comprehension, but I hadn't. Now I was halfway up and at least fifty feet above the water's edge. My descent was more slippery and precarious than coming down the icy slopes of Popocatepetl, and several times it almost developed into a glissade which would have landed me into Srinagar's one and only sewer, the Jhelum.

That the population of Srinagar, 175,000, has on several occasions been decimated by cholera and smallpox, both of which diseases are always present, is not surprising. In the public streets dirt and sanitation are completely disregarded. Pariah dogs are the only scavengers. People empty pails of household filth into the river at one place, while at another you see people drinking and cleaning their teeth with the greatest care. Cholera is regarded as a visitation of the gods.

Back again in the boat, we continued the journey toward the third bridge, occasionally passing a Hindu temple with its dome shining like silver.

Conspicuous by their absence in a predominantly Moslem city of such size as Srinagar are mosques with bulbous domes and graceful minarets. Instead the mosques have pointed steeples made of wood, and the roofs are covered with grass. The largest and most striking is the Jama Mosque, which was built by the Emperor Shah Jehan. Built in the form of a square enclosing the courtyard, the main building with its slender steeples faces Mecca. More beautiful than the Jama Mosque is the Mosque of Shah Hamadan, located close to the river and a favorite object for artists and photographers. It also is built entirely of wood with a pointed steeple. In other Moslem countries bells in mosques are taboo, but not in Kashmir, where many small bells hanging from the eaves made me think of the Buddhist temples of Bangkok.

That journey down the Jhelum River, however odoriferous,

was extremely interesting. There wasn't a dull moment. We saw women, tall and stately, carrying heavy water pots up steep flights of steps that led from the river to their houses. Presumably it was too much trouble for them to walk to one of the numerous standpipes where water that had at least been filtered could have been obtained.

"They probably like their water with more body to it," remarked Sam.

At a place called Harwan, not far from Shalimar Garden, there is a reservoir that supplies Srinagar with drinking water, which is a boon to those who have an even elementary knowledge of sanitation. But most of the townspeople of Srinagar are completely ignorant of it.

Our shikara approached a steep flight of stone steps just above the third bridge. Sewage was trickling down them.

"The factory of Sadak Ali!" exclaimed Dundoo as he leaped ashore and tied the boat to a post.

Zetta held her nose. Sam lit a cigar. "Charming place for lunch," he said. "Shangri-La, my eye."

"We may as well go through with it," said Zetta courageously. "Sadak Ali can hardly be blamed for the state of these steps. It's a public thoroughfare."

Beaming with joy, Sadak Ali met us at the top of the steps and led us up several flights of rickety stairs to his factory, which proved to be his home also.

On entering what I supposed was his living room, we forgot our troubles. Our feet sank deep into a lovely Persian rug, and when our host flung open the windows, the view of Hari Parbat across the river, set against a background of snowy mountains, more than repaid us for our time in getting there.

Clapping his hands to summon a servant, Sadak Ali ordered

luncheon. While it was being prepared he showed us through the many rooms, some of which were for displaying the different kinds of articles he had for sale. Others were workrooms, where the things were actually being made. So far as we could tell, there wasn't a woman in the whole establishment, and when Zetta remarked upon it Sadak Ali replied, "Women's fingers no good for needlework. Good for husking rice and carrying water. Only Kashmiri men have fingers delicate enough for fine work." Then, handing Zetta a little paintbrush, he said, "See, this brush has only three hairs in it."

He summoned a workman and, handing him the brush, ordered him to show us what he could do with it.

"What kind of paint is he using?" asked Zetta as the man started to mix some on his palette. "Precious stones, mem-sahib," answered our host. "They come from Ladakh and Tibet. We grind them into powder and mix them with oil. Look, mem!"

The workman was painting a border on a dish made of papier-mâché. About a quarter of an inch wide, the border appeared to be solid. Sadak Ali handed Zetta a magnifying glass. "Look, mem!"

"Why, it isn't solid at all," said Zetta in amazement. "It is made up of tiny lines so fine that I can scarcely see them, yet they are all parallel and separate."

"Think of a bird, mem-sahib," said Ali.

"How about one of those bright blue kingfishers that are always perching on our boat?" asked Zetta.

In less than thirty seconds by my watch the man had painted a kingfisher beautifully. Body, head, beak, wings, and even its eyes were painted on a space no larger than a dime.

"This man can paint many birds and animals. Another of

my men paints flowers and leaves. One man works only with gold leaf." Then, handing Zetta a gracefully shaped vase, Ali said, "This vase tells the story of the beauty of Shalimar! See the chinar leaves in gold and silver. Look at the bulbuls and the kingfishers and the butterflies. Ah, mem-sahib, you must go to Shalimar."

Turning to me, Zetta said, "Darling, I've simply got to have this vase." But before I could even ask the price Sadak Ali had handed Zetta the vase. "Take it, mem-sahib. You love it. It is yours."

Taking me to one side, Sam muttered, "Ground bait!"

Luncheon was served Japanese style, on the floor. There were two kinds of pilau, one with small pieces of fish and the other with chicken. The well-cooked rice was flavored and colored with saffron. But I must admit that the trip down the Jhelum had caused us to lose our appetites. Turkish coffee, however, soothed us, and as we sipped it from tiny cups I thought the time was opportune to sound out Sadak Ali.

"Which country do you want to join, India or Pakistan?"

Ali looked embarrassed. "I take no part in politics. I'm much too busy with my factory," he replied.

"But you're a Moslem, aren't you? You're wearing a Jinnah hat."

"Indeed I'm a Moslem, but I am not a politician," he insisted.

"Nehru and Abdullah must be pretty tolerant to permit you people to wear Jinnah hats," said Zetta, hoping that she might provoke him into stating his political opinions, but it didn't work. The clever Sadik Ali just smiled as he fumbled with his amber conversation beads.

"Mem-sahib," he said, "how can you think of politics when you are surrounded by such beautiful things as these?" He

228

pointed to the exquisite silk tapestries, the rugs, the carved walnut tables, and the lovely papier-mâché bangle boxes decorated with the birds and flowers of Shalimar. "Come, mem-sahib, let me show you."

Zetta followed him into his showroom.

"He's hooked her!" laughed Sam. "We'd better go and see that she doesn't use up all her traveler's checks."

"How on earth do you propose to get all these things home?" I said testily as Zetta covered a large table with her purchases. "Don't forget, we're flying."

"Now don't get angry, darling. I know what I'm doing. Mr. Ali says that I can pay by check and he'll send everything to us beautifully packed, right to New York."

"All right. It's your funeral," I said. "You know what it says in that guidebook we bought: 'Never be so rash as to arrange for any article to be sent to you after leaving Kashmir.'"

Meanwhile Sam had begun to finger a beautifully carved cigar box made of Shalimar walnut, also an unusually designed pair of nut crackers.

"I see he's got you hooked too!" I said.

Then I found myself gathering together a collection of items that had caught my fancy. "It's no use," I laughed. "These things are simply irresistible."

Together we bought more than a hundred dollars' worth of Sadak Ali's merchandise, to be forwarded to us, "charges paid," to New York.

"Better kiss that good-by," I said as Zetta handed Ali his check.

Four months after our return to America there was no sign of a package from Kashmir. But Zetta's one-hundred-dollar check had long since been cashed at her bank. We had almost given up hope when the postman arrived with a parcel wrapped in sacking. Instead of a label, a piece of white cotton had been sewn to the sacking on which were many stamps and our address.

On opening it, we found only a few of the items we had paid for. "Cheat! Swindler! Scoundrel!" I exclaimed angrily.

Poor old Sadak Ali's ears must have burned as I reviled him and all Kashmiri shopkeepers. But the next day another package arrived just like the first. A few days later, still another one was delivered by the same postman, who happened to be a stamp collector and to whom I gave the unusual stamps.

Those three packages contained every item for which we had paid. Not one was missing, which goes to show that there is at least one honest merchant in Srinagar.

On leaving Sadak Ali's factory, we strolled through the narrow streets of ancient Srinagar, stopping here and there to ask the same question. "Which country do you want to join, India or Pakistan?"

It was surprising how many of those Kashmiris could speak English and still more surprising to find that the majority of the answers could be summed up as follows: "A plague on both countries. What we want is peace and a return to the days of Thomas Cook!" Occasionally a man would sigh for the return of Kashmir's maharajah; not because he was personally popular, but because of the pomp and circumstance with which he was surrounded, especially when he used to make his annual return in the spring to Srinagar from his winter palace in Jammu.

Traveling in the royal barge, a very long boat manned by about fifty rowers dressed in scarlet uniforms, the maharajah was always accompanied by a fleet of boats filled with officials and important state visitors as he made his way along the

Jhelum River. Thousands of cheering spectators lined the banks, and from the windows, jammed with waving women, hung lovely shawls and silks. But most striking of all were the sod-covered roofs of the houses, which at that time of the year were covered with bright green grass, delicate mauve irises, and sometimes scarlet Kashmir tulips.

Needless to say, on such occasions Srinagar would be filled with tourists so that the merchants, from "Subhana the Worst" to "Suffering Moses," made small fortunes.

But not everyone was for independence first and Pakistan second. When I put the question to the Hindu manager of the Kashmir Express Company, who, by the way, claimed to be the representative of Thomas Cook, he spluttered and fumed with fury, so much so that his words tumbled over one another in his excitement.

"Join Pakistan!" He spat on the floor. "A thousand times no! What has Kashmir to do with Pakistan? What has Pakistan ever done for Kashmir, except murder our people, rape our women, and plunder our property? Nehru is the savior of our country. Without the aid he gave us, Srinagar would have been reduced to ashes!"

I thought the man was going to burst a blood vessel.

"No need to get so excited about it. I just asked you a simple question," I said soothingly.

"To that I reply, India, India, India."

"Well," said Zetta as we drove back to the *H.M.S. Pinafore* in a tonga, "being a Hindu, any other opinion from him would have been surprising."

For the first time since we had been in the Vale the highway that skirts Dal Lake was dry and the level of the lake well below the surface of the road. Best of all, the water was no longer muddy, while here and there lotus blossoms were showing on the surface.

Dundoo had already returned in our shikara, for the *H.M.S. Pinafore* was lit from stem to stern.

"Well, my dears, that was one of the most interesting days I've ever spent," said Zetta as we climbed aboard the houseboat just as night was falling.

"Who's the extra place for?" exclaimed Sam as we passed through the dining room. "Candles too!"

"The colonel is coming to dinner," said Zetta. "I'm going to dress. It'll be good for my morale in this gloomy weather. 'By now, see you for snaps." We had one bottle of Swedish snaps which we had bought from the pretty little S.A.S. stewardess just before we left the plane at Calcutta. It's the finest thing in the world for promoting conversation.

"I suppose we had better put on our glad rags too," I said. "If he's what I think he is, the colonel will be wearing a black tie."

Sam agreed with undisguised resignation. "Thank heaven Zetta doesn't want us to wear tails!" he said more cheerfully. "I'd put on a monkey suit for her. I just don't see how she keeps going. She's like a piece of quicksilver."

"I'm rather pleased the old boy is coming," I said. "He will be a good person to include in our poll. He certainly knows his Kashmir."

Our hot baths were ready for us, and within half an hour Sam and I entered the living room, clean and refreshed after our day's prowling about Srinagar. In front of a cheerful fire sat the colonel. He was dressed as we had anticipated, black tie and tuxedo, but wearing a black cummerbund instead of a waistcoat. I could see him looking at me and Sam with an approving eye.

232

"Not much sign of Socialism in this establishment, I notice. I'm told that they don't wear these things very much in Europe nowadays. You cannot teach an old dog new tricks," said the colonel. "My wife and I have dressed for dinner all our lives, and I see no reason for discontinuing the custom in Kashmir."

Just as he spoke, Zetta entered. On his feet in a moment, the colonel greeted her warmly.

She was dressed in a turquoise-blue off-the-shoulder dinner dress. In her hair she wore a red rose. Her long skirt was full and circular, so that when she curtsied to him as though he were a royal prince, all the while holding out her full skirt, she made a charming picture. The old soldier was obviously delighted, and as we skoalled each other with snaps, our spirits rose to the point of gaiety.

"I say," said the colonel after his third glass, "what is this?"

"The moving spirit of Sweden!" I laughed. "But you aren't supposed to sip it. It's down the hatch without moving your Adam's apple."

"What's it made from?" inquired the colonel as he downed his fourth glass.

"Potatoes, I believe."

"Couldn't put them to better use," said the colonel.

It was easy to see that it wasn't going to require much persuasion to get him to talk.

Dundoo was in his element. He loved formality. He reveled in good food, especially when it wasn't included in his contract. The more dinner parties we gave like this one, the better Dundoo was pleased.

He served us delicious soup. (No questions asked.) Roast pheasant stuffed with walnuts, bread sauce and fresh cauliflower formed the main course. For dessert we had *compote de*

233

fruits flambés, after which we had goat's cheese and walnuts.

"I say," said the colonel as we sat around the fire sipping coffee and brandy, "that was a most delicious dessert. What did you use to make it flame?"

"Ah!" said Zetta. "That was going to be a secret, but I'll tell you. It was kirschwasser. I brought a little bottle of it all the way from Europe."

"You must write it down for me," said the colonel. "I must ask my wife to get some. I never liked stewed fruit until to-night."

As usual, it was Zetta who started the conversational ball rolling. "Colonel," she said, "we've been making a poll of what the Kashmiris want in this dispute between India and Pakistan. It may or may not be worth anything, but it was certainly interesting."

"What conclusions did you come to?" asked the colonel.

"None as yet," answered Zetta, "but we did discover that the majority of the Kashmiris we questioned don't want to join either India or Pakistan. They want Kashmir to be a free and independent state, the tourist paradise it used to be."

"From what I gathered," said Sam, "they want nothing to do with politics. It interferes with the shawl trade. Sensible people, these Kashmiris."

"What did you actually ask them?" inquired the colonel.

"I simply asked them this: 'When you have your plebiscite, which side do you want to join, India or Pakistan?' Over 70 per cent didn't want to join either, but when we pressed them, nearly all of them said they would prefer to join up with Pakistan, pointing out that they are Moslems."

Among the better-educated Moslems and Hindus we could tell that they felt very strongly about their future. But many of the poorer people we asked either didn't understand us, or when they did they said they didn't care so long as they were left alone.

One young Hindu woman became quite violent with her outspoken opinions. "Kashmir was invaded by terrorists from the North West Frontier, and the Pakistanis helped them. They almost captured Srinagar, but the maharajah appealed to Nehru for help. India saved us from those devils." Then with flashing eyes she continued: "You ask me about this United Nations plebiscite. Why should we take orders from them? India might as well have stayed under British slavery if the United Nations are going to dictate to us about our internal affairs."

"I'd like to know who she was," I said. "She sounded just like one of those Indian Congress lecturers that used to appear so often before women's clubs in the States."

"Another thing she said," remarked Zetta, "was that Nehru is the greatest living man in all Asia. He is the only leader powerful enough to turn the white imperialists out of Asia. India will never give up Kashmir. Not while Pandit Nehru is alive. He's a Kashmiri himself."

"Must have been quite an excitable young woman," said the colonel dryly, "but there are lots like her, I'm sorry to say."

"Just what is a 'pandit' or 'pundit,' whatever you call it?" asked Zetta.

"In a few words," replied the colonel, "a 'pundit' is an indigenous Kashmiri Hindu or the descendant of one. You see," he explained, "while the majority of present-day Kashmiris are Moslems, they were originally Hindus. It was only in the fourteenth century that they were converted, mostly by force, to become Moslems. Those who succeeded in remaining Hindus are known as 'pundits.' You find them all over India, where they are well known for their acuteness and subtlety of mind, their quick-wittedness and their intelligence. That is a fairly good description of Mr. Nehru, is it not?"

"Awfully interesting," said Zetta. "Please keep on talking."

The colonel smiled indulgently. "Not many people are such good listeners as you, Mrs. Wells. You might be interested to know how the Kashmiris came by their unsightly clothes. It all goes back to the days of the Mogul, Akbar the Great. Like all the Mogul emperors, Akbar loved Kashmir as a country, but he had little use for the Kashmiri men. One day, disgusted at his failure to make soldiers out of them, he said, 'You Kashmiris have stomachs to eat, but not to fight. You call yourselves men, but you have faint hearts, not lions' hearts. Therefore, you shall henceforth wear skirts.' From that day onward he made them eat their food cold and discard their beautiful clothing for the loose, shapeless garment hanging to the ankles, which they still wear. But clothing has a lasting effect on the mind. Today a Kashmiri man would far rather do needlework than go into battle."

"Carveth," said Sam, "d'you remember that United Nations observer you asked about the probable outcome of the plebiscite?"

"Yes, I certainly do. When I said that I felt sure that the Kashmiris, being about 80 per cent Moslems, would vote for Pakistan, he laughed. 'Not if they hold the kind of police-state plebiscite that Nehru demands,' he said. 'He wants the Indian Army to remain here during the plebiscite. That's no way to hold a free and secret plebiscite.'"

It was now the colonel's turn. "If you people had been through it all as I have, you'd understand the bitterness on both sides," he said. "I've learned to take it all with relaxed emotion."

"What was it that you began to tell us the other afternoon about some Hindu sticking his sword through a Moslem woman?"

"Oh yes, I remember the incident quite well. Nedou and I were lunching together one day during the trouble when a young Hindu friend said, 'I love to thrust my sword through a Moslem woman and hear her scream.' Nedou was terribly shocked. I remember him saying, 'Are you a man or a beast?' The Hindu replied bitterly, 'The Moslems murdered my wife, my three children, my father, and my mother. They cut them to pieces before my eyes while three of their soldiers held me down. And now you ask me whether I am a man or a beast!' "

Changing the subject, I said, "Do tell us about dear old Nedou himself. What does he think about the Kashmiris as a people?"

"Nedou has always been one of the Kashmiris' best friends. When the invaders chased them out of their homes he turned over one of his hotels in the mountains to them. He fed them and harbored them. They returned his kindness by stripping the building when they left. Not a piece of silver, not a dish, not even a bit of furniture remained. They stole everything." Then with a stern look on his face the colonel said, "Mr. Wells, the Kashmiris are the scum of the earth."

To say that we were all three shocked is to put it mildly, but we could see that the colonel meant what he said.

"Yet," said Zetta, "you tell us that you plan to stay here for the rest of your life and that Kashmir is your Shangri-La. If the Kashmiris are such terrible people, why do you stay here? The world is large. Nehru hasn't lowered the Iron Curtain, not yet, anyway."

"My dear lady," said the colonel good-naturedly, "the only

thing wrong with Kashmir is the Kashmiris. But they cannot spoil the scenery. They cannot destroy Dal Lake or the Himalayas. Living is easy and inexpensive, and before Kashmir became a bone of contention between India and Pakistan the world came to the Vale, so that we were continually meeting new and interesting people. I still love the place and hope that peace and prosperity will soon return. Unless I'm kicked out, I shall remain here for the rest of my life."

Dundoo entered the room. "Sahib's shikara waiting!"

"Good heavens," muttered the colonel, "how time flies. Midnight. Good thing my wife's in New Delhi!"

"How about one for the road?" said Sam.

"I don't mind if I do. It's chilly on the water." The colonel downed a brandy. "Getting a bit low," he said, looking at our precious bottle of Courvoisier.

"Good night. Good night. Delightful evening."

"There goes one of the most charming men I've ever met," said Zetta. "He's found his Shangri-La. I wonder whether we shall ever find ours."

CHAPTER ELEVEN

"I wonder what is keeping Zetta," said Sam the next morning as we sat down to an early breakfast. "She's unusually late this morning."

"Titivating!" I laughed. "I think she has some plan about going into town shopping. Let's surprise her with a decent cup of coffee for a change."

Sam chuckled. "Americans and British are both in the same boat when they go world traveling. You people complain about the coffee and we do the same thing about tea." Then, tasting his coffee, Sam said with a grimace, "This is worse than usual!"

"Dundoo!" I shouted rather gruffly.

Dundoo appeared in the doorway, where he stood first on one foot and then on the other, looking obviously nervous.

"Your food is fine, but your coffee is like ditchwater," I exclaimed. "Take this coffee away and tell the cook to bring in a pitcher of boiling water. I'm going to make my own coffee this morning."

While Dundoo fetched the hot water I slipped into my bedroom to get a jar of Nescafé which I had hidden away in my suitcase for just such an emergency as this. Dundoo watched me curiously as I placed three teaspoonfuls of the precious coffee powder into a clean teapot for want of a better receptacle. I had just finished pouring in the boiling water when Zetta appeared, singing, " 'Oh, what a beautiful morning, Oh, what a beautiful day, I've got a wonderful feeling, everything's coming my way.' "

Zetta is one of those rare people who never have an early-

239

morning grouch, and on this occasion she was clearly feeling on top of the world.

"What's that I smell?" she said "Real coffee?" Zetta poured out a cup and sniffed the fragrant aroma of freshly made coffee.

"What a wonderful surprise!" she said happily as she leaned over and gave me my morning kiss. "And here's one for you, Sam."

Sam and I looked at one another, smiled knowingly, and said simultaneously, "Zetta, you've been drinking! I thought you were a sundowner."

A puzzled look crossed Zetta's face. "Don't be silly. You know perfectly well that I never touch a thing before sunset. Smell my breath," she said.

We both took a sniff.

"If that isn't alcohol, then I'm Sheikh Abdullah!" said Sam.

Zetta scratched her head and then burst out laughing. "I completely forgot. I brushed my teeth with brandy this morning."

Sam exploded: "My God! What a thing to do! What a crime! Our last few drops of precious Courvoisier! Suppose you get 'Delhi Belly'? Suppose one of us gets cholera? Suppose—— Oh, we ought to throw you into the lake!" Sam continued to erupt. "What a menace women can be! You go and use our precious brandy to brush your teeth when Dal Lake is full of water!"

"Have you finished?" said Zetta coldly. "Dal Lake has plenty in it besides water. I saw the water boy throw the sewage from our bathrooms in it this morning. Then I saw the cook dipping up a pitcher of water just afterward, only a few feet downstream."

Sam's face fell. "What else did you see?"

"Since you're interested," continued Zetta, "I saw the water boy place three little pitchers of water in the bathrooms, and one was in yours. That was when I decided to brush my teeth with brandy. I'll admit I swallowed a teeny-weeny bit just to make sure that my throat was disinfected."

"That calls for another round of Nescafé," said Sam. "We forgive you." Then, as an afterthought, "Any Courvoisier left?"

"Just enough to disinfect your throat tomorrow morning. It's yours," said Zetta.

Of course Dundoo insisted that every drop of water used on *H.M.S. Pinafore* was brought from shore and boiled before use. But for the sake of peace and harmony I let the matter drop before Dundoo burst into tears. Kashmir is no different from any other part of the world where the inhabitants have little or no knowledge of sanitation. The best advice with regard to water is never to drink it except in the form of hot tea or coffee.

Dundoo's face brightened immediately when Zetta announced that all three of us would be dining out that night.

"With whom?" asked Sam, who hated parties.

"With some of the United Nations observers," replied Zetta. "It will give us another opportunity to find out just which way the wind's blowing. One of them has a lovely houseboat, and there are sure to be lots of people there like the colonel who really know the score out here."

Zetta's plan was to leave me on board the *Pinafore* so that I could write my weekly newsletter, *Geographically Speaking,* and get it air-mailed to my office in Los Angeles. She and Sam would take Dundoo and go by shikara to Srinagar, where they could do some shopping and get our return reservations from the Indian National Airways. They also had to get our permits to leave Kashmir. Time was getting short. Sam would soon be due back at his job in Bermuda, and I had a number of lecture engagements to fill in America. The weather was obviously breaking, and from the look of the sky, snow might fall at any moment.

"D'you realize that we haven't yet reached Shalimar?" I reminded Zetta. "Tomorrow's our very last chance. It's Shalimar or bust, rain or shine."

"Now don't get all hot and bothered," said Zetta soothingly. "I've prayed for a fine day tomorrow and I just know that my prayer will be answered. You write your newsletter and I'll tie up the loose ends in Srinagar. We'll be home in time to dress for dinner."

They piled into *Happy Best New Sunlight* and, having settled themselves down on her "full spring seats," glided off to town with Dundoo squatting in the bow, a grin on his face like the one on the cat that has swallowed the canary. Dundoo was to be Zetta's guide and take her to the best places for bargains. And if I knew anything about Dundoo, he would get his commission on every purchase.

As far as Shalimar was concerned, provided we didn't get snowed in, the longer we waited for the climax of our journey to Kashmir, the better. Dal Lake was not yet back to normal water level, but the flood had receded rapidly, and it really looked as if tomorrow would be the day of days.

What a mistake I made in letting Dundoo go to town soon became evident. Within fifteen minutes of his leaving with the shikara a regular fleet of hawkers' boats advanced toward the *Pinafore,* and before I had written a line, heads began to appear at different windows.

When I closed the windows, they came on board the boat. If I chased one out of the bow, another entered by the stern. To curse them in English was a waste of time. They didn't understand. In despair I finally made a bargain with one of the most insistent hawkers to stand guard as Dundoo did and shoo his brethren away. Arming himself with a pole, he pushed their boats away and occasionally threatened them with a stick.

I was afterward told that the only way to keep hawkers from annoying you is to surround your houseboat with a fence of piles driven into the lake bottom. But as this also keeps away people you do want to see, very few houseboat owners isolate themselves so effectively.

At four o'clock Zetta and Sam returned.

"Bad news?" I asked, noticing their gloomy faces.

"More than a hundred Indians were waiting at the airport. Five planes had arrived from New Delhi, but all were grounded because of fog in the Pass," said Zetta, "and we heard at Nedou's that so long as there are Indians to be accommodated there will be no seats for Europeans."

"But what about our return reservations?" I asked in dismay.

"You didn't look at them carefully, darling," said Zetta. "All you got when they sold you your return ticket was a voucher which you have to exchange for a return reservation, if and when they have any. So long as there are any Indians waiting to get back to New Delhi, they will get first choice."

You can hardly blame the Indians for adopting this attitude of preference for Indians. There was a time, we were told, when the shoe was on the other foot and the preference was given to Europeans.

"Something drastic must be done about this," I said. "Unless we act quickly, winter will be upon us and we may be stranded here for weeks. I'm going to send an S O S to Ambassador Henderson."

That night on our way to dinner with our United Nations

243

observers we wired the Embassy in New Delhi that we were stranded and needed help to get out of Kashmir.

"May as well cable for my skis," said Sam hopelessly. "We'll probably be here for Christmas!"

His downcast mood wasn't improved when he discovered that the only drinks at the dinner party were scotch and sodas and sherry. As all three of us loathe scotch, we drank only sherry. "Excellent blotting paper," said Sam as he helped himself at frequent intervals to canapés.

"There's one advantage to scotch," I remarked. "It loosens the tongue and promotes conversation. What we've got to do is to steer the conversation along the right channel."

"Now's your chance," said Sam, glancing toward a tall, distinguished-looking European who was expounding on the Kashmir dispute before a couple of rather pretty girls. "Ask him about the plebiscite."

Introducing ourselves all around, we decided to move out of the living room and go up on the sun deck. "Too much noise down there," I said to our tall friend. "We want to hear your views on the Kashmir question."

I shall always remember that little conference on a houseboat in Dal Lake. Below we could hear the laughter of the guests, whose main interest was in scotch. On all sides of us were the twinkling lights of boats going and coming on the lake, whose waters were as smooth as oil, forming a perfect mirror for the moon.

"Can that be a star?" said Zetta softly, pointing to what appeared to be the reflection of a large star. "No," said our friend, "that's the light of Takht-i-Suliman, an ancient Hindu temple. See," he said, pointing to a light that seemed to be right over our heads, "it's on the top of a hill exactly one thousand feet above the lake. Pilgrims come from all over India just to visit the Throne of Solomon."

"Tell us about this plebiscite business," I said.

"If one is ever held," said our friend, "it's almost a sure bet that Kashmir will choose Pakistan. Most of the people are Moslems, and with the world in the state that it is today, this is one case where the adage, 'Blood is thicker than water,' isn't going to prove true. The Kashmiris are going to stick by their brothers in Islam, despite the fact that they themselves were once Hindus."

Finding that he had an interested audience, he continued: "To understand why Pakistan simply dares not permit Kashmir to fall under the control of India or any other power, you must understand a little of her geography. If it were not for the water that comes from Kashmir, West Pakistan would be a desert. Every Pakistani knows that his very life depends on water from Kashmir, and he's going to fight to the last gasp to prevent India from endangering that water supply. From Liaquat Ali Khan down to the humblest laborer, the Pakistanis are united by the common bond of Islam, and they claim that they have the whole Moslem world behind them. All that is necessary to spark the fire of a holy war is to suggest that the struggle with India is religious rather than political."

"Wouldn't that mean another blood bath in India?" asked Zetta.

"Inevitably," answered our tall friend. "There are still about forty million Moslems left in India whose lives would be endangered the moment Pakistan became engaged in war with India."

At this point Sam joined the discussion. "What beats me is that two great leaders like Nehru and Liaquat Ali Khan, both of whom are highly intelligent university graduates, cannot evolve some plan by which the Kashmir problem can be settled."

"Politics," I said. "Blot out politics, eliminate pride and sentiment, then consider the problem from the point of view of common sense, and a solution of the problem would be found quickly. Nehru and Liaquat should take a little time off to make a study of our international parks."

Now that I had the audience, I continued: "Have you ever heard of Big Bend National Park? Part of that is in Mexico and part in the United States. There's another international park on the Canadian border which overlaps into the United States. The citizens of both countries have the right to enjoy those parks, and they do. Why on earth cannot Kashmir be taken completely out of the realm of politics and made into an international park for health and recreation, with its neutrality guaranteed by both India and Pakistan, backed up by the United Nations?"

It was now the tall man's turn to become interested. "By Jove!" he exclaimed enthusiastically. "That would be the solution. India and Pakistan would have special privileges, such as free entrance into the park for all their citizens, while the rest of the world could pay an admission fee."

"Precisely," I said. "I would have gladly paid ten dollars just to have the privilege of hiring a houseboat on Dal Lake. That would have meant thirty dollars from our party alone. Think of the revenue that would accrue when the Vale of Kashmir once more became known as the 'Playground of the World.' All such a scheme needs is the good will of both India and Pakistan, a first-class park superintendent responsible to a board of park directors, and a top-notch force of park rangers and park police. All roads entering Kashmir would become park entrances, just as they have at Yellowstone, where visitors would have to register, pay their entrance fees, and be given a park passport. This passport would permit them to travel anywhere in Kashmir. But the passports would be no good for exit without a visa from the country the visitor wished to enter. Srinagar would be cleaned up and provided with proper main drainage and a sewage-disposal system. Nedou's could be outfitted with modern plumbing and made the headquarters of the tourist trade and A.A.A.

"First-class guest houses similar to Finnmark's 'mountain huts' or Sweden's Bjorkliden should be built all over Kashmir so that the distance between each would not exceed one day's journey. Less elaborate climbers' huts could be built on some of the most famous mountains to attract mountaineers. Unlike the national parks of the United States, the Kashmir International Park would be open for hunting at regular seasons. Hikers' trails would be staked out and clearly marked. Filling stations would be built for motorists. Ski lifts would be constructed, ski jumps, toboggan courses laid out close to some comfortable park hotel which would specialize in winter sports. With such improvements, Kashmir would become a Mecca for tourists from all over the world. The world's air lines would soon be competing with one another for Kashmir's business, and with 'package tours' enabling them to lower their fares, they would soon be flying thousands to Kashmir from every point of the compass.

"Both India and Pakistan could co-operate with world-cruise liners and fly special excursion parties to Srinagar from Calcutta or Karachi. Then instead of Kashmir being a financial millstone around the necks of both Pakistan and India, it would be a source of large revenue. The money spent in one day on their armies would pay for these developments. The Kashmiris themselves would prosper. They could get back to their sewing and weaving and, if not too late, rescue the art of making cashmere shawls so fine that they pass easily through an ordinary wedding ring."

"You seem to be quite enthusiastic about this idea of yours," said a deep voice out of the darkness. "Your plans sound fine. Your ideal for a neutral Kashmir may be praiseworthy, but you have apparently forgotten that the United Nations has already ordered that a free plebiscite shall be held in Kashmir."

"Who's the newcomer?" I whispered to Zetta.

"He's a lawyer," answered Zetta. "One of the United Nations crowd, I suppose. He just came up from the party to have a smoke."

"As you all seem to be serious up here," said our lawyer friend, "perhaps I might be permitted to point out to you, Mr. Wells, that unless the orders of the United Nations are carried out, then the whole usefulness of that organization ceases. In my opinion, you are suggesting that the decision of the United Nations be ignored and that Nehru and Liaquat Ali Khan take the matter into their own hands. The only legal course is for both those men to accept the decision of the Security Council, remove their forces from Kashmir, and then, with a United Nations police force to maintain order, a free plebiscite could be taken."

"What about Sheikh Abdullah?" I asked. "Is he going to do what he's told and let the Kashmiris vote the way they want to vote?"

"Abdullah will probably take his orders from Nehru."

Zetta now joined in the discussion. "It seems to me that for

India and Pakistan to go to war would be playing right into the hands of Russia. Lowell Thomas was right when he warned that the Communists would soon be in Tibet. They're there now, and they'll soon be in Kashmir if they aren't stopped."

Apparently word had spread that there was a lively political discussion on the sun deck, for the audience suddenly seemed to grow.

"Who's going to do the stopping?" asked a voice. "How do we know Pakistan or India wouldn't join up with Russia?"

Zetta gave me a nudge to join in the discussion.

"Surely you don't think that a deeply religious nation like Pakistan would join up with the Reds? They know as well as anybody that Russia is out to destroy all religion."

"When your back is up against a wall, you're not too particular about anyone who offers to help," said the lawyer with a grunt. "We had an example in our countries when we were fighting Hitler. We knew Russia's bloody history. We knew her aims for world revolution, yet in our extremity we accepted her as an ally. Today we are only beginning to pay the price for her help in the blood of those who have been killed in Korea."

As no one else seemed to want to enter the discussion, the lawyer continued: "Now I'm not saying that either Pakistan or India would voluntarily join up with Russia, but it is not impossible. If the United Nations does not prevent these two nations from going to war, anything can happen."

"Changing the subject," I said, "do you think that Nehru is really going all out for 'Asia for the Asiatics,' to the exclusion of all Westerners?"

I had addressed my question to the lawyer, but the answer came from a very blond man with a typical Scandinavian accent.

"D'you think a man can spend fourteen years of his life in prison and not hate his jailers? Why shouldn't Nehru develop Asia for the Asiatics? Nehru is a great leader. He wants peace, and if he can inspire the peoples of Asia, he may be able to influence Russia in the direction of peace. Nehru is clever. He knows that India is rich in natural resources which the West needs. With Nehru at the head of a Socialist government, he would turn those resources into riches. Then he would raise the standard of living for the millions who have suffered dreadful poverty during the reign of capitalism, when the British imperialists exploited India for the benefit of the Western world."

"I disagree with you completely!" bristled a man who had hitherto remained silently puffing his pipe. His accent was decidedly Oxford. "Nehru is emotionally unstable. Attribute it to his imprisonment if you wish, but the fact remains that he's unstable. Just read his books and his speeches. They are filled with contradictions. And look at India. Although Nehru is a Socialist, you find less Socialism there than in many capitalist countries. You probably noticed that you can buy almost anything in the shops of New Delhi, Calcutta, or any other of India's large cities. There are no controls like there are in England. Indians love their private enterprise, and I doubt if Nehru or anyone else could deprive them of it, even if he tried."

The Englishman looked around him and continued: "It won't be an easy job to regiment millions of Indians, to say nothing of the rest of Asia. The trouble with Nehru is that he's like some Irishmen: he doesn't know what he wants and he won't be happy till he gets it. Nehru's a queer mixture of Hinduism, Gandhiism, theosophy, and Marxism. He was a disciple of Annie Besant, the theosophist and Socialist. Lots of people have forgotten that it was Annie Besant who established the

Indian Home Rule League and that at one time she was the president of the Indian National Congress.

"As for Nehru's Marxist tendencies, there again he is contradictory. He supports Russia on many international issues, but he doesn't hesitate to throw his own Communists in jail and keep them there. Nehru makes flowery speeches about non-aggression and India's peaceful aims, but that didn't deter him from seizing Hyderabad. If that wasn't an example of aggression, then I don't know what the word means."

Evidently the Englishman had a sympathetic audience as he continued: "There are many able men in Nehru's own government who don't go along with him by any means. They accuse him of running with the hare and hunting with the hounds. They say that he spends his energy in setting himself up as the 'Great Leader of Asia' while he lets millions of his own people rot in poverty. All over India you'll hear Nehru criticized for giving the best government jobs to his own relatives." Then, with his voice filled with sarcasm, the Englishman concluded, "India is suffering from 'Nehruitis.'"

"Then you don't think that Nehru can be trusted?" I inquired.

"Trusted!" he snorted. "I wouldn't trust him as far as you can throw an elephant by its tail."

"But surely Nehru doesn't think that a policy of 'Asia for the Asiatics' will bring peace and prosperity to Asia," I said. "That was Japan's slogan, and we all know that one of the bloodiest wars in history was fought over that idea. A good many Asiatics helped us Westerners to win that war: Chinese, Filipinos, and an army of two million Indians, including Moslems, Hindus, Sikhs, and others. India's was the biggest army of volunteers the world has ever seen.

"Hitler had a similar idea. His brave new world was to be for Aryans only. We all know what happened to the Japanese militarists and the Hitlerites. If only Nehru would come down to earth, he couldn't help seeing that without the friendship and help of all free nations, especially those of the industrialized West, Asia's millions cannot possibly prosper."

At this point dinner was announced. It was just as well, for tempers were beginning to rise as the conversation returned to the controversial subject of the Kashmir plebiscite.

Had we not known how cheaply one can entertain in Kashmir, we might have thought our host was guilty of extravagance at the expense of the United Nations, for we had a most delicious dinner in a veritable flower garden.

Sitting next to Zetta was an elderly man who made us think of the colonel. He turned out to be a retired civil engineer who had spent almost thirty years in Indian government service.

"My husband's a member of the Institution of Civil Engineers!" I heard Zetta say proudly. "His hobby is natural history."

"So's mine," said the engineer. "I love birds especially."

"I suppose you must have some lovely birds here in Kashmir?"

The engineer beamed. He was in his element. "Birds! We have many, many kinds, but my favorites are the golden orioles, kingfishers, water wagtails, bulbuls, thrushes, and paradise flycatchers."

"How about mynah birds?" asked Zetta. "We have one at home that we got from Malaya. He talks beautifully and whistles several tunes, including 'The Star-Spangled Banner'!"

"Mynah birds," he said. "We have thousands of them, Mrs. Wells. I'm surprised you haven't noticed them."

"Not where we live!" laughed Zetta. "The only birds I've

noticed on Dal Lake so far are the kingfishers. Aren't they beautiful? We have one that spends most of his time perched on the top of a pole just outside the dining room. He's the most exquisite blue I've ever seen."

The engineer smiled. "So you're living on Dal Lake. Then you ought to know that if it weren't for a mynah bird there wouldn't be any Dal Lake! Let me tell you the story. Of course it's just a legend," he started, "but if you like mynah birds so much, then you certainly ought to know it.

"In bygone ages the Vale of Kashmir was a vast lake inhabited by a demon who fed on human beings living in the highlands. Aroused to pity by their distress, a certain sage named Kashyapa prayed to the goddess Sharika to deliver them from the demon. One day the goddess, having changed herself into a mynah bird, picked up a pebble, which she dropped on the demon from a great height. Suddenly the pebble grew into a mountain which smothered the demon and killed it.

"Kashyapa then set to work, and by cutting a gap in the mountains near a place named Baramulla, he was able to drain the valley until, instead of one vast lake, it contained a chain of lovely smaller ones, of which Dal Lake was the most beautiful. Henceforth the people of Kashmir settled down to a peaceful life making beautiful things which were inspired by the beauty that surrounded them. Prosperity reigned supreme."

"Call out the mynah bird," said Sam. "Evil days have again fallen on Kashmir."

Time always flies too fast when you are in the right company, and it was midnight before we took our leave. Having exchanged addresses with our new-found friends, we boarded our shikara and started back to the *H.M.S. Pinafore.*

253

"Just look at that moon!" exclaimed Sam. "It looks like a stage one that the scene shifter has suspended from a nail on the backdrop."

"Looks encouraging for tomorrow," I said. "Shalimar!"

"Say a little prayer for fine weather, darling."

The next morning we were up with the dawn. There wasn't a cloud in the sky. Our kingfisher was there on his pole top, eying us solemnly as we arranged our camera equipment for the expedition to Shalimar.

" 'Not a cloud in the sky, not a wave on the sea, the ship was as still as she could be.' I learned that at school," said Sam genially as he sat down to breakfast.

I had just returned to my bedroom to pack some film when I heard a voice coming from the dining room: "Where is Big Sahib?"

Peeping through the doorway, I saw Sadak Ali's head and shoulders framed in the window of the dining room. He was standing up in his shikara, which was moored alongside.

"Dundoo is in the kitchen," replied Sam.

"No, no!" persisted Sadak Ali. "I not want Dundoo. I want see Big Sahib. Mr. Carveth Wells."

Zetta and Sam snickered as I entered the room.

"Ah! Big Sahib!" exclaimed Sadak Ali joyfully, his face still framed in the dining-room window. "I was with an officer of United Nations last night," he said breathlessly. "He told me you very big sahib; you write books, you explore the world, you talk on radio in America."

"What on earth do you want? We almost bought your whole store the other day!"

Sadak Ali's head disappeared, but in a moment he was climbing on board with a piece of writing paper in his hand. I thought he was going to burst into tears as he said, "Oh, big sahib, I come to beg a favor. You said many nice things about my factory and my workmen. You admired the work of my artists. You buy many things. Just write me one short letter, please, and I will be forever grateful."

"Big Sahib very busy now," said Zetta impishly. "Big Sahib is going to Shalimar. When Big Sahib comes home, Big Sahib will write a letter."

"But," pleaded Sadak Ali, "it will only take him three minutes to write testimonial. I come six miles in my shikara to catch you."

Zetta relented. "All right. Big Sahib can write testimonial."

"May as well get it over and done with," I muttered as I wrote the usual testimonial, praising Sadak Ali and all his works. Then, having drawn an elephant after my signature, I handed the letter to the merchant.

He read it. "This is worth thousands of rupees to me, big sahib. Thank you, thank you, may heaven bless you."

Then, recognizing the elephant, Sadak Ali smiled happily as he fumbled in his pocket. "Here, big sahib, a present!" he said, handing me a small red seed about the size of a pea but as flat as a lentil. At the very most it could not have measured more than a quarter of an inch wide and an eighth of an inch thick.

Removing a small stopper from the seed, Sadak Ali emptied into my hand some white substance which looked like coarse grains of salt.

"Elephants!" he cried triumphantly. "Twenty elephants for Big Sahib!" Handing me a magnifying glass, he told me to examine the white substance in my hand. They were beautifully carved ivory elephants, twenty of them.

Sadak Ali, beside himself with joy, hurried back into his shikara and was gone.

"What a line that chap has!" said Sam. "He could charm the wig off a dummy. Better not go near his store again, Zetta, or it'll cost you another hundred bucks."

It was nine o'clock. Our shikara was loaded with cameras, tripods, and baskets full of food. Dundoo was squatting in the bow, inhaling and exhaling smoke from his hubble-bubble. We had two boatmen to paddle in the stern, while the three of us lounged comfortably on the "full spring seats" of *Happy Best New Sunlight*.

Zetta gave my hand a squeeze as she whispered, "Your mother's prophecy has come true!"

"Yes, I'm gliding over the Lake of Cashmere with my loved one by my side!" I said.

"Big Sahib's happy," said Zetta, grinning at Sam.

Sam salaamed before me. "Big Sahib like walnut?" handing me a sackful.

I could see that it would be a long time before they let me forget the "Big Sahib" episode. They wrote home to my daughter and many of our friends, tipping them off to call me "Big Sahib" and salaam when they met me on my return from Kashmir. Even today the three of us have many laughs about Big Sahib and Sadak Ali.

For the next hour we glided over and through a fantastic fairyland of flowers and reflections. Still considerably above normal water level, Dal Lake was not covered with masses of pink lotus, as is usually the case in late September. Here and there were many gorgeous lotus blossoms floating on the surface, but when we looked down there were thousands of them waving gracefully in the crystal-clear water. If you have ever tried arranging flowers in an "aquaflorium," those big glass bubbles that look like inverted goldfish bowls, you know how air, sticking to the petals, often makes flowers appear to be silver-plated. Dal Lake was a gigantic aquaflorium filled with countless pink and silver lotus blossoms.

Swimming among the long white stalks of the lotus, many different kinds of fish could be seen. Often as we watched them, one of the fish would turn on its side and take a peep at us.

I have seen the submarine gardens of Bermuda, Nassau, and Catalina Island, but none can compare with the bottom of Dal Lake in lotus time. No glass-bottomed boat was necessary, for the water, completely devoid of ripples, might as well have been solid plate glass. So gently did we glide toward Shalimar that the surface of the lake was never broken by spray or splash. Only the distortion of the reflections showed that we were causing the lake surface to undulate.

Under ordinary circumstances the rooflike cover of our shikara would have interfered with our view of the surrounding scenery, but with Dal Lake acting as a perfect mirror, we merely watched the water in order to see the snow-capped Himalayas, the flower-decked meadows, little hamlets nestling among fruit trees, a rickety three-storied wooden house set among poplars and willows, masses of red peppers drying on its roof, no windowpanes, bedraggled-looking children with huge silver earrings and necklaces playing on a floating island, avenues of immense chinar trees sloping toward the lake front, boats loaded with vegetables on the way to the market in Srinagar, a woman perched precariously on the very prow of an empty dugout drifting with the stream, a heart-shaped paddle trailing idly behind her, and a man towing a long floating island covered with red and yellow tomatoes. These were just a few of the things we saw as we glided toward the north end of Dal Lake.

Suddenly Dundoo stopped smoking.

"Shalimar!" he shouted, pointing to a large group of chinar trees that were surrounded by a brick wall. Behind them, against a blue sky filled with huge cumulus white clouds, we could see one of the loveliest bits of mountain scenery it is possible to picture. Snow-capped and very broken and rugged, they made me think of Wyoming's Tetons at their loveliest. Sloping toward the great avenues of chinar trees were valleys filled with violet haze.

Then our shikara entered a rather narrow canal lined with houseboats and small wooden cottages. Scattered over the roofs of the houseboats were more quantities of peppers drying in the sun. Some were bright green, others yellow, but most were scarlet. Standing here and there among the houses were Kashmiri women in their long, shapeless Mother Hubbards, husking rice with long, heavy wooden pestles which they thumped into the wooden mortars with monotonous regularity. Squatting on the bank of the canal or in boats were elderly men contentedly drawing on their hubble-bubble pipes.

As we approached our journey's end and tied the shikara alongside the canal we noticed three small boys sitting beside a large pile of freshly gathered walnuts that reached higher than their heads.

"Dundoo," said Sam, "have our sack filled with walnuts."

It was no sooner said than done. "How much?" asked Sam.

"Half a rupee, sahib."

"Expensive!" said Sam. "That sack only holds ninety nuts! Now what's happening?" he asked as the boys started loading walnuts into the boat.

"I buy all the nuts for Sahib. No more money. Half rupee!"

"I'm going into the walnut business," said Sam delightedly.

258

We landed within a few yards of the entrance to the garden, which was a simple archway through a brick wall about eight feet high. Beside the gate and nailed onto the wall was a large painted sign: SHALAMAR.

"That settles all our arguments," said Zetta as she focused her Contax on me and Sam standing beneath the sign. "Shalamar is spelled with an *a* and not with an *i*."

That's what she thought, but instead of settling the argument, it started all over again. When checking this with our editor, this is what she said, "In spite of the photograph (which we're not going to use anyway) we're spelling it 'Shalimar.' Everybody in the place called to tell me 'Shalamar' looked funny and sounded unhappy to hear it was correct. The poem, the song, the perfume—all use *i*. So I called the Indian consulate. They said the *a* was correct—*shala* means 'a garden'— but an hour later they called me back, said they were stunned but one source, the Indian Yearbook, published in India, lists it as 'Shalimar.' So I think we should stick to the *i*. If we use *a* many people will be sure we're wrong, possibly some reviewers."

Before entering the garden we stood for a few moments and looked at it through the gateway. The first impression is of a lovely shady park with velvety lawns under enormous trees, of long straight flower beds filled with brightly colored blossoms and bordered by some low-lying plant of vivid yellow. The garden is rectangular, ascending in steps toward the snow-capped mountains that provide an ever-changing backdrop of beauty as they change their colors from dawn to sunset. There are long lines of fountains that run down the center of the garden toward a beautiful pavilion, itself set in an artificial lake and surrounded by fountains. Beyond the pavilion we could see another, set on a wide terrace; and still farther back toward the mountains yet another pavilion on a terrace. Flowing completely through the garden and underneath the pavilions with their fountains and square pools was a sparkling mountain stream.

And as we walked toward the pavilions we could feel the cool air rushing down the center of the garden toward the lake. To me it was clear that the Mogul Emperor Jehangir, who laid out Shalimar, was a pioneer in air conditioning. In fact, the Moguls' conception of a garden was not necessarily a place filled with flowers, but a shady retreat where they could not only feel a cool breeze but also hear the water that caused it. And the time to use the garden was at night, when its lovely fountains, waterfalls, and trees could be illuminated.

The total length of Shalimar is about six hundred yards, arranged in four terraces, on three of which are built the pavilions already mentioned. At the far end of the garden is the most beautiful pavilion, with exquisitely carved pillars of black marble. It was here that the royal ladies of the harem rested in cool seclusion while members of the court roamed about under the trees.

"You know what used to roam about Kashmir before the dawn of history? Mastodons, eleven different kinds of elephants, six species of rhinoceroses, and a colossal four-horned ruminant called a sivatherium. There were giraffes, camels, wild oxen, buffalo, chimpanzees, orangutans, and baboons. Kashmir had them all once upon a time, although all that is left of them nowadays are their fossils."

"Where's Zetta?" Sam asked suddenly as we were about to photograph a bulbul with a telephoto lens.

"There she is," I said with relief. "See her red parasol? She is walking along the last terrace, which was reserved for the ladies of the harem."

By that time the bulbul had of course disappeared, so swinging the camera around, we photographed Zetta walking in the steps of Nur Jahan, Light of the World, beloved wife of Emperor Jehangir, whose son, Shah Jehan, built the Taj Mahal for the remains of his own beloved Queen, Mumtaz Mahal, Glory of the Palace.

It seemed strange to think that this garden in which we were about to have a picnic lunch had been the favorite resort of Jehangir and Shah Jehan. If only the stones of those pavilions could have spoken, they would have told of the vast cortege of elephants, pack horses, and gaily decorated sedan chairs containing the ladies of the harem that used to arrive there after a long trek from Delhi, accompanied by as many as thirty thousand coolies to wait upon man and beast.

For five hundred elephants to arrive at Shalimar in one day was by no means an unusual event in the days of the Moguls. They had their traffic accidents, too, in those days. On one occasion fifty elephants fell over the side of a precipice just before reaching Srinagar.

Dundoo gave us a grand luncheon under one of the largest chinars. The best description I can give of a chinar tree is to call it a giant maple. For not only are chinar leaves very much like maple leaves, although much larger, but they also change to the most brilliant colors when autumn comes.

It seemed almost sacrilegious to wash down a hearty lunch with iced beer in Shalimar, but we didn't feel so bad about it when I reminded Sam that Emperor Jehangir had the same motto as he did, "Work is the curse of the drinking classes." Although wine was forbidden by the Prophet, Jehangir is said to have had a weakness for the bottle. In his own journals he recorded his failing and the debt of gratitude that he owed his favorite wife, Nur Jahan, who used to persuade him to be more abstemious.

Having finished our picnic, picked up our trash with the utmost care, and left a generous tip for the Shalimar gardener, we re-embarked and returned in time for dinner on board the *H.M.S. Pinafore*.

"Well!" I said as we sat around the fire after dinner. "What's the verdict?"

"The end of a perfect day!" we chimed in unison.

And so to bed.

Next morning Dundoo appeared wearing his kangra under his skirt. "Snow, sahib! Look, the mountains."

There was no doubt about it, they were sparkling as they never had before, being covered with fresh snow. Our gaiety was gone. So was our firewood. Sam looked doleful, and Zetta was anxious because we had had no reply to my cable to New Delhi.

"We shall freeze to death here. Dundoo!" I shouted. "Pack our things. We're going to move into Nedou's."

It was Dundoo's day of reckoning. His bill was to be paid, and then there were all the extras and, last but not least, baksheesh for the servants. Our contract called for only five servants, but to judge from the number of people, male and female, who suddenly appeared with anxious looks upon their faces, the servants must have had their wives and mothers-in-law with them.

Fortunately my pocket was filled with Indian money, which had a way of accumulating as pennies do in America. Soon our baggage was piled in two shikaras, and the baksheesh having been distributed, we waved good-by to the good old *H.M.S. Pinafore* and her trusty captain, Dundoo. Without a doubt we had spent the most enjoyable time in the loveliest surroundings and at the least expense of any holiday we had ever had.

On arrival at Nedou's we practically threw our baggage into our rooms and dashed off on different errands. Sam and Zetta went to the office of the Indian Airways, where the crowd of waiting passengers was bigger than ever.

"If I don't get a reply to my telegram to Ambassador Henderson," I said, "I'll cable Washington direct for help!"

"Only President Truman or Winston Churchill could expect such aid," moaned Sam. "Who are we to be given special treatment?"

Leaving Sam and Zetta in the lobby of Nedou's, I went to my room to write. I had scarcely closed the door when there was a sharp knock. In walked a smartly dressed American officer. He had an open telegram in his hand.

"Good morning. I'm Major Keogh. I have just received orders to fly you and Mrs. Wells and a Mr. Tatem out of Kashmir, over the cease-fire line into Pakistan, and then on to New Delhi. The plane will be leaving first thing tomorrow morning. I'll have a jeep here for your baggage."

I could have kissed that major.

The next thing I heard was Sam moaning and groaning to Zetta as he stood outside my bedroom door. "I'll miss the opening of Parliament! That's something I haven't done for years."

Flinging open the door, I showed them the telegram. Both of them embraced me.

"Who said only Truman or Churchill could do such a thing?" taunted Zetta. "Now you can see what happens when you have a government that is a servant of the people instead of the people being servants of the government. If my father hadn't taught me that when I was a little girl, I would never have had the courage to appeal to the government for help."

Evidently we made so much noise in our excitement that we attracted the attention of our next-door neighbor on the same floor. The door opened, and out walked a charming American woman.

"I'm Mrs. Henderson, wife of Ambassador Henderson," she said. "I've heard my husband speak of you. Won't you join me for coffee after dinner?"

It appeared that she and Ambassador Henderson had been marooned by the flood while motoring from New Delhi to Srinagar. The Ambassador had flown out, but he had left Mrs. Henderson and his chauffeur with their car, to wait until the roads permitted their return to New Delhi.

Soon we were all sitting around a blazing fire roasting chestnuts and cracking walnuts. In a surprisingly short time we ran out of walnuts.

"Sam has a whole sackful," said Zetta.

Sam looked dumb. "Finished the whole lot yesterday," he said without blinking.

Zetta and I looked at one another. We knew perfectly well that Sam had a sack of walnuts in his room. "No understanding these Bermudians," I thought to myself. While Sam is thrifty, I have never known a more generous person. I just couldn't understand why he wouldn't give Mrs. Henderson any of his walnuts.

Six months later, when we arrived at our Bermuda home for a rest, Sam conducted us to a sheltered spot in the garden, where he had four Kashmiri walnut trees growing. They were about eighteen inches high and were already branching out nicely.

"So that's why you refused to share your walnuts with Mrs. Henderson that night in Srinagar!" I said joyfully.

Much too excited to sleep that night, we practically watched the clock as we sat, fully dressed, before the fire in our bedroom.

Promptly at six o'clock the jeep arrived, and by six-thirty we reached the Srinagar airport.

If you have ever had the thrill of seeing the Statue of Liberty after having been absent from the United States for any great length of time, then you know just how we felt when we saw awaiting us on the runway a DC-3 flying the Stars and Stripes.

"All ready to go!" exclaimed Captain Hoke as we drove across the field and deposited our baggage right at the plane.

"The Brigadier," I remarked, reading the name painted on the nose of the plane.

"Great guy, that Canadian brigadier," said Captain Hoke. "We named our plane for him after he was killed in that plane crash in the Banihal Pass. I suppose you heard about it."

"The weather doesn't look very promising," said Zetta as she scanned the sky and saw the low ceiling that covered the mountains on all sides.

Perfectly level, the low layer of white cloud which covered the airport made me think of the "tablecloth" which periodically covers South Africa's Table Mountain. Standing by the hangar were five passenger planes of the Indian National Airways, their covered engines denoting that they were not likely to take off for some time, perhaps days or even weeks.

Around the terminal building, looking very cold and discouraged, stood a crowd of Indians. There must have been at least one hundred of them.

"No knowing when they'll get out of here," said Captain

Hoke. "The Pass into India has been either fogbound or snow-bound for days." Then, pointing to a V-shaped notch in the mountains, he said hopefully, "We may be able to get through if the ceiling doesn't get any lower. That pass leads over the cease-fire line into Pakistan." After a few words with his engineer he added, "We'll have a try at it. If we don't get through we'll come back, wait awhile, and try again. We have just enough gas for three attempts."

"What d'you mean by three attempts?" said Zetta anxiously.

Captain Hoke then explained that in flying through the Pass, which narrows rapidly, he had to be sure that he did not fly too far in, so that in the event the ceiling closed down before he had actually flown through the Pass there would be room to turn around and fly back to the airfield.

"I've got to be able to see through that Pass and beyond to Pakistan before I dare fly through it," he explained. "Once the ceiling in front of us touches the ground, we must turn back quickly. Too dangerously narrow to trust to instruments only!"

The next ten minutes were spent in lashing down our baggage to the floor of the plane while the pilot raced his twin engines, preparing to take off. There was a crew of five men, consisting of Captain Hoke, his co-pilot, a navigator, a radio engineer, and a mechanic. Zetta soon spotted all five as Southerners, and much to her delight she learned that the radioman was from Norfolk, Virginia, her home town.

The interior of the plane was quite empty except for our big pile of baggage and the canvas bucket seats which lined the sides. Sam sat on one side, while Zetta and I sat on the other.

"Ready?" shouted the pilot as we snapped our belts.

"Okay, here we go!"

With a deafening roar the plane raced down the runway and

266

in a few seconds left the ground and headed straight for that V in the mountains. All five of the crew kept their eyes straight ahead. At frequent intervals the navigator looked at his map. The mechanic told us that it was very doubtful if we would be able to get through.

"Okay?" inquired the pilot.

"Okay so far," answered the navigator as he looked at the ground, then at the converging sides of the mountains, and then at his map.

"We're going through," said Captain Hoke.

Zetta and Sam were tense with excitement, and my heart was beating like a sledge hammer.

"We've made it! We're through the Pass!" shouted Captain Hoke with a sigh of relief.

"What a thrill that was," said Zetta as she placed her hand gently in mine.

"Penny for your thoughts, darling," she said as I was gazing thoughtfully out of the window. "You've seen your Shangri-La. I hope it wasn't too much of a disappointment. As for me, I wouldn't have missed it. One look at the Vale of Kashmir as we flew over the Himalayas was worth our whole trip halfway around the world."

"Disappointment?" I said. "Not by any means. And while Kashmir is far from being a Shangri-La right now, it might be in time to come, but I fear that time is a long way off." Then putting my arm around Zetta, I continued, "I've spent most of my life in search of Shangri-La, and you, my dear one, have been by my side for these last twenty years. I'm still convinced that somewhere there is a real Shangri-La, and if you still love travel and adventure as much as I do, I think we can find it."

PAKISTAN

LAHORE   With a population of slightly more than one million, Lahore is the second largest city of Pakistan. Home of the Pubjab University, with more than forty colleges and institutions, Lahore is the principal cultural and academic center of the nation. Here you can see the exquisite Shalimar Gardens which were laid out by the Mogul Emperor Jehangir, whose son was responsible for the Taj Mahal at Agra. However, Lahore's Shalimar Gardens must not be confused with Shalimar, "The Garden of Love," which the same Emperor created on the shore of Dal Lake in the Vale of Kashmir. Both are masterpieces of landscape gardening, but the Lahore garden is much more formal and does not have the magnificent background of the Himalayas or the glorious chinar trees for which Kashmir's Shalimar is so famous.

Not far from Lahore is the beautiful tomb of Jehangir, the father of Shah Jehan. Aurangzeb, who succeeded Shah Jehan on the imperial throne of Delhi, gave to Lahore the beautiful Royal Mosque.

Thoroughly up to date, Lahore might be termed the Hollywood of Pakistan, for here a number of fine film studios are situated. But unlike California's Hollywood, where maps are sold showing the location of the homes of the most famous film stars, Pakistan's "Hollywood" stars shun publicity, so that the last thing you will be able to discover is where any of them live.

With wrestling such a popular sport in America, promoters might do well to investigate the matter of wrestling in Pakistan, for this new country has some of the best wrestlers in the world. Should Gorgeous George or Man Mountain Dean ever visit Lahore, they will have to look to their laurels. The present champion wrestler of Pakistan, whose name is Bhollu, would like to make their acquaintance.

Lovers of Kipling will be interested to see in the office of Lahore's *Civil and Military Gazette* a plaque which records that Rudyard Kipling once worked there. Kim's gun, Zam-Zammah, still stands outside the Museum, where Kipling's father, Lockwood Kipling, used to be curator. There is much to see and do in Lahore. The best time to visit the city is during the winter season, from October to March, when life is at its gayest.

MURREE   Winter sports are not usually associated with the Indian subcontinent, yet at the town of Murree in West Pakistan the snowfall provides ideal conditions for all kinds of winter sports. Thirty-seven miles from Rawalpindi and connected by an excellent motoring road, Murree is also one of the most popular summer resorts of Pakistan. It is 7525 feet above the sea and commands a fine view of the Himalayas' towering peaks. Good hotel accommodations are available all the year round.

SIALKOT   Speaking of sports, it would be interesting to know how many tennis champions realize that many of the rackets they wield in their tournaments came from Pakistan. Yet for three quarters of a century the name Sialkot has been synonymous with sports goods. Not only tennis rackets but badminton rackets, shuttlecocks, hockey sticks, golf clubs, footballs, cricket balls and bats, basketballs, and volley balls are manufactured by the tens of thousands in this ancient city which has been identified with Sagala, the capital of the Indo-Greek ruler Menander two thousand years ago.

Sialkot is also famous for the excellence of its surgical instruments. At a critical stage of World War II, when surgical instruments were unobtainable elsewhere, Sialkot came to the rescue and made a notable contribution to the Allied war effort, saving many thousands of lives.

The town is easily reached by rail or motor and is well worth seeing.

HYDERABAD Not to be confused with the great Indian state of the same name, Hyderabad is in the province of Sind, about 111 miles from Karachi. The town is famous for its lovely silk, gold, and tissue embroidery. Here the historic tombs of Kalhoras and Talpurs, who once ruled Sind, can be seen. Incidentally, the tall galvanized iron ventilators which are seen on the tops of Hyderabad houses are for drawing in the fresh cool sea breeze. Air conditioning is an old story in Pakistan.

SUKKUR The name Sukkur is better known to engineers than tourists, for here the huge Sukkur Barrage is located, built across the river Indus and supplying water to an irrigated area that is about one quarter the size of England. The irrigation canals that are fed from the Sukkur Barrage would encircle the globe twice.

Another marvel of engineering to be seen at Sukkur is the Landsdowne Bridge over the Indus. Reminiscent of the Forth Bridge in Scotland, this huge structure is the longest single-span railway bridge in the East.

QUETTA If you want to play a round of golf fifty-five hundred feet above sea level in a region where the air is crisp and the countryside rich with peaches, grapes, pomegranates, and other delicious fruit, just take a plane or train to Quetta, the capital of Baluchistan. To many people Baluchistan is just another name in a geography book, but since it has become a part of Pakistan, this rugged region is rapidly becoming a popular resort for tourists.

RAWALPINDI Situated at the foot of the Himalayas, Rawalpindi, the principal town of the Punjab, has for hundreds of years been a military center. It is now the headquarters of the Pakistan Army and one of the largest military depots in the country.

PESHAWAR   There are few more historic cities than Peshawar, capital of the North West Frontier Province. Only a dozen miles from the entrance to the Khyber Pass, Peshawar, with a population of 200,000, is an important center of trade between Afghanistan and Pakistan. For centuries Afghan merchants have brought their caravans from Kabul, Bokhara, and Samarkand to Peshawar. In the days before Partition the caravans could travel through the Khyber Pass only between certain hours on only two days a week, when, as a result of an arrangement with the British, the tribesmen did not fire upon them. But during the rest of the week there was an open season for snipers. Nowadays, however, the caravans pass through unmolested.

You can no longer buy the lovely embroideries, silk rugs, and other works of art made in Bokhara, however, because in 1922 the Red Army of Soviet Russia captured the city and massacred a large part of its population. As for the Emir of Bokhara, he managed to escape to Kabul, where he became just another rug seller in the bazaar. Thus did the Soviet torch of "freedom" not only scatter the craftsmen of Bokhara but bring ruin to the merchants of Peshawar as well.

Time has healed many of the wounds inflicted by Communism, however, and Peshawar itself has become famous for the beauty of its handicrafts, particularly gold embroidery and beaten copperware.

About ten miles from the city is the celebrated Jamrud Fort which commands the entrance to the Khyber Pass, through whose rugged ravines have flowed countless hordes of foreign invaders. But now that the British have gone, peace reigns for the first time in more than a century and the Khyber Pass is actually open to tourists.

How long this happy state of affairs will last depends largely on the settlement of the Kashmir dispute between Pakistan and India. Unless a just settlement is reached soon, war may break out and bring in its wake the chaos for which Russia is waiting. Then history may repeat itself and the Khyber Pass may witness hordes of Communists invading Pakistan en route to India.

BAHAWALPUR   Bahawalpur is the capital of the state of the same name. It is also known as Baghdad-ul-Jahid, or "New Baghdad," because its present ruler, who acceded to Pakistan, is a direct descendant of the caliphs of Baghdad. His name is almost as interesting as the city itself. Just what his wife calls him, I cannot say, but his official title is Lieutenant Colonel Dr. Al-Haj His Highness Rukn-ud-Daula-Nusrat-i-Jang Saifud Daulla Haflzul-Mulk Mukhlisud-Daula, Wa-Muinud-Daula Nawab Sir Sadiq Mohammed Khan Sahib Bahadur Abbasi the Fifth.

Bahawalpur is the richest of the states which acceded to Pakistan at the time of Partition. It has an area of twenty thousand square miles and produces large quantities of wheat and cotton. For tourists, its chief attraction is its fine embroidery work and the delicacy of its pottery.

MULTAN   This historic city, once the headquarters of Alexander the Great, who invaded Pakistan in 116 B.C., can be reached by railway from Karachi. A detailed description of Multan is extant in the writings of historians. Here you can see a famous old fort and several Moslem shrines. But if you are looking for something to buy, you will find in Multan's market all kinds of lovely things, from enameled trinkets to silk carpets.

KASHMIR

THE VALE AND ITS PEOPLE   Kashmir is slightly smaller than Great Britain and about the same size as Hyderabad. Situated in the north of India, it extends over 84,471 square miles.

The high plain through which the Jhelum flows is the world-famed Vale of Kashmir. Eighty miles long and twenty to twenty-five miles in breadth, the valley rises six thousand feet above sea level. It has been described as an emerald set in pearls, for the valley is evergreen, and during nine months of the year the hills that encircle it are covered with snow. To the north of the valley are the mighty Himalayas rising in several parallel ranges, culminating in some of the tallest peaks in the world. The loftiest of them is Mount Godwin-Austen, 28,250 feet, second only to the great Mount Everest in height and grandeur.

In the third century B.C. Asoka held his court in Kashmir, introduced Buddhism, and founded the first city of Srinagar. Buddhism and Hinduism existed side by side for several centuries. In this Hindu-Buddhist period many fine temples and monasteries were erected. One of the greatest of Kashmir's rulers was Lalitaditya. He conquered the neighboring lands of the Pubjab and central Asia and built the famous temple of Martand. Sultan Zain-ul-ab-din, who is often compared with Akbar for his tolerance, ruled Kashmir in the early part of the fifteenth century. Akbar conquered it in 1586. Jehangir and his son Shah Jehan deeply loved this picturesque land and laid out a number of lovely gardens, known as the Mogul gardens of Kashmir.

Most of the people of Kashmir are tall and fair, with regular features. They are tolerant, intelligent, and pleasing to talk to, and have a keen sense of color harmony and make excellent craftsmen.

275

HANDICRAFTS   The glorious surroundings of Kashmir have bred in the Kashmiri an instinctive feeling for beauty, and his deft fingers can turn raw material into articles of exquisite delicacy. His artistic genius finds its best expression in shawls woven from a fine wool called pashm. The pashmina, as this finely woven material is called, is then embroidered by hand in beautiful patterns and colors. In the nineteenth century Kashmir shawls were greatly prized in Europe and are in demand in India to this day. Among the other industries for which the craftsmen of Kashmir are justly renowned are woodwork, silver, engraving, metalwork, embroidery, silk weaving, papier-mâché work, and carpet making.

NATURAL RESOURCES   The Kashmir Valley is very fertile. Rice and wheat are staple crops. Among vegetables, cucumbers, turnips, radishes, cabbages, tomatoes, peas, carrots, beans, asparagus, and spinach grow in abundance. Fruits, which are plentiful, are exported in large quantities. These include apples, peaches, plums, apricots, walnuts, and green almonds. The principal trees are cedars, pines, spruces, poplars, willows, and the famous chinar.

WILD LIFE   Kashmir has a very abundant animal life. Among the wild animals are ibexes, foxes, black bears, chamois, goats, Kashmir stags, snow leopards, flying squirrels, and many other smaller animals. There are countless birds, including pheasants, many different kinds of ducks, geese, and partridges. Along the northern tributaries of the Jhelum, wild goats, birds, and deer haunt the silent glades. The gooral, or Himalayan chamois, frequents the crags and forests of the low ridges.

WHAT TO EXPECT WHEN YOU GO TO KASHMIR   Sir Francis Younghusband once compared Kashmir and Switzerland as follows: "The country with which one is most apt to compare Kashmir is, naturally, Switzerland. And Switzerland, indeed, has many charms and a combination of lakes and mountains in which, I think, it excels Kashmir. But it is built on a smaller scale. There is not the same wide sweep of snow-clad mountains. There is no place where one can see a complete circle of snowy mountains surrounding a plain of anything like the length and breadth of the Kashmir Valley, for the main valleys of Switzerland are like the side valleys of Kashmir. And above everything, there is at the back of Kashmir, and visible in glimpses from the southern side, a region of stupendous mountains surpassing every other in the world."

Kashmir's appeal is not merely limited to scenery, nor is there just one particular season of the year to go there. Kashmir may truly be called "an all-year resort," for it caters to many different tastes. For the botanist there are flowers of many different kinds, from the lovely lotus on the lakes to the rarest of alpine flora. The archaeologist will find, in the ruins of ancient cities, temples, and monasteries, subjects of absorbing interest. For the geologist there is the story of the Himalayas to unravel from the great mass of fossils, from oysters to mastodons, and from the great variety of rocks, many of which are of volcanic origin. For the artist and photographer, Kashmir has exquisite landscapes and an abundance of extraordinary types of human beings and habitations.

The connoisseur of art will find plenty of shawls, carpets, papier-mâché, wood carvings, embroideries and needle point, jewelry and carved precious stones. Hunting, shooting, and fishing await the sportsman, while for those who love sheer adventure, mountaineering and hiking are without a peer, not to mention wonderful skiing.

But if it is just rest you seek, nothing can beat life on a houseboat on Dal Lake or a summer camp in cool, invigorating Gulmarg, eighty-seven hundred feet high.

YOUR KASHMIR CALENDAR   The right time to go to Kashmir
depends entirely upon what you want. If you arrive about New
Year's Day, the valley will probably be covered with a few inches
of snow. You will be able to skate or ski. There will be a variety
of shooting and hunting to be had. The temperature will be anywhere from a minimum of 15° to 45° F. in the shade. February is
similar to January, but as March approaches, the valley warms up
suddenly, and by the middle of the month spring has arrived,
willow trees begin to burst into leaf, and the gardens of Srinagar
are gay with crocuses and daffodils. The hardiest of the wild
flowers now begin to bloom. "April showers bring May flowers"
is true of Kashmir, and by the end of the month spring is fully
established and the valley presents a wonderful sight, with
apricot, almond, peach, and early apple blossoms. In May the
mean temperature in the Vale is 65° F., but the midday heat is
not oppressive. May is the time to see the chinar trees in all their
glory of fresh green foliage. Dal Lake in May is very beautiful,
with drooping willows and graceful poplars providing cool shade
for the houseboats which now begin to fill with visitors.

Flower boats in May are a wonderful sight, loaded with masses
of sweet peas, roses, and mauve irises. In June many people leave
the lake and go to Gulmarg, twenty-nine miles from Srinagar,
where they stay in hotels or bungalows within reach of one of the
finest golf courses. June is "fruit month" in Kashmir: strawberries,
mulberries, cherries, apricots, and raspberries, followed by pears
and apples.

In July and August the Vale is definitely hot, with shade temperature ranging between 80° and 95° F., but these are the best
months to see the lotus blossoms on Dal Lake. Having seen them,
most people prefer to spend these months in one of the many
mountain camping grounds which are easily reached from Srinagar by car. September marks the beginning of autumn in the Vale.
Evenings get chilly, log fires are welcome, but the weather in

general is very much like an Indian summer, fine, clear, and sunny. From October to Christmas the leaves change color and fall, yet it is hard to say which is the more beautiful season of the year in the Vale: autumn, when the chinar trees are ablaze with brilliant color, or spring, when the air is filled with the fragrance of many blossoms.

SPORTS   Information with regard to hunting, shooting, and fishing may be obtained from the Office of the Game Warden at Srinagar, from whom licenses may be secured. For general information, contact the Visitors' Bureau, Srinagar, whose cable address is BUREAU KASHMIR.

There is always some kind of sport to be obtained in Kashmir, but, like other countries, there are open and closed seasons to be observed.

Two of the commonest words heard in Kashmir are "shikara" and "shikari." A "shikara" is a small boat. A "shikari" is a professional hunting guide. Beware of engaging a shikari merely on the strength of his testimonials; the best shikaris are registered with the Game Department. A good one can take charge of your expedition, arrange for transport and obtain supplies, employ local coolies, guide you to the best hunting grounds, and generally make himself useful. Your shikari needs watching, however. His astonishing greed for money may tempt him to swindle and cheat over even the smallest sums. But the cost of living in Kashmir is so fantastically low that even if he systematically overcharges you double, your expenses will be far less than they would be in America.

SHOOTING   Big game includes red bear, black bear, snow leopard, antelope, and various kinds of mountain goat, sheep, ibex, and Kashmir stag. Some of the finest duck shooting in the world is to be had on Wular Lake. The season usually opens on September 16. Many different kinds of ducks, geese, teal, and snipe spend the fall, winter, and early spring in the Vale. Partridges and quail are also exceedingly numerous. Other game birds that are likely to be met with include pheasants and blue rock pigeons.

FISHING The lakes of Kashmir provide excellent sport for followers of Izaak Walton. The most famous indigenous fish that puts up a valiant fight is the mahseer, which runs as high as sixty-five pounds. Brown and rainbow trout have been introduced and multiplied exceedingly. Ten-pound trout are not uncommon, while fish of more than fourteen pounds have been caught. Trout streams may be booked at the Office of the Game Warden. Tackle and tents may be hired in Srinagar.

HIKING AND MOUNTAINEERING The season lasts from May to October, headquarters usually being at Srinagar, Gulmarg, and Pahalgam. Camping equipment may be rented, but it is advisable to carry your own mosquito net. Warm clothes, really dark glasses, and nailed boots are necessary when hiking in snow-clad mountains.

SKIING Ski enthusiasts will find skiing in Kashmir a unique experience. The season usually begins in December. The intending visitor is advised to apply to the Secretary of the Ski Club of India for membership. The subscription is very moderate, and membership will save expense and greatly simplify the arrangements. Address Srinagar, Kashmir.

SRINAGAR AND ITS ENVIRONS   Srinagar lies between Hari Parbat and Takht-i-Suliman. An ancient city, it was first built by Asoka the Great in the third century B.C. Today it has a population of nearly 200,000 and is the political and cultural center of Kashmir. The Jhelum flows right through the heart of the city, cutting it into two parts which are joined together by seven bridges. A trip down the river in a swiftly gliding shikara will give the tourist a good view of the city's picturesque balconies, busy ghats, mosques, and temples. Among the places of interest are:

THE MUSEUM Located on the left bank of the Jhelum, the Museum has fine specimens of Kashmir art and interesting antiques and curios.

SHANKRACHARYA TEMPLE This is a stone temple of great archaeological interest, built about 400 B.C., on the top of a hill about one thousand feet high, called the Takht-i-Suliman, or Throne of Solomon.

JAMA MASJID Half a mile from the fourth bridge you can see the largest mosque in Kashmir, which was built in 1404.

PATHAR MASJID One of the most interesting mosques in Kashmir. Built on the left bank of the Jhelum, this remarkable mosque of polished stone was erected by Nur Jahan, wife of the Mogul Emperor Jehangir. Because it was built by a woman it was never used, the status of women in Islam being inferior to that of men.

SHAH HAMADAN This graceful mosque situated close to the riverbank is a favorite object for artists and photographers. Like most Moslem structures in Kashmir, it is built of wood with a pointed steeple. On its beautifully carved eaves hang many bells.

PANDRETHAN About three miles up the river from Srinagar is the site of what is probably the original city of Srinagar founded by Asoka, the Buddhist king. Here you can see a very interesting medieval temple which was built in the tenth century and dedicated to Vishnu.

HEALTH RESORTS GULMARG An ideal place for camping during the hot summer months, Gulmarg is one of the vast meadows on the northern slopes of the Pir Panjal range. Eighty-seven hundred feet high, it is covered with snow for seven months of the year. In June, however, it suddenly springs to life with the influx of visitors from Srinagar. The climate is exhilarating. Gulmarg's golf course is said to be the best in the East. Gulmarg is about twenty-nine miles from Srinagar, all of which distance is motorable except for the last four miles, which is an uphill footpath running through groves of pines. Accommodations may be had in hotels or furnished bungalows.

KHILENMARG Ten thousand feet high and a four-mile climb from Gulmarg. There is an excellent camping site. Here is a botanist's paradise with many different kinds of wild flowers.

PAHALGAM Sixty miles from Srinagar, Pahalgam, seven thousand feet high, is in many ways the counterpart of Gulmarg but without its sophistication. Pahalgam is on the pilgrim route to the Cave of Amar Nath where there is a frozen spring which is the object of worship for the many Hindu pilgrims who go there. The distance from Pahalgam to Amar Nath is about forty-one miles, but the hike is one of the most beautiful and thrilling in Kashmir.

KOKARNAG About fifty miles from Srinagar, this place is well known for the refreshing and curative waters of its springs. Among other attractions are a camping ground and trout fishing. Board and lodging are available.

ACHHABAL About forty miles from Srinagar, it has a garden with one of the largest springs in Kashmir. Near the garden is a government trout hatchery.

GANDERBAL A camping site on the bank of the Sind Nallah. Thirteen miles from Srinagar.

LAKE WULAR This is the largest fresh-water lake in India. The Jhelum flows into and out of the lake. Fishing is excellent, especially mahseer. The lake can be reached either by road or by river, in a shikara or a houseboat.

MANASBAL LAKE Eighteen miles from Srinagar and surrounded by low hills. This lake is famous for the transparency of the water and the beauty of its lotus gardens.

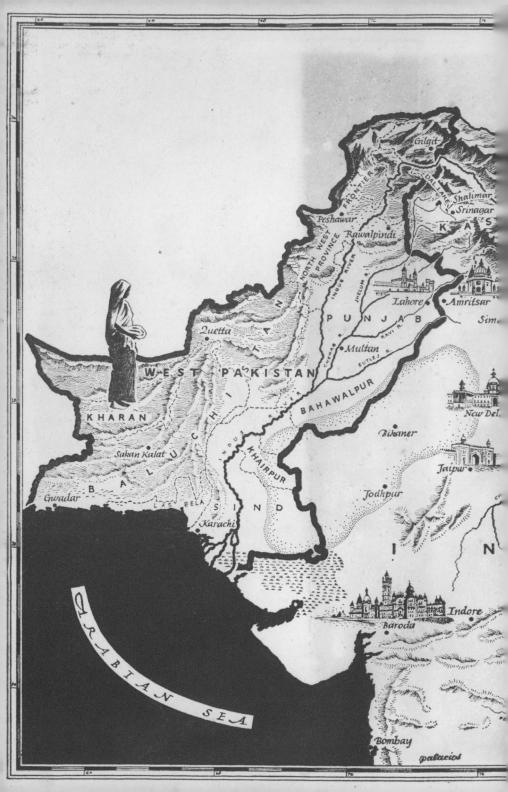